Now Hiring!
Jobs in Eastern Europe

Also in the Now Hiring! series:

Now Hiring! Jobs in Asia
Now Hiring! Ski Resort Jobs
Now Hiring! Outdoor Jobs
Now Hiring! Destination Resort Jobs

Now Hiring!
Jobs in Eastern Europe

The Insider's Guide to Working and Living in the Czech Republic, Hungary, Poland, and Slovakia

Clarke Canfield

PERPETUAL
P R E S S

Seattle, Washington

Printed in Canada

Library of Congress Catalog Card Number 94-74013
ISBN 1-881199-62-2

First edition
10 9 8 7 6 5 4 3 2 1

Cover: Michelle Lustgarten at Allegro Design
Interior: Lynne Faulk Design
Maps: GreenEye Design

Publisher's note: The purpose of this book is neither to encourage nor discourage anyone from seeking employment as an English teacher in Eastern Europe. *Now Hiring! Jobs in Eastern Europe* is designed to give you the most accurate information possible; we have made every effort to be objective and present both the positive and the negative aspects of teaching in Eastern Europe. We have also attempted to ensure that the information in this manual is accurate and up-to-date. Prices, wages, employer information, and hiring policies can change quickly, however, so be sure to double-check all information before making any final decisions about pursuing overseas employment.

The struggle of man against power is the struggle of memory against forgetting. . . .

We will never remember anything by sitting in one place waiting for the memories to come back to us of their own accord! Memories are scattered all over the world. We must travel if we want to find them and flush them from their hiding places!

Milan Kundera
from The Book of Laughter and Forgetting

CONTENTS

ABOUT THE NOW HIRING! SERIES

Most people need to scrimp and save for a while before they can travel. With Now Hiring! we thought to turn that concept on its head: why not earn money while you travel? Why work at the local greasy spoon when you could spend a summer in Yellowstone National Park working outdoors? Or why work retail at your hometown mall when you could travel to South Korea for a year to teach eager students English?

Now Hiring! says that if you have to work, then work a fun job in a really cool place. In fact, the hundreds of people we've talked to in compiling these guides actually have made, and sometimes even saved, money while traveling. They've held positions like SCUBA instructor, wildlife biologist, snowboard instructor, and private tutor everywhere from Kenai Fjords to the Caribbean and Prague to Taipei. Their experiences confirmed what we already knew: you don't need extraordinary skills or training to get jobs in exciting places around the world. You just need motivation, dedication, a bit of luck, and a few good leads.

The jobs we cover in our books give you the chance to earn a living while broadening your horizons. You'll have fun, gain new skills, meet people from around the world, and perhaps make a difference in the lives you encounter along the way.

As you should expect, we do our best to make sure all our information is accurate and up-to-date. For every book we talk to countless industry insiders about how to get hired, which are the best jobs, where to work, and how to have fun and save money once you're there. But because change is one of life's few constants, you are bound to encounter phone numbers that have been disconnected, organizations that have folded, or changes due to late-breaking political or economic developments. For those reasons, it's a good idea to call ahead.

Thanks for your interest in the Now Hiring! series. Feel free to drop us a line here at Perpetual Press about your adventures, and bon voyage!

FOREWORD

You should like your job. It should give you the satisfaction of gaining experience while earning money. It should also enable you to live the kind of life you want to live. Otherwise, what's the point? Life's too short.

Yet, many of us find ourselves withering away in jobs that have lost their meaning. Or we find ourselves hesitant to even enter the "real world" of nine-to-five work. Most of us realize that it's not always easy to find jobs that offer excitement and support an adventurous lifestyle. With *Now Hiring! Jobs in Eastern Europe*, it just got easier.

The Czech Republic, Slovakia, Hungary, and Poland all are working hard to emerge from decades spent behind the Iron Curtain of Soviet communism. All of these countries have been aggressively dismantling their old social, political, and economic systems and replacing them with open, democratic, and market-based systems, modeled after those of the West. Some countries are succeeding more readily than others. And all of them are taking advantage of the expertise and experience of people from Western Europe, the United States, and Canada.

Now Hiring! Jobs in Eastern Europe provides the up-to-date information you need to understand the evolving working and living conditions in Eastern Europe. This book consolidates a wide range of information that will save you time and energy in making your decision to go to Eastern Europe.

We have included contact information for teacher recruitment organizations, EFL training programs, study-abroad and internship programs, and such general travel organizations as ticket consolidators, airlines, youth hostels, and hospitals. We've also given you tips on how to make travel arrangements for an extended trip, how to obtain the necessary travel and work papers, and how to successfully prepare and apply for a teaching position. There are tips on how to save money and plan wisely, as well as sources of further information. Most importantly, we give you lists of schools in each of these countries that hire native English language instructors. We provide addresses and phone numbers for all the schools listed, as well as information on hiring requirements, starting wage, and application procedures, whenever available. In addition, there are first-hand accounts of people who have done these jobs, as well as those who have started their own businesses in Eastern Europe.

With all this information at your fingertips, *Now Hiring! Jobs in Eastern Europe* should provide you with the means to begin your decision-making process and to continue on in pursuit of a positive expatriate experience. If you decide to spend time living and working in Eastern

Europe, we are confident that our book will be useful throughout the length of your stay. Don't forget to pack it!

And don't forget to write. Let us know about your experiences in Eastern Europe. Tell us when you were there and how long you stayed. And regale us with some of your adventures searching for work, the job you eventually found, and what you did in your spare time.

We would like to incorporate your comments and suggestions into future editions of *Now Hiring! Jobs in Eastern Europe*. If we do, we'll send you a copy of the Perpetual Press title of your choice. Use the form at the back of the book to let us know what you were up to. Feel free to attach a letter if you need the extra space.

—The Editors

PREFACE

This book was written after much preliminary brainstorming, long hours of research, and a hell of a lot of hoofing around Eastern Europe. My goal was to get to the heart of the "expat" experience—to find out what common traits and experiences move people to drop their careers or simply give up their customary routines to go east into the center of Europe.

During the course of my travels, I discovered many of the motivations that drive young people to live and work in Eastern Europe. For many, the land that once lay behind what Winston Churchill called the "Iron Curtain" remains a frontier despite the ravages of its long and complex history—perhaps the last frontier in all of Europe.

The Czech Republic, Hungary, Poland, and Slovakia hold promise for those who are frustrated by the economic stagnation that grips much of the First World. Though these countries have economic and political frustrations of their own, they are not necessarily beset by the strict rules and regulations that prevent foreigners in many European and Asian countries from pursuing interesting employment opportunities. Because the governments of these four countries are still struggling to stabilize their fledgling market economies, they often welcome various forms of assistance from the West. For the eastwardly mobile and energetic North American, this can translate into an English teaching job, the beginnings of an entrepreneurial endeavor, or other kinds of work opportunities.

This book explains the "how to" and illustrates the "why" of the expat experience in Eastern Europe by providing hard-core information, including addresses of employers and other useful contacts, along with a narrative derived from research, personal observation, and interviews with the folks who breathe and sweat in cities like Prague, Budapest, Bratislava, and Krakow. This guide book provides the link between your desire to travel and the many possibilities that await you inside the borders of Eastern Europe.

ACKNOWLEDGMENTS

I owe many thanks and much credit to those on both sides of the Atlantic who helped me to research and write this manual.

First and foremost, I would like to thank my wife, Daisy, for all her assistance and inspiration.

For sharing personal experiences, a big thank you to: Levi Hansen, Gregory Niedokos, Karyn Panitch, Paulina Mrazova, William Corley, Stephen Lynch, Nicholas Wingfield, Alex Lash, John Doyle, Peter Dibuz

For research, advice, editorial support, and photos: Robert Beck, Julie Hansen, Marilyn McCune, Renata Susser, Ania Burczynska, Alice Egyed, Jana Klepetarova, Anja Jakubowski, Gabriella and Lorant Szabo, Maurice and Sondra Lustgarten, Scott Andrews, Dennis Hart and Colette Toddy Hart, Brenda Spoonemore, Jennifer DuBois, Derek Edwards

For project management: Thom Votteler

And thanks to everyone at Perpetual Press, who have stuck by this project throughout its sometimes difficult evolution.

A special word of appreciation to the many schools and organizations that generously gave of their time and resources to help bring this project to life. Most importantly, thanks to the people of the Czech Republic, Hungary, Poland, and Slovakia, whose tireless pursuit of freedom and democracy have inspired the world.

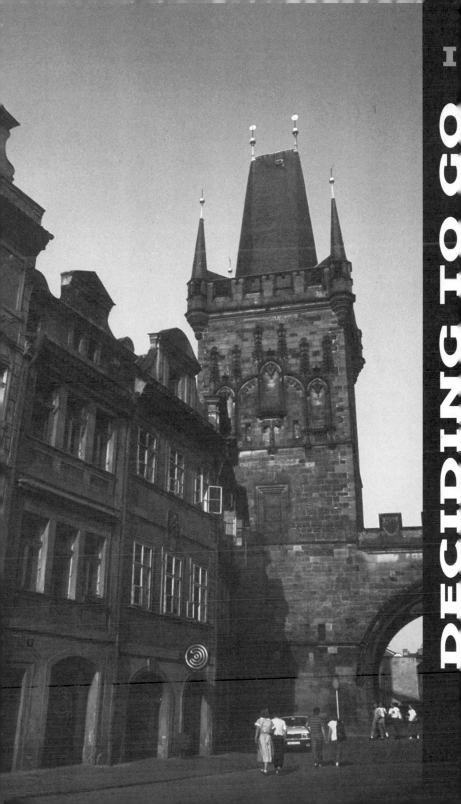

Why work in Eastern Europe?

THE REWARDS OF LIVING AND WORKING IN EASTERN EUROPE

Living and working in countries such as the Czech Republic, Hungary, Poland, or Slovakia for any length of time can be an unforgettable and enriching experience. Imagine teaching English in Budapest or starting your own small business in Prague. Think of consulting for a growing Polish company in the field of computer graphics or standing in front of a classroom full of eager students in one of the oldest universities in all of Europe. Any one of these possibilities could be part of your new adventure.

Now Hiring! Jobs in Eastern Europe provides a broad range of information. Such considerations as history, language, culture, economic stability, quality of life, employment availability, and local customs are important when trying to determine which Eastern Europe destination is best suited to your needs. Understanding these aspects of Eastern European life will help make your sojourn a rich and fruitful experience.

Now Hiring! Jobs in Eastern Europe helps you find employment in an exciting and evolving part of the world. Because positions in the field of English-language instruction are widely available, they are the focus of this manual. Yet, this book also provides valuable information on opportunities in other fields of employment, whether you want to start your own business or just get by.

No matter what your designs on work and travel in Eastern Europe, *Now Hiring! Jobs in Eastern Europe* will assist you in planning and following through.

WHERE IS EASTERN EUROPE?

A knowledge of European geography and a clear understanding of the region's history are important parts of your preparation. For the purposes of this manual, Eastern Europe encompasses the Czech Republic, Hungary, Poland, and Slovakia, though this is certainly not an all-inclusive list. Other countries that are commonly considered part of Eastern Europe—Romania, Bulgaria, the former Yugoslavia, and the Baltics—are not covered here.

The centrality of the Czech Republic, Hungary, Poland, and Slovakia places the region in an interesting geographic and historical position in relation to the rest of the former communist bloc, known as Eastern or Central Europe. With Romania lying further east and the former Yugoslavia, Bulgaria, Albania, and Greece situated to the south and southeast, Eastern Europe extends from the Baltic Sea in the north to the Mediterranean in the south, and from the German border in the west to the shores of the Black Sea in the east.

The four countries we're using to define Eastern Europe, with the possible exception of Slovakia, are increasingly referred to as being part of an emerging Central Europe. "Central" is a useful term here because it implies, among other things, a state of being in the middle of something—at a crossroads or a juncture. In this way Europe, in its entirety, is composed of more than just East and West. The history of Europe certainly fits this description.

At the treaty of Yalta in 1945 after the Second World War, the Allied leaders—Roosevelt, Churchill, and Stalin—determined the borders of the new Europe. Their agreements subsequently created the division between East and West that inspired the "Iron Curtain" image evoked by Winston Churchill, an image that effectively lumped together the countries of the Eastern Europe into a seemingly amorphous mass in the minds of many Westerners. That the Soviets liberated Hungary, Poland, and Czechoslovakia at the end of the war seemed to inextricably tie all of their histories to the Soviet Union's, rather than keeping them within the long, complex storylines of European history.

At the end of the war, after the Allies and the Soviets had time to take inventory of their spoils and recognize their ideological differences, the Cold War set in between the U.S.S.R. and the countries of the West. The relationship between the United States and the U.S.S.R. entered a dangerous phase that would last nearly forty-five years. During this time, Czechoslovakia, Hungary, Poland, Romania, Bulgaria, and other Eastern European countries were used by the U.S.S.R. as "buffer states." In these countries the Soviets established military bases and required citizens to learn and speak Russian. By subverting the cultures of all these nations, the effect was to create quasi-Russian societies throughout Eastern Europe.

By the mid-1980s, it became clear that the Soviet Union could not stay on course, economically or ideologically. During the course of a remarkable series of events, perhaps most significantly the rise to power of Soviet leader Mikhail Gorbechev, the centralized government based in Moscow collapsed. This paved the way for the countries of Eastern Europe to move forward on their own and reassert their independence without economic or ideological directives from the former Soviet Union.

Western foods and products are increasingly available in the larger Eastern European cities.

The governments of the West, especially that of the United States, made every attempt to decorate the fall of communism with the slogans of a wartime victory. Hence, the capitalist/democratic system "defeated the evil empire" and "won the Cold War." Couching the demise of the Eastern European governments in the rhetoric of the Cold War often served to isolate their identities from the rest of Europe, to which they are nevertheless historically connected.

Given the modern tendency to view the world through easily digested media bites, many North Americans envisioned Europe to be divided neatly in half prior to the revolutions of 1989, with one side belonging to the adherents of democracy and the other to the followers of communism. Politicians and journalists exploited all the convenient dualities—good versus evil, East against West—in order to further their own interests and sell newspapers. Of course, the interests of educating the general public or improving international understanding frequently took a back seat to these personal ambitions. As a result,

Americans often held biased opinions about the countries and peoples of Eastern Europe. While Western Europe shared with Americans both a similar heritage and a similar vision for the future, according to the common media perspective, Eastern Europe lurked off in the distance, a dark and little-understood place.

In fact, though pervasively used, the term "Eastern Europe" contributes to the world's misunderstanding of this region: Prague actually lies further west than Vienna, though Vienna has long belonged to the domain of Western Europe. Yet, until recently, Prague was relegated to the nether world known conveniently as "the other Europe," a euphemism for the former Eastern bloc. It's an odd situation. As one observer, long involved in the reform movements of the Czech Republic prior to the revolution of 1989, stated:

❝ *Russia is as strange to us here in the Czech Republic as it is to people in America, even though it is perceived as being nearby."*

THE REWARDS OF TEACHING ENGLISH

Teaching English is a challenging proposition certain to bring both frustration and reward. Imagine an entire classroom of students weighing your every word, intent upon gleaning some grammatical tidbit that will bring them closer to fluency! Seriously, by teaching the language employed by much of the international business world, you are assisting in the economic transition of an entire region. Achieving proficiency in English means greater opportunities for the people of the countries of the former Eastern bloc. In fact, in Hungary, for example, English-language competency is a common requirement for many Hungarian government positions.

Eastern Europeans prize education. Some of the oldest universities on the European Continent are located here and stand as testament to the grand educational traditions of the region. Students at all levels are known to be both courteous and committed. Dedicated teachers garner respect and gratitude for their efforts, not to mention a decent wage. Because twenty classroom hours per week is considered full-time, well-organized teachers can find ample time to pursue leisurely activities.

A long-time teacher in southern Poland observed:

❝ *You come in here as a teacher and you're automatically upper-middle-class. It beats working at some entry-level job in the United States. Entry level is nothing anymore.*"

Teaching English effectively requires dedication, discipline, and imagination. Standing in front of a class wagging your native English tongue doesn't qualify as instruction. Teaching strategies and skills are important tools for any competent teacher. In many cases, you will be expected to prepare lessons in advance. You will also be the catalyst for most of the interaction in the classroom. To a large degree, your ability to inspire students will influence their willingness to learn. Ultimately, the gratification you and your students derive from teaching will come from your hard work, creativity, and patience. The teacher in Poland continued:

❝ *I experienced the hard way. When I first came here, I was one of those unqualified people. You know, I thought—well, I'm a writer so I'll just come here and do it [teach]. For my first class, I brought in a short parable by Franz Kafka. It was in simple English, only one paragraph. Then I realized my students didn't understand anything I was saying. So, I just threw it out, and started over. That was my cold shower.*"

Some native speakers of English teach in Eastern Europe for adventure, while others do it to accumulate credentials for their careers in education. Many who initially approach teaching as a temporary adventure discover the long-term satisfaction that it can bring. These are the people who go to Eastern Europe on a lark and come back with a new and exciting vocation. No matter what your take on teaching, you are likely to return from Eastern Europe with new skills, friends from all over the world, and a broadened perspective.

About working in Eastern Europe

IS IT FOR YOU?

Let's be honest: Living and working in the Czech Republic, Hungary, Poland, or Slovakia is not for everyone. Language barriers and cultural differences are serious considerations. Bureaucratic red tape and lack of sufficient infrastructure are frequent complaints of those who are used to the fast-paced life of the West.

Pollution is also a serious concern. After decades of unrestrained Soviet-backed industrialism, much of Eastern Europe's beauty is shrouded in a haze of air pollution and undermined by water and ground contamination. Although these issues are recognized and being addressed as best they can by the new governments of these countries, it will take years, probably decades, to clean up what's already there and make the necessary, and expensive, adjustments to industrial practices and standards to prevent further contamination.

Food can be a sensitive issue, too. A steady diet of meat and potatoes complemented by soggy vegetables and an infrequent serving of fruit is for many people the fodder of nightmares, not healthy living.

Teaching presents frustrations of its own. Though not physically demanding, any form of classroom instruction can quickly sap your stores of mental energy, leaving you feeling spent and exhausted. One grueling hour-long session in front of a room full of disinterested students is often enough to make you want to pull out your hair. And setting aside the time to prepare for your classes requires discipline.

And yet, while life in Eastern Europe is a definite departure from life in North America, there are many positive aspects to living in such world-renowned places as Prague, Budapest, Bratislava, Krakow, and Warsaw, or in the surrounding cities and towns.

Eastern Europe ultimately draws people who are interested in the rich historical and cultural traditions of the region. The region's culture speaks through the breathtaking architecture of its premier cities, the stoic lifestyles of its rural people, and the spectacular castles and churches that dot its countryside. If you are willing to give a little of yourself and open up to the differences that surround you, immersion in the cultures of Eastern Europe will enhance your understanding of your own culture, as well as of yourself.

In the words of one North American living in the Czech Republic:

❝ *This is my journey to the East. It's a kind of initiation experience, like you might find in older cultures. Life is here. I have lost hold of the structure that used to exist in my life in the West. I am no longer that person I was when I lived in the United States. My senses and values, old criteria, my worries have changed. I've exchanged them for new ones. . . . I came here hoping to be able to share something [by teaching English]. It is the richness of the personal relationships that keeps me here.*❞

THREE COMMON QUESTIONS

Q: Will I be able to find a job?

A: When you arrive at your Eastern European destination, you will discover that many people are interested in learning to speak English. Young people, especially, understand the need to learn English in order to compete in a rapidly evolving job market. Business people of all ages are concerned about their place in the evolving marketplace. Everyone seems to realize that English is the emergent language of international business and diplomacy. Private English-language schools have been widely established, and they need teachers.

Q: What if I've never taught before?

A: Ask yourself these questions: Can I speak English correctly? Am I genuinely interested in teaching in Eastern Europe?

If you answered "yes" to both questions, you are qualified to teach in any of the four countries. A sturdy command of spoken and written English combined with a willingness to teach is your greatest asset. Although you don't need a degree in English or a teaching certificate, formal qualifications always come in handy. With them, you will have an advantage over the competition. As a general rule, the further you get from the more popular expat destinations—larger cities like Prague and Budapest—the less you will need to rely on teaching certificates and degrees. If you are lacking in the "papers" department but have demonstrable teaching experience, you will likely be a convincing and attractive job applicant. But it depends on whom you talk to. Some employers favor experience, while others stress the importance of a teaching certificate or a related college degree.

Q: How can I possibly teach in Hungary, Poland, Slovakia, or the Czech Republic if I don't speak Hungarian, Polish, Slovak, or Czech?

A: As a teacher in any of these countries, you likely will be focusing on conversational English. Your students will have a fundamental grasp of spoken and written English so that your lack of foreign language skills will not impede your ability to teach effectively. You will be hired to teach solo when your employer has determined that your students have an appropriate level of English language facility. Or you will teach in tandem with a native speaker who handles the intricacies of grammar and translation when the going gets tough. Either way, you are bound to encounter occasionally difficult and perhaps embarrassing classroom situations. Inadvertent errors and assorted faux pas come with the territory. Accept the challenge of teaching: be patient with yourself and your students, innovate in tight spots, and learn to laugh a little when all else fails.

 here to go?

THE CZECH REPUBLIC, HUNGARY, POLAND, OR SLOVAKIA

Although closely situated to one another, the Czech Republic, Hungary, Poland, and Slovakia possess remarkable differences. Each country has much to offer, but choosing a final destination requires careful consideration. Don't fret too much, though, because travel within Eastern Europe is both inexpensive and efficient. Should you change your mind after selecting your first destination, it would not be unreasonable to pack up your belongings and move on.

There are a few noteworthy traits shared by all four countries: public transportation is generally efficient (especially in the larger cities), violent crime is virtually nonexistent, the cost of food is relatively low, and housing costs are generally reasonable, with the notable exceptions of Prague, where housing costs have risen sharply in recent years. Yet, in Prague or Budapest, it's still easy to step out your door, catch a tram, transfer to the subway, and arrive at your destination without spending much or getting mugged. Thieves and pickpockets are not unheard of, though. Common sense and street smarts are invaluable in any part of the world.

On the downside, the vestiges of the communist era still weigh heavily on anyone who wants to achieve something quickly. It's virtually impossible to get any official business accomplished without running into dull-headed career bureaucrats. No matter whether you are applying for a work permit or merely trying to send a package home, you are bound to encounter resistance on some level. Waiting in lines for one rubber stamp or another is part of the daily routine almost anywhere in Eastern Europe. The daily groove you take for granted in North America will be steadily chipped away and replaced by a distinctly different version of the everyday grind.

Perhaps the most formidable obstacle to settling down in any of the countries of Eastern Europe is finding a place to stay. Housing shortages are common throughout most of the major cities. This is something to consider early on in your decision-making process, though it shouldn't dissuade you from going. Persistent apartment-hunters are usually successful. Since an adventure into the heart of Europe is not designed for the lazy or those of weak resolve, the search for accommodations should merely be taken in stride and looked upon as part of the package.

Trying to determine what sets each country apart from the others is not always an easy task, not to say that they are all the same. The Iron Curtain that separated Eastern and Western Europe did act as something of a common denominator, but there are more than a few subtle differences between each country. Real opportunities for both enriching experiences and employment exist throughout these countries. It is up to you to decide how much effort you want to expend during your time in Eastern Europe. In general, there are several points and questions worth considering, regardless of which country you choose to visit:

- Hungary is the only non-Slavic country under discussion here. Hungarian (Magyar) and Slavic cultures (in general) are fundamentally different, given their divergent histories and dissimilar languages.
- Are you interested in language? If so, how do you want learning a new language to be part of your immediate experience as well as part of your future?
- University or college towns generally offer more social and employment opportunities for young people regardless of the type of work you seek or the type of social circles you want to investigate.
- If politics are important to you, small towns and rural areas are usually more conservative, and perhaps more constricting.
- What sort of support system do you require? Are you comfortable confronting new situations on your own? Or, do you expect to have access to an expat community of like-minded people?

The following summaries should give you some specific ideas as to which country might be best suited to your needs and expectations.

Czech Republic

The Czech Republic, primarily Prague, is the most popular destination in Eastern Europe for young Americans. In fact, the media has already come up with the moniker YAP to mean Young Americans in Prague. The YAP phenomenon has become a hot topic in the media over the last few years. A number of magazines and newspapers have published articles on all the goings-on in "the Paris of the nineties." Some estimates put the number of American expatriates in Prague at 20,000, though only about 2,000 are officially registered with the government.

Situated in the heart of Europe, the Czech Republic lies at the crossroads of the new Europe, brought to life after the revolutions of 1989. The right-leaning government of the two Vaclavs—President Havel and Prime Minister Klaus—has quickly brought the country to the forefront of the reform movement in Eastern Europe. Economic shock therapy has been their answer to making the transition to a market-oriented economy. Arguably, they have been more successful than any of the other governments in the region. The Czech Republic's government has been relatively stable, its low foreign debt is the envy of its neighbors, and its projected entry as the first Eastern European member of the European Economic Community bodes well for the future of the country.

Because the government is dedicated to creating a prosperous future for its citizens, it has invited assistance from the West. This has made it relatively easy for Western investors to get involved in developing the country's infrastructure. Consequently, many Western business people, particularly Germans and Americans, have made profitable in-roads into the Czech Republic.

The cost of living remains low in the Czech Republic by Western standards, but is on the increase compared to the rest of Eastern Europe. Inflation has been kept under control to a much greater extent than in Poland, Slovakia, or Hungary and unemployment is the lowest in the region. As of October 1, 1995, the Czech crown is fully convertible.

Though it's likely that the governments of Central and Eastern Europe will eventually begin to clamp down on foreigners who want to live and work in their countries, the Czech Republic stands as one of the more inviting places to settle. Americans are treated well, and the Czech government still seems amenable to their continuing presence. The Czech government seems to recognize the need for foreign financial and intellectual involvement in its drive toward a burgeoning free-market economy. A young American who ventured to Prague and ended up staying for several years remarked:

> **66** **The Czechs are generally friendly toward Americans, especially when compared to Germans and other Europeans. Prague is easy and relaxed. Even for white-collar people, it's an enjoyable place. It's a new market—13 million people in the Czech Republic. And just look at the map. Prague is so central."**

Because Prague is such a popular destination, you can expect to run into other native English speakers on a regular basis. Sometimes it seems that there is more English or German spoken on the streets of

Prague than there is Czech. It is easy to understand why this could be viewed as either a plus or a minus. If you like to know that many of your compatriots reside nearby, then Prague could be the place for you. On the other hand, you might be turned off by the prospect of being lumped together with countless other Americans and dealing with the opinions many Europeans have about people from the United States.

It's clear from spending time in the four countries covered in this book that the Czech Republic has the most opportunities for foreigners to work. The demand for English teachers is still on the upswing and the opportunities afforded Americans in other fields are more numerous than in either Poland, Hungary, or Slovakia.

Hungary

Hungary stands out in stark contrast to the Czech Republic, Poland, or Slovakia. Ten and a half million people inhabit a country whose language, culture, and history have very little in common with any of its neighbors. Hungarian is a Finno-Ugric language that has nothing in common with Slavic languages, like Czech, Slovak, Polish, or Serbo-Croatian. It is reputedly one of the world's most difficult tongues. A day on the streets of Budapest very quickly illustrates this linguistic nightmare. One Hungarian educator long involved in language and cross-cultural studies said:

66 *The problem here in Hungary for foreigners is not culture shock, it's language shock. The culture isn't so different that it takes any enormous adjustment, but the language is another story."*

Budapest is easily the second most popular destination for expats in Eastern Europe. It rivals Prague on many counts. Expats here teach English, start their own businesses, and generally have a good time. Though not as commonly as in Prague, English can be heard on the sidewalks. Evidence of Western commercial influence is everywhere. There are many popular bars and nightclubs that act as second living rooms to many in the expat community. Western businesspeople have been welcome in Hungary for a number of years, so Hungarians are accustomed to the presence of Westerners.

The old regime in Hungary was more lenient and more genuinely oriented to market reform than elsewhere in the former Eastern bloc. Its policies, known as "goulash communism," mixed aspects of Soviet-style government with dashes of free-market liberalism. Consequently, Hungary has been open to the West for a longer period of time than any of the other countries under discussion. The Hungarian people seem more open and gregarious than their neighbors to the north. The climate, too, is more forgiving and at times can almost seem Mediterranean.

Work is available, but the requirements and qualifications are often more demanding. Hungary has entered its second phase of English language education. That is, there are more people in Hungary who are advanced in their English language studies than in the other countries of Eastern Europe. The support structure for English-language instruction is better developed. One long-time educator at the university level stated:

❝ *It is clear that qualified and talented teachers are what is needed here in Hungary. Of course, it is possible for a native speaker of English to find work teaching, but it is unusual for them to be effective—and they often do more harm than good. . . . There remains a definite demand for qualified English teachers to teach and work in various English-related positions."*

Nevertheless, many uncertified teachers find work in Budapest and elsewhere. The pay can be good, while the cost of living remains low by Western standards. It just might take a little more determination and hard work to get settled into a good teaching job because Hungarians are fond of formal papers, such as college diplomas and teaching certificates.

Poland

Of the four countries under discussion, Poland—along with Slovakia—is a less-frequented destination for North American expats working in Eastern Europe. However, this shouldn't dissuade you from working there. With larger cities like Warsaw in the north, and Krakow in the south, plus a host of other interesting destinations, the home country of the Pope should be considered by anyone attracted to Eastern Europe.

Krakow, for example, has just about as much natural charm and romance as Prague. Warsaw, though much larger and perhaps less attractive to Westerners because it feels like a generic metropolis, is a major world city with a dynamic and cosmopolitan atmosphere. Other larger cities, like Wroclaw and Gdansk, are rich in history and architecture, if less visited because they simply are not yet familiar destinations to many Westerners.

Teaching opportunities abound throughout the country, if you know where to look. Pay is comparatively good, and the Polish people are generally friendly and welcoming. One American worked as an English teacher for several years and saved up enough *zloty* to establish his own English language school without any infusion of cash from back home. Here is what he had to say about his experience:

66 *Making this school has been a big accomplishment. I worked my ass off. I did this all on Polish money. I worked two and three jobs, I saved up, and I got a lucky break. I started with one room, last year we had four rooms, and now we have seven. I started with thirty-one students (several years ago) and now we're past 300 students. And it's not easy."*

Poland is perhaps the most Catholic country in the world and certainly the most devout in all of Europe. Consequently, traditional values run deep and strong in much of the population. Behavioral norms are more strict here than in the rest of Eastern Europe. It wouldn't be wise, for example, to wait until the last moment to see if you can find a condom. And don't wear a hat into the local church. You could be scolded by a nun for not removing your beret as you gaze up at one the most beautiful stained-glass windows you'll ever see.

Slovakia

Slovakia shares a seventy-four-year history with the Czech Republic. Prior to their formal separation on January 1, 1993, the two republics formed the now-defunct country of Czechoslovakia. Since that time the two countries have taken decidedly different paths, and Slovakia desperately wants to maintain a separate identity from the Czech Republic, while pursuing economic reform.

Because the Soviets chose Slovakia as home for many of their large-scale industries in the former Czechoslovakia, the Slovaks must now contend with the often unwieldy problems that these businesses present. Consequently, the downsizing and dismantling of these monoliths will undoubtedly impede Slovakia's progress toward economic reform.

Slovakia's slower resolve in the reform arena, combined with a greater tendency toward provincialism, makes prospects challenging for prospective English teachers and other job hunters. In addition, red tape is more prevalent in Slovakia than in the Czech Republic. This is not

The expatriate life allows you the opportunity to meet other adventurous spirits from around the world.

to say that Slovakia should not be considered as a destination. Patience, determination, and a hankering to get off the beaten track bring more than a few expats Slovakia's way. The capital, Bratislava, has a certain allure that might charm you away from Prague's well-beaten paths. It is only an hour or so away from Vienna and just a three-hour train ride from Budapest. The smaller cities and towns spread over eastern Slovakia provide relief from places like Prague and Bratislava and a little obscurity. For this reason, prospects for English teaching jobs in these areas are good. Both public and private schools frequently search for the elusive native speaker of English who is willing to forgo a big city lifestyle for a quieter existence.

Of working in a smaller town, one American expat said:

 ❝ *In smaller communities, foreigners are often more respected and well liked. The legacies of Americans and Canadians who once lived in these small towns often follow them. Everyone assumes that their successors will know them. Life may not be as glamorous in these places, especially when compared to a place like Prague. But at the same time, you are finding people who have heads on their shoulders and a clear vision of what they are doing here and why. They don't seem to be trying to escape from something. I think you definitely find more of that in Prague and Budapest."*

Before you make a decision, read other books and magazines, talk to people you know who have traveled, find a native from your country of interest, then choose the destination best suited to your interests. The chapters in this book on each of the four countries contain more information that will help you decide.

COUNTRY OR CITY?

Should you set your sights on Budapest, Prague, Krakow, Warsaw, or Bratislava, or aim for an off-the-beaten-track town in southern Bohemia, the great plains of Eastern Hungary, or the Carpathian mountains that form the border between Poland and Slovakia? Will the teaching experience be the same no matter which you choose? Here are some hints from an American woman who taught English and worked for a volunteer organization:

❝ *The availability of teaching jobs is dependent upon the economy. Consequently, the larger cities generally have higher-paying jobs, but the cost of living is higher, too. Within the smaller cities and rural towns, it is necessary to create your own possibilities by convincing a local school or college headmaster to take you on as the local native speaker."*

Living in the less-populated areas will afford you a slower-paced lifestyle. It does not mean, though, that life will be easier. While the cost of living may be lower, you will often have greater demands made on your time because you are teaching, performing other school duties, and acting as the local foreign ambassador. Schools in rural towns and smaller cities often have less money to pay their teachers, so you may find yourself accepting a combination of cash and room and board as compensation for your efforts.

Because larger cities like Prague and Budapest attract the bulk of the expat communities, you often won't see one of your compatriots for several days or even weeks. In some places, you will be the only foreigner for miles around. Though this may be an expedient way of immersing yourself in the local culture and language, you must be willing and able to handle all the trappings of isolation. Remember that the larger cities are never really that far away. You might be able to find a perfect balance between rural responsibilities and big-city anonymity if you choose a smaller town that is only a few hours' train ride from a major metropolis.

Teaching English

Teaching English is the most widely available form of employment for North Americans living in Eastern Europe. Private language schools and public schools are the most common sources of jobs in the field of English-language instruction. Private tutoring of both individuals and groups is becoming popular, too. Even larger companies are hopping on the English-language bandwagon by paying native speakers of English to tutor their management teams in the world's most dominant business tongue.

As a general rule, the larger your employer, the more structured your approach will have to be in the classroom. Most schools will provide you with lesson plans or at least general guidelines to follow. When you tutor privately, you are usually on your own. Even with a good amount of experience, devising your own lesson plans and teaching strategies can be a daunting task.

Students usually range in age from school-age to their late thirties and early forties, though you will also encounter a few older students. Up until the revolution of 1989, Russian was the second language taught in most of the schools in Eastern Europe, and many of those old enough to have lived during the Second World War speak German.

SOME GENERAL CONSIDERATIONS

Most schools hire teachers locally. It is uncommon for all but the largest English-language schools in Eastern Europe to recruit internationally, or even outside their area. This means, of course, that your best bet is to find a job once you arrive at your intended destination. Because it is reasonably inexpensive to travel to Eastern Europe and even less expensive once you arrive, the advantage you gain from presenting yourself in person far outweighs the convenience of attempting to find work in advance through the mail or over the telephone. Moreover, it is in your best interest to feel as comfortable and at home as possible in your chosen destination. Living large in Prague may sound intriguing when your friend describes her experience there, but you may find that you are better suited to a smaller, less touristy village once you arrive. If you arrange employment before you go, you may find that you end up spending time and money extricating yourself from a sticky, and potentially time-consuming, situation.

Said one school director in Poland about the need for teachers:

❝ *I am looking for people who are talented and committed, and I'm not as concerned about whether or not they're certified. It's getting to the point where I am having to consider advertising or even recruiting teachers in the States because I can't meet the demand here [in Krakow]. But that would be both expensive and a hassle. I hope it doesn't come to that."*

If you can't bear the thought of winging it, you may be able to find a job through someone who has personal connections in Eastern Europe, a teacher recruitment organization, or even your college or church. Though not always the best approach, it is possible to find work in this way via letters and phone calls. You will need to prepare a small portfolio of personal information, including a cover letter, a resume, copies of any relevant diplomas or teaching certificates, and perhaps a picture of yourself. After you collect this information, select a specific location, or at least a geographic area, and write to a few schools there. Aside from documenting your qualifications, be sure to give some indication of why you are interested in a particular area. The more you demonstrate familiarity with the region, the more convincing you will be. Most employers in Eastern Europe are tired of English teachers who turn out to be more interested in chugging the local brew than teaching the local kids.

If you have some money set aside—say, US$500 or more beyond the price of your airplane ticket—and you are willing to just set your sights and go, you are almost assured of finding a teaching position. Of course, it would be wise to do some research and follow the advice in this book. The length of your job search will depend primarily on your destination and your timing. Other factors that are important to consider include:

- Qualifications. Teaching certificates, related degrees, and experience all will be considered by your prospective employer.
- Demand. Depending upon the population and economic strength of your chosen area, demand for teachers will fluctuate throughout the year. Cities are a better bet based on sheer scale, but the competition is greater, too. Because of the difficulties inherent in moving and adapting to a foreign land, teachers tend to come and go throughout the school year. It is not uncommon for a teacher to resign on short notice. This forces employers to find replacements at odd times during the school term.
- Requirements. The rules and regulations of immigration in the

English language schools provide the greatest number of job opportunities for North Americans in Eastern Europe.

countries of Eastern Europe are constantly changing. Laws may not actually exist at any given time, so it is up to the local immigration official or interior office to decide whether or not to stamp your passport. Of course, many expats work "black," which means that they don't apply for a work permit and work under the table. Depending upon your intended length of stay and your destination, this may be a reasonable alternative to jumping through all the bureaucratic hoops when you apply for your residence status and work permit. In recent years, however, there has been an increase in "spot" checks targeted specifically at undocumented workers. Working "black" is risky and can lead to deportation if you're caught.

• Personality. Your ability to market your strengths and downplay your weaknesses will be crucial to succeeding in your job search. If you seem personable and cheerful, you stand a much better chance of finding work:

WHEN TO APPLY

When is the best time of the year to look for teaching employment in Eastern Europe? It depends on where you're going and what type of teaching job you are interested in. Overall, the best time to go to Eastern Europe and look for a job is later in the summer in order to find work for the school term that begins in late August or September.

Aside from being the high season for travelers, logistically it is the easiest time to travel given the usually favorable weather conditions and the likelihood that you will have a little fun starting out on your new adventure.

Alternatively, new school sessions often begin in January, so arriving in the dead of winter has its advantages. In this case it would be wise to start your job search before the holidays of late December. Everything slows down, so you might find yourself sliding (not stomping) along the icy pavement in vain, only to find that your prospective employers are enjoying hot toddies at home rather than giving interviews in the office.

Another time to consider is the late spring or very early summer. When school is out there are a number of summer camps and short-term intensive language programs. Frequently, teachers are in short supply because this is the time when many of them travel or return home between sessions. Many of these jobs do not require work permits or formal credentials, although this is increasingly risky, and finding well-qualified teachers on short notice can be a difficult task.

Keep in mind that many schools hire on an as-needed basis. It certainly is possible to find work throughout the course of the year. If you are not set on working for a larger private school or a public institution, then your chances are better for getting hired at times other than in August and September, or December and January. If you want to tutor on a private basis, then your options are wide open. Remember, though, it takes time to establish yourself. This approach requires more financial planning and forethought. You are less assured of securing a solid teaching schedule. Private students are notorious for canceling their lessons at the last minute or simply not showing up at all. If self-sufficiency is not your objective and you are willing to supplement your travel budget with money from home, this approach allows you the greatest overall flexibility.

No matter when you go, plan to spend a few weeks getting situated. Finding accommodations and searching for work at the same time can be tiring. It would be wise to give yourself some time to adjust to your new surroundings and to meet people who can give you valuable tips on the local job market and social scene.

FOR EXPERIENCED EDUCATORS

Prague, Bratislava, Budapest, and Warsaw are enticing destinations for adventuresome teachers of English as a foreign language (EFL teachers). American and international schools in Eastern Europe have many opportunities for motivated, professional teachers. But it is generally experienced teachers who have the best shots at lining up teaching jobs before traveling abroad. Nevertheless, there are opportunities for inexperienced native speakers, as well. In fact, some of the recruitment agencies listed below specialize in placing inexperienced but motivated teachers.

The following sections review a few main types of teaching opportunities available to native English speakers in Eastern Europe.

Schools affiliated with the Department of State

American schools funded in part by the Department of State hire staff on a school-by-school basis, not through government channels. School curricula are usually patterned after the American model, but the student body may be international. For more information, contact:

Office of Overseas Schools, C/OS
U.S. Department of State
Room 245, SA-29
Washington, DC 20522-2902
Phone: (703) 875-7800

Public schools

These are state-run schools, much like public schools in the United States. There are opportunities for North Americans to teach at these institutions and requirements vary. Many inexperienced teachers find teaching jobs in the public system. To find out more, contact one of the teacher recruitment organizations listed below, or consult the public school listings for each chapter.

Private schools

Private schools can be affiliated with a company, church, volunteer organization—like the Peace Corps—or just plain private. These schools probably present the greatest opportunity for inexperienced teachers. Private schools tend to pay the most money and provide the best chances for you to cultivate private tutoring sessions on the side. For more information on employment with a private school, contact one of the teacher recruitment organizations listed below, or consult the school listings for each chapter.

Teacher recruitment organizations

A variety of organizations recruit teachers for employment in overseas schools. They hire for positions in many countries at recruitment fairs held around the United States. Generally, these organizations are looking for qualified, experienced EFL teachers, though not always. Application proceedings do take time, so consult the organization you are interested in well in advance of your planned date of departure. Depending upon the recruiter, the application process could take six months or more. Fees vary, with some as high as US$1,000.

Association for the Advancement of International Education (AAIE)
Thompson House
Westminster College
New Wilmington, PA 16172
Phone: (412) 946-7192

City University
919 SW Grady Way
Renton, WA 98055
Phone: (800) 426-5596, ext. 3907
Fax: (206) 637-9689

East European Partnership
Carlton House
27A Carlton Drive
London SW15 2BZ
England
Phone: (441-081) 780-2841 (24-hours)

Education for Democracy
P.O. Box 40514
Mobile, AL 36640-0514
Phone: (205) 434-3889
Fax: (205) 434-3731

English for Everybody (USA)
655 Powell Street, Suite 505
San Francisco, CA 94102
Phone: (415) 789-7641
Fax: (415) 433-4833

English for Everybody (Czech Republic)
Spanielova 1292
Prague 6 16 300
Czech Republic
Phone/fax: (02) 301-9784

Foundation for a Civil Society (USA)
The Masaryk Fellowship Program
1270 Avenue of the Americas, Suite 609
New York, NY 10020
Phone: (212) 332-2890
Fax: (212) 332-2898
Email: 73303.3024@compuserve.com

Foundation for a Civil Society (Czech Republic)
Jeleni 200/3
Prague 1 118 00
Czech Republic
Phone: (02) 451-0873
Fax: (02) 451-0875
Email: FndCivSoc@ecn.gn.apc.org

Foundation for a Civil Society (Slovakia)
Kapitulska 7
Bratislava 811 01
Slovakia
Phone: (07) 333-539
Fax: (07) 333-544
Email: Carrie@fcs.sk

Friends of World Teaching
P.O. Box 1049
San Diego, CA 92112-1049
Phone/fax: (619) 275-4066

Hungarian Chamber of Language Schools
Rath Byorgy u. 24
Budapest 1122
Phone/fax: (01) 155-4664
(Has database of qualified English

teachers that are consulted by member schools)

InterExchange
161 16th Avenue
New York, NY 10013
Phone: (212) 924-0446
Fax: (212) 924-0575

International Educators Cooperative
212 Alcott Road
East Falmouth, MA 02536
Phone/fax: (508) 540-8173

International Educators Institute
P.O. Box 513-A
Cummaquid, MA 02637
Phone: (508) 362-1414
Fax: (508) 362-1411

International Schools Services
P.O. Box 5910
15 Rozel Road
Princeton, NJ 08543
Phone: (609) 452-0990
Fax: (609) 452-2690

Language Methodology Centre (JODM)
ul Dombatantow 20
Walbrzych 58 302
Poland
Phone/fax: 48-47-8694

Overseas Academic Opportunities
949 29th Street, Second Floor
Brooklyn, NY 11210

Search Associates
P.O. Box 636
Dallas, PA 18612
Phone: (717) 696-5400
Fax: (717) 696-9500
Email:
    74721.2500@compuserve.com

Soros English Language Program
888 Seventh Avenue, Suite 1901
New York, NY 10106
Phone: (212) 757-2323

Southern Illinois University
International Employment Service
University Placement Center
Woody Hall, Room B-204
Carbondale, IL 62901
Phone: (618) 453-2391
Fax: (618) 453-1924

Students for Central and Eastern Europe, Inc. (SFCEE)
3421 M Street NW, Suite 1720
Washington, DC 20057
Phone: (202) 625-1901
Fax: (202) 333-1147

Teach Hungary and the Central European Teaching Program
175 High Street, Suite 433
Belfast, ME 04915
Phone/fax: (207) 338-6852

U.S. Information Agency (USIA)
English Teaching Fellow Program
301 Fourth Street SW
E/ALP, Room 304
Washington, DC 20547
Phone: (202) 401-6016
Fax: (202) 401-1250
Email: Fellows@USIA.GOV

Volunteers Exchange International
134 W 26th Street
New York, NY 10001
Phone: (212) 206-7307
Fax: (212) 633-9085

World Learning
School for International Training
(SIT)
Kipling Road, P.O. Box 676
Brattleboro, VT 05302-0676
Phone: (802) 257-7752, ext.
2052 or (802) 258-3311
Fax: (802) 258-3210
(The USIA (see above) sponsors
and supervises the English Teach-

ing Fellow Program. SIT admin-
isters the program.)
WorldTeach
Harvard Institute for Interna-
tional Development
1 Eliot Street
Cambridge, MA 02138-5705
Phone: (617) 495-5527
Fax: (617) 496-8899

TESOL

TESOL is the world's largest organization of ESL instructors, with over 19,000 members worldwide. TESOL membership costs US$71 per year and includes subscriptions to the *TESOL Quarterly*, a research publication; the *TESOL Journal*, containing news of interest to ESL teachers; and *TESOL Matters*, a bimonthly newsletter. TESOL also offers its members a placement service for US$20, which includes a bimonthly bulletin of currently available teaching positions. A master's degree and ESL teaching experience are required. TESOL provides reduced-rate memberships for students and other reduced-rate membership options, and hosts an annual convention of members at which many overseas English schools recruit new teachers.

Teachers of English to Speakers of Other Languages (TESOL)
1600 Cameron Street, Suite 300
Alexandria, VA 22314-2751
Phone: (703) 836-0774

International recruiting fair sponsors

The following organizations sponsor international teacher recruiting fairs. Contact each for verification of dates, registration deadlines and procedures, registration fees and/or placement fees, schools attending, qualifications required or preferred, and additional services.

**European Council of
International Schools**
ECIS Staffing Services Officer
21B Lavant Street
Petersfield, Hampshire GU32 EL
England
Phone: (441-07) 30 26 82 44
**International Educators
Cooperative**
212 Alcott Road

East Falmouth, MA 02536
Phone/fax: (508) 540-8173

International Schools Services
Education Staffing
P.O. Box 5910
Princeton, NJ 08543
Phone: (609) 452-0990
(Credential files must be set up six weeks prior to fair dates.)

Ohio State University
Student Academic and Career
  Center
110 Arps Hall
1945 N High Street
Columbus, OH 43210
Phone: (614) 292-2741

Queen's University
Placement Director, Faculty of
  Education
Kingston, ON K7L 3N6
Canada
Phone: (613) 545-6201

Search Associates
P.O. Box 100
Mountaintop, PA 18707
Phone: (717) 696-5400
Fax: (717) 474-0380

**Teachers of English to
  Speakers of Other
  Languages (TESOL)**
1600 Cameron Street, Suite 300
Alexandria, VA 22314-2751
Phone: (703) 836-0774
(Master's degree and ESL teach-
ing experience required.)

University of Northern Iowa
Overseas Placement Center
Career Development and
  Placement
Student Services Center
Cedar Falls, IA 50614
Phone: (319) 273-2083

WHO GETS HIRED?

You don't necessarily need formal credentials or past teaching experience to find employment teaching English in Eastern Europe. There
are plenty of people without credentials who get hired to teach because there are not enough prospective teachers to meet the demand.
Though a teaching certificate, past experience, or a related degree will
attract the attention of employers, it won't necessarily guarantee you a
job. Often, demonstrating desire, good communication skills, and an
interest in the culture and language of your chosen country will be
enough to get you hired.

As a general rule, the closer you get to the more popular, larger city
destinations, like Budapest and Prague, the more likely it is that employers will expect you to possess a teaching certificate, teaching experience, or both. By the same token, the larger and better known the
English school, the greater the possibility that applicants will be required to possess a TEFL certificate or a degree in education in order
to even be considered.

Interviews with employers

An American in Poland

Q: What do you look for in an English teacher?

A: In our case we don't necessarily look for someone with credentials, as we offer teacher training here on our premises. We want people who get enjoyment from working to help others, who are gregarious, and who have it together. Teaching is a challenge, especially when you take into consideration your surroundings here. It's not home, it's not like living in the States.

Q: What problems do new teachers face?

A: That's a tough question because everyone is different, of course. All newcomers to the area face a difficult housing situation. Though this is not directly related to teaching, it certainly affects how settled a person feels. Accommodations are available, but usually it takes connections to find an apartment or a room. And you don't just waltz in here and pick up connections immediately. You have to get to know people. Beyond that, teaching is very demanding, and not everybody who packs their rucksack in the United States and comes over here is aware of that. If you think you can just show up and improvise in front of an entire class, you're either exceptional or high on yourself. It takes work. I didn't just come here, teach English for a while, and then start a school. I worked my ass off, and I still am—every day.

A Briton in Budapest

Q: What do you look for in a teacher?

A: Because of our reputation and our size, we only hire teachers who have RSA or TEFL certificates and the like. That's not to say that every school here in Budapest has requirements as demanding as ours . . . . We simply want people who are willing to make the commitment, and having a teaching certificate demonstrates that they are just that . . . . Of course, we want to hire personable and effective teachers who will be good with the students and good for the school.

Q: Are the prospects still good here in Hungary for teachers?

A: Well, Hungary is getting into its second phase of English-language education and there isn't the demand that there used to be. And there are more Hungarians who are actually qualified to teach English than in the other countries around here. But this is not to say there isn't still a demand for teachers. There definitely is. It's just getting harder to find work, especially if you don't have experience or teaching credentials . . . . The farther you get outside of Budapest, the better chance you have of finding a teaching job that doesn't demand qualifications.

●●●●●●●●●●●●●●●●●●●●●●●●●●●●●●●●●●●●●●

DEVELOPING YOUR QUALIFICATIONS

Having a teaching certificate will definitely increase your chances of getting hired. At the very least, it puts you in a more competitive position in the applicant pool. Having a TEFL (Teacher of English as a Foreign Language) or RSA (Royal Society of Arts) certificate should also give you a certain amount of confidence. Knowing that you are formally qualified will let you rest assured that you have much of what it takes to find a good teaching job just about anyplace in Eastern Europe.

Because of Britain's proximity to the European continent, more employers will recognize RSA certification than the American equivalents. Though this should not necessarily dissuade you from pursuing certification in the United States, you may want to consider taking the six-week RSA course in Europe, if that option is available to you. There are also a growing number of United States certification programs that offer the RSA.

The schools listed in the following section offer short-term TEFL training courses. If you are not able to attend one of these courses before you go, there are schools in Eastern Europe that offer teacher training courses. If getting a certificate is not an option, you can prepare yourself in other valuable ways for your overseas teaching adventure. The following activities will increase your chances of getting hired:

- Advertise your services as an English tutor for international students. Contact the TEFL program or the organization of international students at your local university or college. Or simply put up a flier in the international student lounge.
- Volunteer with a foreign-exchange program or a refugee organization in your community. Make sure to find a tutoring position that does not require a lengthy time commitment. Many of these

organizations and programs welcome volunteers for conversational sessions with TEFL students.

- Review several TEFL course books before you leave, and use them to familiarize yourself with the various methods of English-language instruction. When you interview with prospective employers, you will be able to demonstrate some valuable knowledge. If you are serious about landing a job, you might design your own sample lessons to show your interviewer. See the In the Classroom chapter of this book for more teacher preparation tips.
- Request an informational interview with the director of an EFL program (or even an EFL teacher) here in North America. Find out what they look for in a teacher and what the teaching jobs overseas actually entail. This way you will at least be prepared for your interviews once you arrive in Eastern Europe.
- If you have ever studied a foreign language, include that in your resume. Your own experience should qualify you to attest to what makes a language teacher effective. If the language is German, Hungarian, or Slavic, you might find that you can share some words with your prospective employer, which is usually a plus in the eyes of another linguist.
- Think creatively about your skills and past experience. Does any of it relate to the demands of teaching? If you have given public presentations, acted, or otherwise shown off in front of audiences, you will likely have the gumption to stand up in front of a classroom full of students. Evidence of solid communication skills and of an ability to hold your own before an audience is all good gravy in the eyes of a hungry employer.

Understanding ESL terms

The field of English as a second language is rife with confusing acronyms, and teachers themselves are often confused about what to call their profession. TEFL, TESL, CTEFLA, and TESOL are the most common designations and are often used by teachers interchangeably, even though they do have slightly different meanings depending on who's being taught. ESL schools usually distinguish between the terms, though, so it's good to know the difference.

TEFL stands for Teaching English as a Foreign Language, and correctly refers only to teaching English to pupils who are in a non-English-speaking area, such as the Czech Republic, Hungary, and most Eastern European countries. When checking out ESL schools, make sure that they teach TEFL instruction if you want to teach overseas.

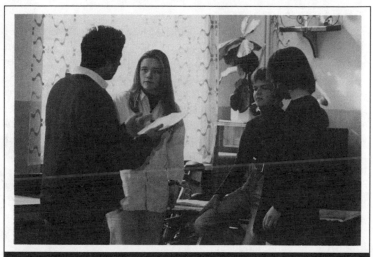

Enthusiasm and people skills are key characteristics of successful EFL teachers.

TESL means Teaching English as a Second Language, and describes the teaching of English to non-native students in countries like America, where the students need to learn English to function in everyday society. TESL can also refer to teaching English in a country like Singapore or Hong Kong, where English is an official language but most residents have a different first or "home" language such as Mandarin Chinese that they use in the home or most social situations.

TESOL, meaning Teachers of English to Speakers of Other Languages, is a good catch-all term, since it refers to pretty much any kind of English teaching as long as it's to non-native English speakers. This term can be confusing though, since it also refers to TESOL, Inc., which is the world's largest organization of ESL instructors.

CTEFLA stands for Certificate for Teaching English as a Foreign Language to Adults and is generally used in reference to the certificate given to successful participants in the Cambridge certificate program. This certification is also known as RSA (Royal Society of Arts) certification, RSA Cert, RSA Cambridge CTEFLA, or RSA/CTEFLA. This program is the most widely recognized EFL program in the world, and courses are offered at universities and training centers all over the world. Courses last either one month (full-time) or two months (part-time), and instruction is aimed particularly at English teaching in foreign countries (EFL). We've noted schools below that offer the Cambridge program.

TEFL training

Teacher training programs in the United States rely predominantly on the TEFL program that was developed in the States. More and more schools, though, are offering RSA certification, which is sanctioned by the Cambridge University in England. In Eastern Europe, the RSA program is more widely recognized than any other certification program. Though this shouldn't necessarily dissuade you from entering another program, having an RSA certificate simply means that you will be asked fewer questions regarding your qualifications by your prospective employer. Expect to pay between US$1,500 and $2,000 for four- to six-week intensive teacher training programs. In Europe, schools such as International House may discount their programs if you agree to sign a contract to teach at their school after you complete your RSA course.

The following United States schools offer certification in teaching English as a foreign language:

United States

Alabama

University of Alabama at Huntsville
Department of English
203 Morton Hall
Huntsville, AL 35899
Phone: (205) 895-6320

California

Azusa Pacific University
Department of International Studies
901 East Alota
Azusa, CA 91702
Phone: (818) 969-3434, ext. 3226

University of California at Berkeley
Education Extension
2223 Fulton Street
Berkeley, CA 94720
Phone: (510) 642-1171

Fresno Pacific College
Language Development Specialist Program
1717 South Chestnut
Fresno, CA 93702
Phone: (209) 453-2054

California State University at Fullerton
Department of Foreign Languages and Literature
835C Humanities Building
Fullerton, CA 92634
Phone: (714) 773-3534

University of California at Irvine
University Extension ESL
P.O. Box 6050
Irvine, CA 92716
Phone: (714) 824-8205

California State University at Long Beach
Department of Linguistics
MHB 408
1250 Bellflower Boulevard
Long Beach, CA 90840
Phone: (310) 985-4210

Monterey Institiute of International Studies
TESOL/MATFL Program

425 Van Buren Street
Monterey, CA 93940
Phone: (408) 647-4182

**California State University at
Northridge**
ESL Minor and Certificate
Program
School of Humanities
18111 Nordhoff Street
Northridge, CA 91330
Phone: (818) 885-3302

**William Carey International
University**
Division of Applied Linguistics
and TESOL
1539 E Howard Street
Pasadena, CA 91104
Phone: (818) 797-1200

**University of California at
Riverside**
UNEX-Intensive English
Program
1200 University Avenue
Riverside, CA 92507
Phone: (909) 787-4346

Sonoma State University
Department of Anthropology/
Linguistics
1801 East Cotati Avenue
Rohnert Park, CA 94928
Phone: (707) 664-2312

**California State University at
Sacramento**
Department of English
Sacramento, CA 95819-6075
Phone: (916) 278-6586

San Diego State University
PLC Department, College of
Education
San Diego, CA 92181
Phone: (619) 594-1184

English International
655 Sutter Street, Suite 500
San Francisco, CA 94102
Phone: (415) 749-5633
Notes: CTEFLA courses are offered
every month except December.

New World Teachers, Inc.
P.O. Box 420425
San Francisco, CA 94142-0425
Phone: (800) 644-5424
Email: teacherssf@aol.com

**St. Giles Language Teaching
Center**
1 Hallidie Plaza, Suite 350
San Francisco, CA 94102
Phone: (415) 788-3552
Notes: CTEFLA courses are offered eight times a year for the
full-time program and twice a year
for the part-time program.

Transworld Teachers, Inc.
683 Sutter Street
San Francisco, CA 94102
Phone: (415) 776-8071

San Jose State University
Linguistics Program
San Jose, CA 95192
Phone: (408) 277-2802

**University of California at
Santa Barbara**
TEFL Certificate Program
University Extension
Santa Barbara, CA 93106
Phone: (805) 893-3450

Coast Language Academy
501 Santa Monica Boulevard,
Suite 403
Santa Monica, CA 90401
Phone: (310) 394-8618
Notes: Four-week and eight-week
CTEFLA courses are offered four
times a year.

Connecticut

Fairfield University
Department of Bilingual/
  Multicultural/
  ESOL Education
127 Canisius Hall
North Benson Road
Fairfield, CT 06430-7524
Phone: (203) 254-4000, ext.
  2139

District of Columbia

American University
Department of Language and
  Foreign Studies
326 Asbury Building
4400 Massachusetts Avenue NW
Washington, DC 20016
Phone: (202) 885-2381

Georgetown University
School of Languages and
  Linguistics
Washington, DC 20057
Phone: (202) 687-6045

Florida

Florida Atlantic University
ESOL/Bilingual Education
  Teacher Training Program
418 Fleming Hall
College of Education
Boca Raton, FL 33431
Phone: (407) 367-3000

Missouri

**Central Missouri State
  University**
Department of English
Martin Hall, Room 336
Warrensburg, MO 64093
Phone: (816) 543-4425

Montana

University of Montana
Department of Linguistics

201 Liberal Arts Building
Missoula, MT 59812
Phone: (406) 243-5231

North Carolina

**University of North Carolina
  at Charlotte**
College of Education and Allied
  Professions
3117 Colvard South
UNCC Station
Charlotte, NC 28223
Phone: (704) 547-2531

**University of North Carolina
  at Greensboro**
Romance Languages/Education
338 Curry Building
Spring Garden Street
Greensboro, NC 27412
Phone: (910) 334-5000

Nebraska

**University of Nebraska at
  Omaha**
Department of English
Omaha, NE 68182
Phone: (402) 554-2635

New Jersey

Montclair State University
Linguistics Department
G418 Partridge Hall
Upper Montclair, NJ 07043
Phone: (201) 655-4000

William Patterson College
Bilingual/ESL Program
Wayne, NJ 07470
Phone: (201) 595-2535

New York

**State University of New York
  at Buffalo**
Intensive English Language
  Institute
320 Christopher Baldy Hall

Buffalo, NY 14260
Phone: (716) 645-2455

**The Center for English
Studies**
330 Seventh Avenue
New York, NY 10001
Phone: (212) 620-0760
Notes: CTEFLA courses are offered four times a year.

Ohio

Wright State University
Department of English Language
and Literatures
438 Millet Hall
Colonel Glenn Highway
Dayton, OH 45435
Phone: (513) 873-3136

Oregon

Portland State University
Department of Applied
Linguistics
P.O. Box 751
Portland, OR 97207
Phone: (503) 725-3000

South Carolina

University of South Carolina
Linguistics Program
Columbia, SC 29208
Phone: (803) 777-2063

Utah

Brigham Young University
Department of Linguistics
2129 JKHB
Provo, UT 84602-6278
Phone: (801) 378-2937

University of Utah
Department of English
LNCO 3500
Salt Lake City, UT 84112
Phone: (801) 581-3392

Vermont

St. Michael's College
Center for International Programs
Winooski Park
Colchester, VT 05439
Phone: (802) 655-2000, ext.
2300

Washington

Seattle University
School of Education, Program in
TESL
7210 First Avenue NW
Seattle, WA 98117
Phone: (206) 296-5760

Wisconsin

**University of Wisconsin at
Green Bay**
Department of Communication
Processes
2420 N Nicolet Drive
Green Bay, WI 54311-7001
Phone: (414) 465-2348

Canada

**Columbia College CTEFLA
Program**
6037 Marlborough Avenue
Burnaby, BC V5H 3L6
Canada
Phone: (604) 430-6422
Notes: This school offers a
CTEFLA program.

**Vancouver Community
College**
TESL Certificate Program
Continuing Education
1155 E Broadway
P.O. Box 24785, Station F
Vancouver, BC V5N 5N2
Canada
Phone: (604) 871-7070

International Language
Institute
1496 Lower Water Street
Halifax, NS B3J 1R9
Canada
Phone: (902) 429-3636
Notes: This school offers a
CTEFLA program.

Canadian Cooperative
Language and Cultural
Studies, Inc.
635 Markham Street, Second
Floor
Toronto, ON M6G 2M1
Canada
Phone: (416) 588-3900
Notes: This is a nonprofit organi-
zation offering an 80-hour TESL
course. Emphasis is on adult in-
struction and understanding stu-
dents from other cultures.

George Brown College
TESL Department Casa Loma
Campus
2 Dartnell Avenue
Toronto, ON M5T 1M3
Canada
Phone: (416) 944-4953
Notes: This school offers a part-

time, one-year program and is
currently considering daytime
courses.

Humber College
88 Industry Street
Weston, ON M6M 4L8
Canada
Phone: (416) 763-5141
Notes: A sixteen-week graduate-
level program is offered once a
year, usually in September.

Concordia University
Center for TESL
Montreal, PQ H3G 1M8
Canada
Phone: (514) 398-6982
Notes: This school offers a TESL
course.

University of Saskatchewan
CERTESL Program
Kirk Hall, Room 326
Saskatoon, SK S7N 0W0
Canada
Phone: (306) 966-5563
Notes: This school offers ESL cor-
respondence courses to students
worldwide.

TEFL/RSA training in Eastern Europe

The following foreign schools and organizations offer teaching certification, usually RSA, in or convenient to the Czech Republic, Slovakia,
Poland, or Hungary:

International Language House
(RSA)
Bimbo u. 7
Budapest H-1022
Hungary
Phone: (01) 115-5275

International House-Krakow
(RSA)
ul. Czapskich 5
Krakow 31 110
Poland
Phone: (012) 21 94 40
or (012) 22 64 82

International House (RSA)
Moravske Namesti 2
Brno 602 00
Czech Republic
**International Language
 Centers (RSA)**
International House
Lupacova 1
Prague 3
Czech Republic

Transworld Teachers (TEFL)
683 Sutter Street
San Francisco, CA 94102
Phone: (800) 241-8071
 or (415) 776-8071
Fax: (415) 441-1326
Recorded newsletter hotline
 (415) 995-2554

There are several schools in Eastern Europe that train native speakers of English to teach using their own methods and programs. Berlitz is probably the best known of these. These schools are not listed here because their specially designed training programs are not recognized universally by private English language schools or public employers. They are geared specifically to fit the structure of the school's particular teaching methods. If you consider taking a job in any of these schools, just be aware that down the road your experience will come in handy, but another employer may not consider you certified to teach as he would if you had RSA certification.

Exploring other opportunities

FREELANCE WORK

Teaching English is not the only work available to Americans in Eastern Europe (though it is by far the most common source of employment in all of the four countries and thus the focus of this book). If you want to look for other kinds of jobs, you must be more selective in your choice of destinations and more diligent in your job search. Yes, there are those who, with little preparation, are lucky to find positions in their chosen fields soon after their arrival, but they are the exception rather than the rule. William Corley of Seattle related his early experience in the Czech Republic:

> ❝ I came to Prague to teach English, and then discovered that it wasn't the best use of my time, so I moved on to a press agency. I corrected and proofread all the important documents in English. It was there that I began to study Czech. When I could make my own way with the language, I started to peruse the want ads in Annonce [Prague's classified ad newspaper], and I found a job with an import/export company. ❞

The advantage that many skilled North American job applicants in Eastern Europe have over their native counterparts is greater experience with advanced technologies. The former Socialist regimes did not foster economic progress like their democratic, capitalist counterparts in the West. Consequently, many skilled Eastern Europeans lag behind their Western colleagues in computer programming, advertising and marketing, and business management, to name a few areas. There are obstacles, though. Because of economic hardship and rampant unemployment in certain areas, it can be difficult to get formal residence status or a work permit, which makes finding work difficult, if not impossible. You will need to prove that you are not taking a job away from a Pole, a Hungarian, a Czech, or a Slovak. In other words, your prospective employer will have to document your unique skills in order to convince the rubber stamp-wielding bureaucrats down at the local city hall that your employment doesn't translate into "one less job for a local."

For more information on jobs other than teaching English, consult each country's Other Opportunities section.

INTERNSHIPS

College students or graduates may choose to pursue an internship in Eastern Europe. If you have a special area of expertise (engineering, marketing, or computer programming, for example) and an interest in applying your expertise overseas, consider an internship as an alternative to teaching English or searching for a job independently once you arrive. Internships range in length from a couple of months to a year or more. Often, credit is available through colleges and universities, though you must arrange this well in advance of your departure.

Although internships may be low-paying, they are often used as stepping stones to more permanent, higher-paying positions. It also is more likely that they can be arranged in advance, taking care of any anxieties you might have going abroad without an established job.

Inquire through your college or university, or contact any of the following organizations:

Association for International Practical Training
10400 Little Patuxent Parkway, Suite 250
Columbia, MD 21044-3510
Phone: (410) 997-2200

People-to-People International
501 E Armour Boulevard
Kansas City, MO 64110-2200
Phone: (816) 531-4701

Worldwide Internships and Service Education (WISE)
303 Craig Street
Pittsburgh, PA 15213
Phone: (412) 681-8120

Georgetown University Internship Programs
P.O. Box 2298
Washington, DC 20057
Phone: (202) 687-5055

AISEC–US

AISEC (a French acronym for The International Association of Students in Economics and Commerce) is a worldwide association offering short- and long-term internships abroad for students at colleges or universities with AISEC chapters. Internships are offered to students studying economics, business, marketing, and computer science.

For more information, contact:

AISEC-US
135 W 50th Street, 20th Floor
New York, NY 10020
Phone: (212) 757-3774

AIPT student exchanges program

The Student Exchanges Program of the Association for International Practical Training offers three- to twelve-month placements and summer opportunities for juniors, seniors, and graduate students from accredited colleges. Positions are taken mainly by students studying engineering, architecture, mathematics, and computer and other sciences.

IAESTE Trainee Program
10 Corporate Center, Suite 250
10400 Little Patuxent Parkway
Columbia, MD 21044-3510
Phone: (410) 997-2200
Fax: (410) 992-3924

STUDY ABROAD PROGRAMS

Study abroad programs are another possibility for students interested in living in Eastern Europe. Living the life of a student while considering all the other possibilities of living and working in Eastern Europe may be just the ticket for those who are a little daunted by the idea of up and leaving for foreign destinations without the benefit of a planned itinerary. Study abroad programs send individuals and groups overseas for a quarter, a semester, or a year. Intensive language programs often precede departure. Be sure to do your research and select the program best suited to your needs and interests.

Czech Republic and Slovakia

Penn in Prague
Penn Summer Abroad
College of General Studies
University of Pennsylvania
3440 Market Street, Suite 100
Philadelphia, PA 19104-3335
Phone: (215) 898-5738

Penn Abroad
International Programs
Office of International Studies
University of Pennsylvania
133 Bennett Hall
Philadelphia, PA 19104-6275
Phone: (215) 898-4661
Fax: (215) 898-2622

Northern Illinois University
Foreign Study Office
Northern Illinois University,
    Winston Hall 100
De Kalb, IL 60115
Phone: (815) 753-1501

**Northwestern University
Summer Study Abroad-
Prague**
Northwestern University
    Summer Session
2115 N Campus Drive
Evanston, IL 60208
Phone: (800) FINDS-NU
Email: SUMMER95@nwu.edu

Study Abroad in Prague
IntelCross, Inc.
822 College Avenue, Room 791
Kentfield, CA 94914

Phone: (800) 788-3922
   or (415) 331-3151
Fax: (415) 331-3153
Email: intelcrs@well.sf.ca.us

Hungary

Beaver College Center for Education Abroad
450 S Easton Road
Glenside, PA 19038
Phone: (800) 755-5607

Beloit College
World Affairs Center
700 College Street
Beloit, WI 53511-5595
Phone: (608) 363-2269
Fax: (608) 363-2689
Email: bigalket@beloit.edu

Northern Illinois University
Foreign Study Office

Northern Illinois University,
   Winston Hall 100
De Kalb, IL 60115
Phone: (815) 753-1501

University of Wisconsin-Madison
Office of International Studies
   and Programs
261 Bascom Hall
500 Lincoln Drive
Madison, WI
Phone: (608) 262-2851
Fax: (608) 262-6998
Email: abroad@macc.wisc.edu

Poland

The Global Campus
University of Minnesota
106 Nicholson Hall
Minneapolis, MN 55455
Phone: (612) 625-2571

University of Wisconsin-Stevens Point
International Programs
108 Collins Classroom Center
University of Wisconsin–Stevens Point
Stevens Point, WI 54481
Phone: (715) 346-2717

Sopot School of Polish
Al. Niepodleglisci 763
Sopot 81 838
Poland
Phone: (58) 51 41 31

Penn in Warsaw
Penn Summer Abroad
College of General Studies
University of Pennsylvania
3440 Market Street, Suite 100
Philadelphia, PA 19104-3335
Phone: (215) 898-5738

OTHER RESOURCES

There are several magazines, newsletters, and books geared toward independent international travel and employment. These are often good sources of opportunities to work, study, and travel abroad, including opportunities in the countries of Eastern Europe. Some of the more useful publications are listed below.

Also below are Internet addresses for a few of the better sites for general information on the countries of Eastern Europe. These sites are characterized by high-quality information, snappy presentation, and links to other related sites. (A list of recommended Eastern European travel guides appears later in this chapter.)

Magazines

International Travel News
520 Calvados Avenue
Sacramento, CA 95815
Phone: (800) 486-4968

Transitions Abroad: The Guide to Learning, Living, and Working Overseas
Department TRA
Box 3000
Denville, NJ 07834
Phone: (800) 293-0373

Newsletters

Consumer Reports Travel Letter
Box 53629
Boulder, CO 80322-3629
Phone: (800) 234-1970

International Employment Gazette
1525 Wade Hampton Boulevard
Greenville, SC 29609
Phone: (800) 882-9188

International Employment Hotline
P.O. Box 3030
Oakton, VA 22124
Phone: (703) 620-1972
Fax: (703) 620-1973

Books

Transitions Abroad Alternative Travel Directory: America's #1 Guide to Living, Learning, and Working Overseas, 1995. Clayton A. Hubbs, ed., Transitions Abroad Publishing, 1995. 256 p.

People to People: Czech-Slovakia, Hungary, Bulgaria. Jim Haynes. Zephyr Press.

People to People: Poland. Jim Haynes. Zephyr Press.

Work Your Way around the World. Susan Griffith. 7th ed. Vacation Work; distributed in the United States by Peterson's Guides, 1995. 512 p.

Internet resources

The gopher and USENET sites are text-based, while the http:// sites are graphics-based and require an Internet browser, such as Netscape, Mosaic, or Netcruiser.

General

http://reenic.utexas.edu/reenic.html
http://www.itaiep.doc.gov/eebic/cdceec.html

Czech Republic and Slovakia

http://reenic.utexas.edu/reenic/Countries/Czech/czech.html
gopher://inic.utexas.edu/11/reenic/Country-Dir/Slovakia
USENET newsgroup: soc.culture.czecho-slovak

Hungary

http://www.fsz.bme.hu/hungary/homepage.html

Poland

http://reenic.utexas.edu/reenic/Countries/Poland/poland.html

Travel preparations

YOUR PAPERS, PLEASE

No, you can't leave your thick pocketbook or heavy wallet at home. International travel requires that you keep your papers in order, and in some cases on your person at all times. It's worth the hassle, though. You won't regret being organized and on top of your game when an immigration officer interrupts your snoozing on the train to check your passport or when a prospective employer wants to make sure you've actually taken all the coursework you boast about.

Passport

All international travelers need a passport valid for at least six months beyond their planned date of return to the United States. Contact your nearest passport agency for information and an application. Make sure you apply well in advance of your planned date of departure because the application process can take several weeks (sometimes longer during busy times). Passports usually are valid for ten years from the date of issue. If you were younger than eighteen when you were issued your first passport, make sure to check the expiration date because these passports expire five years from the date of issue. As a precaution, leave a photocopy of the first page of your passport with a friend or family member at home and carry another copy with you, but be sure to keep it separate from the original.

Passport photos

If you are applying for a new passport, consider getting some extra passport-size photos taken. (If you have your passport already, it would be wise to get some photos taken anyway.) They will come in handy when you submit visa applications, job applications, and when you apply for a work permit or residency status. Not all countries in Eastern Europe require photos for applications, but it is sensible to carry a few spares with you just in case.

International driver's license

Driving a car abroad over an extended period may require an international driver's license. You must be over eighteen and have a valid United States driver's license. To obtain an international driver's license, bring two passport-size photos to your nearest American Automobile Association (AAA) office. The license is valid for one year and costs US$10 for members and $15 for nonmembers. Make sure that you become familiar with the different driving laws of the countries you'll be traveling through, since it's very likely that they will be different from traffic laws in the United States.

The Student Identity Card

Available at student travel organizations (Council Travel, STA, etc.), the international Student Identity Card can get you sizable discounts on airfares as well as many transportation and admission costs. It also identifies you as a student, which could come in handy when you apply for a work permit. The Youth Identification Card is similar, but for non-students under the age of twenty-six. (Don't bother going out of your way to get a youth card because your passport proves your age as well as anything.) It's not as easy, however, to get youth discounts in some areas of Eastern Europe as it is in Western Europe.

College diploma or transcript

If you can get original copies of your transcripts or an official document from your college or university stating your date of graduation and degree, bring them. They will come in handy during interviews, especially if you don't have a teaching certificate. If your degree or a good portion of your coursework is related to the various demands of English teaching, your prospective employer will likely take an interest in you. Or at the very least, you will be able to prove your level of education.

Teaching certificate and resume

A teaching certificate, such as TEFL or RSA, is the single most valuable document for those looking for work in the English-teaching field in Eastern Europe. If you have one, bring it. Make copies, too, just in case. If you have teaching (or related) experience, an up-to-date resume is essential. Letters of recommendation also will prove helpful, especially if they give your interviewer evidence of your potential or proof of your experience. In an increasingly competitive job market, any of these documents will bolster your chances of getting hired.

Information to go

Embassies, consulates, and tourism offices offer a wealth of information (most of it free) to prospective travelers. Take the opportunity to get as much information as you can prior to your departure. It will save you time, money, and potential hassles later on. (Embassies and consulates for each country are listed in the section below. Tourism offices are listed in the individual country chapters.)

VISAS, WORK PERMITS, AND OTHER FORMALITIES

Though each of the four countries differs in the way that it treats foreigners with respect to issuing work and residency permits, it is important to note several common points:

- Citizens of the United States do not need visas to enter the Czech Republic, Slovakia, Poland, or Hungary. Canadian citizens, on the other hand, might require entry visas. Since the laws change frequently, consult the nearest consulate or embassy. (Visas are made available through the nearest embassy or consulate in Canada, or may be granted either at a Czech, Slovak, Polish, or Hungarian consulate in another nearby European country with a Canadian consulate, or sometimes at the border prior to travel into one of the four countries. However, do not rely on visas being available at all border crossings. For example, in the Czech Republic no visas are available on trains or buses. You can get a visa at the airport, or at larger border crossings if you are traveling by car.)
- The laws that regulate a foreigner's ability to legally reside and work in these countries change constantly. This is due to (among other things) instability in the labor markets and inconsistencies in the legislative machinery of the governments of Eastern Europe.
- Bureaucratic red tape is rampant, so the work permit application process often takes several months.
- Work permits are issued for individual jobs via a specific employer. You cannot randomly transfer work permits if you decide to take a job with another school or company.

Though it is recommended that you abide by the laws of the land, many American expats choose to work without a permit and stay for months or even years without applying for residency status. Be advised, however, that this is risky business. Despite rumors of people working in the "black," within the past two years the countries of Eastern Europe have stepped up their efforts to seek out individuals or companies employing illegal workers. Large financial fines or deportation could result if you're caught; therefore, correct working papers are sought increasingly by both officials and companies looking to hire new employees.

Because of the various employment taxes and social security benefits tied to work permits, it is usually the employer's responsibility to see that their workers apply for the proper documentation. They may be subject to fines if they are caught hiring and employing foreigners

The cities of Eastern Europe are closely situated. Most are not more than a few hours' train ride away from each other.

under the table. Moreover, there are certain advantages to having the proper papers: you frequently are covered by the government health care plan and can get certain discounts (on public transportation and bus and train fares, for example) if you possess a residency permit (similar to a green card in the United States).

Czech Republic

The Czech Republic once had the reputation of being one of the most lenient countries in Europe with respect to both American travelers and prospective expatriates. In fact, it used to be that because of the lack of enforcement by the Czech government, many Americans who lived and worked in the Czech Republic never bothered to register with the local authorities for a residency permit or apply for a work permit. Though this was never the recommended approach, there was plenty of evidence to suggest that it was easy to get away with. Even today, Prague is rumored to be home to roughly 20,000 Americans, of whom fewer than 2,000 have actually documented their status with the authorities.

In recent years, however, that leniency has changed. In 1994 the Czech police conducted a number of "sweeps" through the busiest squares of Prague and arrested up to 200 foreigners who could not produce appropriate papers. Although it's a hassle, keep in mind that work permits (often difficult to come by because of bureaucratic red tape) are generally made available to those who persist. On the other hand, it is still true that visas are not required for Americans to enter the country.

The laws and regulations that govern the issuance of work permits and residency permits change constantly. Depending on who is in charge at any given time and place, these permits may take weeks or months to get. The official word from the Czech labor department is:

❝ *Work permits to employ foreigners are issued on the basis of the situation in the labor market and with regard to the prognosis of developments in the labor market.*❞

In other words, if a specific position can be filled easily by a Czech then the government will not issue a work permit to the foreign national seeking that position. For prospective English teachers, this usually does not pose obstacles. There are enough English teaching jobs available and relatively few Czechs capable of filling those positions at the same level as a native speaker.

Having a work permit does entitle you to free medical care and gives you the privilege of paying Czech prices. It also puts you in the position of having to pay taxes. According to one woman who was teaching in a small town in western Bohemia, all of this is "worth it beyond a few months' stay." The formal requirements include a police background check, a physical exam (possibly including an AIDS test), and a contract to work full-time. It takes roughly two months for your papers to clear all the bureaucratic hurdles, desk to desk, office to office. Once the process is initiated through your employer, it's usually no problem to begin working. For the latest information, make sure to contact the Czech embassy.

Czech embassies

United States

Embassy of the Czech Republic
3900 Spring of Freedom Street NW
Washington, DC 20008
Phone: (202) 363-6315

Canada

Embassy of the Czech Republic
541 Sussex Drive
Ottawa, ON K1N 6Z6
Canada
Phone: (613) 562-3875

Slovakia

Compared to the Czechs, the Slovaks seem much more suspicious of foreigners (Americans included) in their country. Part of the problem is the comparative instability of the Slovak government. The Slovaks have not managed to match the economic and political successes of the Czechs. Successive political leaders have been ineffective in converting Slovakia to a stable market economy. A whole host of problems created during the years of Socialist repression, combined with a more gradual approach to economic reform, makes for both confusion and uncertainty. The Slovaks also seem to feel that they have been ignored by the governments of the West in comparison to the Czechs. Needless to say, all of this makes Slovakia a somewhat less-attractive destination for North Americans who want to live and work in Eastern Europe.

United States citizens do not need a visa to enter Slovakia. As in the Czech Republic, work permits and residency permits are required by the local authorities for those who want to stay and work and must be obtained via an employer. Canadian citizens must obtain a visa to enter the Republic of Slovakia (at press time, $55 CDN).

An application for a Long Term Stay Permit is formally required for anyone who intends to work or study in the Slovak Republic. The application (in Slovak) must be accompanied by a preliminary job agreement, notification of acceptance for study or training, legal copy of entry into the commercial register, or legal documentation of a company's origination. Also required are a document stating the source of your income and a document that verifies accommodation (a lease or rental agreement). More specific information on applying for work and residency permits can be obtained from the Slovak Embassy.

Once again, it is not uncommon for American expats to work without ever getting work papers. It is, however, becoming increasingly difficult. Stories circulate about unfriendly and even outright wicked bureaucrats who decide whether or not to issue permits based on their particular mood at the time, rather than according to the laws. There has also been talk of requiring foreigners to take AIDS and other medical tests before they are eligible for residency status.

Slovak embassies

United States

Embassy of the Slovak Republic
2201 Wisconsin Avenue NW, Suite 380
Washington, DC 20007
Phone: (202) 965-5164

Canada
Embassy of the Slovak Republic
50 Rideau Terrace
Ottawa, ON K1N ZA1
Canada
Phone: (613) 749-4442

Hungary

In Hungary, the rules that control the granting of work permits and residency status are stricter and more of an inconvenience. "Working" visa applications must be submitted to a Hungarian embassy or consulate outside the country in the applicant's native country or place of residence abroad. In order to apply for a visa, the applicant must possess a labor permit. The employer must apply for the labor permit, which is issued by the Labor Office in Hungary. Labor permit applications must be accompanied by the applicant's degree or certification, which attests to the applicant's qualifications for the job, and a health certificate. (Certain teaching jobs at institutes of higher education are exempted from the labor permit requirements.)

Requiring a labor permit enables the Hungarian authorities to make sure that there are no unemployed Hungarians who are qualified for the same position. The health certificate requirement assures that foreigners cannot take undue advantage of Hungary's public health benefits.

If someone who has already entered Hungary wishes to obtain a work visa, they must first apply for a labor permit inside the country, and then leave Hungary to pick up their work visa. It's often possible to get this taken care of in Vienna (only a three-hour train ride from Budapest).

Despite the hassle of obtaining working visas and labor permits, many teachers of English obtain all the necessary papers with relative ease, sometimes with assistance from their employers. Even with the government's strict attention to their own visa and work permit laws, Hungary remains a great place for North Americans to pursue employment, especially in the English-teaching field.

Hungarian embassies and consulates

United States
Embassy of the Republic of Hungary
3910 Shoemaker Street NW
Washington, DC 20008
Phone: (202) 362-6730

Consulate General of the Republic of Hungary
223 E 52nd Street
New York, NY 10022
Phone: (212) 752-0661

Consulate General of the
Republic of Hungary
11766 Wilshire, Suite 410
Los Angeles, CA 90025
Phone: (310) 473-9344

Canada

Embassy of the Republic of
Hungary
299 Beverly Street
Ottawa, ON K2P 0V9
Canada
Phone: (613) 230-2717

Consulate General of the
Republic of Hungary
1200 McGill College Avenue,
Suite 2030
Montreal, PQ H3B 4G7
Canada
Phone: (514) 393-1555

Consulate General of the
Republic of Hungary
102 Bloor Street West SW, Suite
1005
Toronto, ON M5S 1M8
Canada
Phone: (416) 923-3596

Poland

As in the other countries of Eastern Europe, Poland's work visa and
residency permit rules are designed to protect the Polish work force
from foreign competition, particularly during these times of high unemployment. Because the Polish government has experienced many
difficulties since 1989—prime ministers have come and gone, scan-
dals are common, and reviving the stagnant economy remains a
Herculean task—don't count on the rules staying the same.

Americans don't need a visa to enter Poland, but they do require
both a work permit and residency status for stays longer than ninety
days. Because of the high rate of unemployment, foreigners who are
looking for jobs often find it difficult to get work papers; however,
not many Poles speak English, so prospective teachers are not perceived by the authorities as being in competition with many people
in the Polish workforce. Expect the permit process to take as long as
it does anywhere else in the region.

Though big business has made quick advances in the largest and most
religious of the countries of Eastern Europe (PepsiCo announced a half-
billion-dollar investment in Poland during the summer of 1993), it is
not as popular a destination among North American expats as the Czech
Republic or Hungary. This is not to say that it isn't an interesting or
appealing choice, it's just not as fashionable as Prague or Budapest.

Polish embassies and consulates

United States

Embassy of the Republic of
Poland
2640 16th Street NW
Washington, DC 20009
Phone: (202) 234-3800

Consulate General of the
Republic of Poland
12400 Wilshire Boulevard,
Suite 555
Los Angeles, CA 90025
Phone: (310) 442-8500

Consulate General of the
Republic of Poland
1540 N Lake Shore Drive
Chicago, IL 60610
Phone: (312) 337-8166

Consulate General of the
Republic of Poland
233 Medicine Avenue
New York, NY 10016
Phone: (212) 889-8360

Canada
Embassy of the Republic of
Poland
433 Daly Street, Suite 2
Ottawa, ON K1N 6H3
Canada
Phone: (613) 789-0468

GETTING THERE

There are many ways of getting to Eastern Europe. Exploring several different options can save you some money and provide you greater flexibility. Regardless of the option you choose, you should plan your trip at least a couple of months in advance in order to get the best available airfares and most convenient flights.

For the budget-oriented, it may be cheaper to fly to larger Western European hubs, such as Frankfurt or Berlin, and then take a train or bus to your final destination. This approach may also allow you greater flexibility if you are undecided about where you will end up. However, this route is most effective when your connecting train or bus ride is relatively short.

As Eastern European destinations have become more popular over the last several years, plane fares have dropped in price, while the number and frequency of flights have increased. This bodes well for those who want to fly directly to their country of choice without many layovers or transfers to buses or trains along the way. It may cost more initially to purchase a ticket to Prague, Bratislava, Budapest, or Warsaw, but it can save time and the hassle of figuring out the best and least expensive way of traveling over land from an airport in Western Europe to your final destination in Eastern Europe.

Unrestricted economy-class tickets

If you want maximum flexibility and are not concerned about cost, check into unrestricted economy-class tickets. These tickets will allow you to change dates or destinations and even postpone your trip for up to one year. Expect to pay at least US$800 to $900 for an Eastern European destination.

Apex tickets

If you're budget-minded and know exactly when you want to travel, you should consider an apex ticket. Though there are some signifi-

Since the fall of communism in 1989, it is rare to find statues of communist heroes still standing in Eastern Europe.

cant restrictions, you can save a lot of money if you don't mind committing to your departure and return dates in advance. Apex tickets are generally nonrefundable and subject to penalties if you want to make changes after you purchase them. There are, however, different kinds of apex tickets so you should be careful to check exactly what restrictions are attached. Make sure to ask what you'll be charged if you need to make changes.

Round-the-world tickets

If you plan to travel extensively for at least a year, a round-the-world ticket can be an inexpensive option. It's important to have an idea of where you're going to stop before you purchase this kind of ticket so that you can compare the price to what it would cost you to purchase individual tickets between each planned destination. Generally, you must travel in the same direction (i.e., east to west or west to east). Round-the-world tickets allow you to make unlimited stops using a combination of airlines for a set price.

Courier companies

If you are short on funds and don't mind packing lightly, you might consider flying as an air courier. As a courier, you are hired by a courier service to accompany packages to an overseas destination. Courier companies need people to accompany packages because unattended luggage is not allowed on international passenger flights. The courier service simply purchases a seat and sells it cheaply in exchange for luggage space. This is completely legal and in most cases you never even see the luggage. If you are heading to Eastern Europe for a stay of a month or more, you will obviously need to take more than you can fit in your carry-on bag (which is all you're allowed as a courier because your luggage allowance is taken by the courier service's package). In this case, you will have to pay an extra charge for any additional personal luggage you need to take. In most instances, though, the total price will be much less than a regular fare. To be eligible, you must be over eighteen years of age.

For more information on courier flights, try *The Courier Air Travel Handbook* by Mark I. Field. This 144-page book is filled with information on the ins and outs of flying as an air courier (available for US$9.95 plus shipping from Perpetual Press, P.O. Box 45628, Seattle, WA 98145-0628).

Courier services

United States

Way To Go Travel (New York)
404 Park Avenue S, Suite 1304
New York, NY 10016
Phone: (212) 840-8851

Halbart Express (Boston)
147-05 176th Street
Jamaica, NY 11434
Phone: (718) 656-5000

Mid-America Travel Marketing (Chicago)
3011 S Wolf Road
Westchester, IL 60154
Phone: (708) 620-8080

Now Voyager (Houston, New York)
74 Varick Street
New York, NY 10013
Phone: (212) 431-1616

Discount Travel International (Los Angeles)
930 W Hyde Park Boulevard
Inglewood, CA 90302
Phone: (310) 672-1100
  or (310) 330-7096

Canada

F.B. On Board Courier Services (Vancouver)
E107 4871 Miller Road
Richmond, BC V7B 1K8
Canada
Phone: (604) 278-1266

F.B. On Board Courier Services (Toronto)
10225 Ryan Avenue
Dorval, PQ H9P 1A2
Canada
Phone: (514) 633-0740

Consolidators and discount agencies

Consolidators contract with various airlines to offer discounted tickets to retail agents and individual customers. They typically offer international flights for twenty to thirty percent less than normal economy fares. Although this is an economical way to travel, be aware that ticket deliveries are notoriously slow, and refunds can be made only through the consolidator. Consolidator tickets can be obtained through your travel agency or directly from discount brokers.

ARIZONA

Cefra Discount Travel
Scottsdale
Phone: (800) 264-5055
   or (602) 948-5055
Fax: (602) 948-6896

Council Travel
Tempe
Phone: (602) 966-3544
Fax: (602) 966-7235

Panda Travel
Phoenix
Phone: (800) 447-2632
   or (602) 943-3383 in AZ
Fax: (602) 943-5984

Southwest Travel Systems
Phoenix
Phone: (800) 787-8728
   or (602) 255-0234
Fax: (602) 255-0220

CALIFORNIA
(Northern)

Airbound
San Francisco
Phone: (415) 834-9445
Fax: (415) 834-9447

Air Brokers
San Francisco
Phone: (800) 883-3273
   or (415) 397-1383
Fax: (415) 397-4767

All Continents Travel
Burlingame
Phone: (800) 325-2553
   or (415) 548-9477 in CA
Fax: (415) 579-7387

All Star Travel
Santa Clara
Phone: (408) 247-9743
Fax: (408) 247-2762

Anglo California Travel
San Jose
Phone: (408) 257-2257
Fax: (408) 257-2664

B.E.T. World Travel
San Jose
Phone: (800) 747-1476
   or (408) 229-7880
Fax: (408) 365-1101

British European Travel
San Jose
Phone: (800) 747-1476
   or (408) 984-7576
Fax: (408) 365-1101

Budget Traveler
Sausalito
Phone: (415) 331-3700
Fax: (415) 331-1377

Char-Tours
San Francisco
Phone: (800) 323-4444
   or (415) 495-8881
Fax: (415) 543-8010

Community Travel Service
Oakland
Phone: (510) 653-0990
Fax: (510) 653-9071

Council Travel
Berkeley
Phone: (510) 848-8604
Fax: (510) 848-8634
Davis
Phone: (916) 752-2285
Fax: (916) 752-3691
Palo Alto
Phone: (415) 325-3888
Fax: (415) 325-4325
San Francisco (Bush Street)
Phone: (415) 421-3473
Fax: (415) 421-5603
San Francisco (Irving Street)
Phone: (415) 566-6222
Fax: (415) 566-6730

Custom Travel
Daly City
Phone: (800) 535-9797
   or (415) 239-4200
Fax: 415-239-0121

Festival of Asia
San Francisco
Phone: (800) 533-9953
   or (415) 693-0880
Fax: (415) 693-0884
Limited tickets available to
Eastern Europe

Global Access Travel Group
San Francisco
Phone: (800) 938-5355
   or (415) 896-5333
Fax: (415) 227-4641

Omniglobe Travel
San Francisco
Phone: (800) 894-9942
   or (415) 433-9312
Fax: 415-433-9315

Overseas Tours
Milbrae
Phone: (800) 323-8777
   or (415) 692-4892
Fax: (415) 692-7450

Scan the World
Palo Alto
Phone: (800) 775-0200
   or (415) 325-0876
Fax: (415) 325-0893

Skytours
San Francisco
Phone: (800) 246-8687
   or (415) 777-3544
Fax: (415) 777-9290

STA Travel
Berkeley
Phone: (510) 642-3000
Fax: (510) 649-1407
San Francisco
Phone: (415) 391-8407
Fax: (415) 391-4105

Sunco Travel
San Francisco
Phone: (800) 989-6017
   or (415) 291-9960
Fax: (415) 291-9950

Sun Destinations
San Francisco
Phone: (415) 398-1313
Fax: (415) 398-1399

Travel Design Unlimited
Mountain View
Phone: (415) 969-2000
Fax: (415) 966-8262

Travel Time
San Francisco
Phone: (800) 235-3253
   or (415) 677-0799
Fax: (415) 391-1856

CALIFORNIA
(Southern)

All Continents Travel
Los Angeles
Phone: (800) 368-6822
  or (310) 337-1641
Fax: (310) 645-0412

ANZ Travel/Australia New Zealand Travel
Laguna Hills
Phone: (800) 281-4449
  or (714) 586-1112
Fax: (714) 586-1124

Cheap Tickets
Los Angeles
Phone: (800) 377-1000,
  (213) 233-6977,
  or (310) 645-5054
Fax: (800) 284-4443

Continental Travel Shop
Santa Monica
Phone: (310) 453-8655
Fax: (310) 453-5093

Council Travel
La Jolla
Phone: (619) 452-0630
Fax: (619) 452-2448
Long Beach
Phone: (310) 598-3338
Fax: (310) 598-7998
Los Angeles
Phone: (310) 208-3551
Fax: (310) 208-4407
San Diego
Phone: (619) 270-6401
Fax: (619) 270-6419
Santa Barbara
Phone: (805) 562-8080
Fax: (805) 562-8740

Discover Wholesale Travel
Irvine
Phone: (800) 576-7770

  or (714) 833-1136
Fax: (714) 833-1176

Fare Deal Travel
San Diego
Phone: (800) 243-2785
  or (619) 236-8869
Fax: (619) 236-0036

Flight Coordinators
Santa Monica
Phone: (800) 544-3644
  or (310) 581-5600
Fax: (310) 581-5620

Jetway Tours
Los Angeles
Phone: (800) 421-8771
  or (818) 990-2918

K & K Travel
Fullerton
Phone: (800) 523-1374
  or (714) 525-4494
Fax: (714) 525-4586

Picasso Travel
Los Angeles
Phone: (800) 247-7283
  or (310) 645-4400
Fax: (310) 645-0412

Rebel Tours
Valencia
Phone: (800) 227-3235
  or (805) 294-0900
Fax: (805) 294-0981

STA Travel
Los Angeles (West Hollywood)
Phone: (213) 934-8722
Fax: (213) 937-6008
Los Angeles (Westwood)
Phone: (310) 824-1574
Fax: (310) 824-2928
Santa Monica
Phone: (310) 394-5126
Fax: (310) 394-4041

Sunbeam Travel (Payless Travel)
Beverly Hills
Phone: (213) 653-6718
Fax: (213) 655-4393

Supersonic Travel
Hollywood
Phone: (800) 439-3030
  or (213) 851-0333 in CA
Fax: (213) 851-0444

TS Travel
Woodland Hills
Phone: (818) 346-8600
Fax: (818) 883-4624

World Link Travel Network
Los Angeles
Phone: (310) 342-1280
Fax: (310) 342-1288
Santa Monica
Phone: (310) 453-8884
Fax: (310) 453-7924

COLORADO

Council Travel
Boulder
Phone: (303) 447-8101
Fax: (303) 447-9798
Denver
Phone: (303) 571-0630
Fax: (303) 571-0718

Fare Deals Travel
Englewood
Phone: (800) 878-2929
  or (303) 792-2929
Fax: (303) 792-2954

Overseas Travel
Aurora
Phone: (800) 783-7196
  or (303) 337-7196
Fax: (303) 696-1226

CONNECTICUT

Council Travel
New Haven

Phone: (203) 562-5335
Fax: (203) 562-8123

FLORIDA

Arnsdorff Travel
Apopka
Phone: (407) 886-1343
Fax: (407) 886-5959

Cosmopolitan Travel Center
Fort Lauderdale
Phone: (800) 548-7206
  or (305) 523-0973
Fax: (305) 523-8324

Council Travel
Miami
Phone: (305) 670-9261
Fax: (305) 670-9266

Direct Line Travel
Miami
Phone: (800) 422-2585
  or (305) 385-2585
Fax: (305) 382-9429

Getaway Travel International
Coral Gables
Phone: (800) 683-6336
  or (305) 446-7855
Fax: (305) 444-6647

Hostway Travel
Fort Lauderdale
Phone: (800) 327-3207
  or (305) 966-8500
Fax: (305) 966-7815

Interworld Travel
Coral Gables
Phone: (800) 468-3796
  or (305) 443-4929
Fax: (305) 443-0351

Mena Tours and Travel
Miami
Phone: (800) 327-4514
  or (305) 649-7066
Fax: (305) 643-4615

Rebel Tours
Orlando
Phone: (800) 732-3588
  or (407) 352-3600
Fax: (407) 352-3609

The Smart Traveler
Miami
Phone: (800) 448-3338
  or (305) 448-3338
Fax: (305) 443-3544

Travac
Orlando
Phone: (800) 872-8800
  or (407) 896-0014
Fax: (407) 896-0046

TFI Tours International
(Miami Travel Center)
Miami
Phone: (305) 895-8115
Fax: (305) 895-4653

GEORGIA

All World Travel
Atlanta
Phone: (404) 458-3366
Fax: (404) 454-6023

Alpha Travel
Marietta
Phone: (800) 793-8424
  or (770) 988-9982
Fax: (770) 988-9986

Council Travel
Atlanta
Phone: (404) 377-9997
Fax: (404) 377-9995

Everest Travel
Atlanta
Phone: (404) 231-5222
Fax: (404) 231-9745

GIT/Travel Wholesalers
Alpharetta
Phone: (770) 518-7060
Fax: (770) 399-6957

JC Tour & Travel
Doraville
Phone: (800) 239-1232
  or (404) 451-1236
Fax: (404) 451-9969

McAbee Travel
Atlanta
Phone: (800) 622-2335
  or (770) 396-9988
Fax: (770) 393-0084

Midtown Travel Consultants
Atlanta
Phone: (800) 548-8904
  or (404) 872-8308
Fax: (404) 881-6322

Skyway Travel
Atlanta
Phone: (404) 525-6528
Fax: (404) 525-6824

Spalding Corners Travel
Norcross
Phone: (404) 441-1164
Fax: (404) 448-1723

HAWAII

Cheap Tickets
Honolulu
Phone: (808) 947-3717
Fax: (808) 284-4443

Pali Travel
Honolulu
Phone: (808) 533-3608
Fax: (808) 524-2483

Riverside Travel & Services
Honolulu
Phone: (808) 521-5645
Fax: (808) 523-2342

ILLINOIS

Austin Travel
Elmwood Park
Phone: (800) 545-2655
  or (708) 452-1010
Fax: (708) 452-9264

Compare Travel
Chicago
Phone: (312) 853-1144
Fax: (312) 853-2446

Council Travel
Chicago
Phone: (312) 951-0585
Fax: (312) 951-7437
Evanston
Phone: (708) 475-5070
Fax: (708) 475-0857

Cut Rate Travel
Deerfield
Phone: (800) 388-0575
    or (708) 405-0575
Fax: (708) 405-0587

Mena Tours and Travel
Chicago
Phone: (800) 937-6362
    or (312) 275-2125
Fax: (312) 275-9927

Overseas Express
Chicago
Phone: (800) 343-4873
    or (312) 262-4971
Fax: (312) 262-4406

STA Travel
Chicago
Phone: (312) 786-9050
Fax: (312) 786-9817

Sunbeam Travel
Chicago
Phone: (312) 263-7664
Fax: (312) 263-0587

Travel Avenue
Chicago
Phone: (800) 333-3335
    or (312) 876-1116
Fax: (312) 876-1254

Travel Core of America
Lincolnshire

Phone: (800) 992-9396
    or (708) 948-1300
Fax: (708) 948-5446

U.S. International Travel & Tours
Chicago
Phone: (800) 874-0073
Fax: (312) 404-2888

INDIANA

Council Travel
Bloomington
Phone: (812) 330-1600
Fax: (812) 332-1628

LOUISIANA

Council Travel
New Orleans
Phone: (504) 866-1767
Fax: (504) 861-9875

Globe Tours
New Orleans
Phone: (800) 374-8352
    or (504) 522-6697
Fax: (504) 522-6703

Uniglobe Americana Travel
New Orleans
Phone: (504) 561-8100
Fax: (504) 525-9020

MARYLAND

AESU Travel
Baltimore
Phone: (800) 638-7640
    or (410) 323-4416
Fax: (410) 323-4498

Fare Deals
Owings Mills
Phone: (800) 347-7006
    or (410) 581-8787
Fax: (410) 581-1093

Hans World Travel
Rockville
Phone: (800) 421-4267

or (301) 770-1717
Fax: (301) 770-0650

Suburban Travel
Rockville
Phone: (301) 770-9300
Fax: (301) 770-5823

MASSACHUSETTS

Amtrack
Boston
Phone: (800) 872-7245
Fax: (617) 589-3708

Council Travel
Amherst
Phone: (413) 256-1261
Fax: (413) 253-3340
Boston
Phone: (617) 266-1926
Fax: (617) 266-7168
Cambridge (Harvard)
Phone: (617) 497-1497
Fax: (617) 876-4830
Cambridge (MIT)
Phone: (617) 225-2555
Fax: (617) 225-0671

STA Travel
Boston
Phone: (617) 266-6014
Fax: (617) 266-5579
Cambridge
Phone: (617) 576-4623
Fax: (617) 576-2740

Up and Away Travel
Boston
Phone: (601) 236-8100
Fax: (617) 247-2920

MICHIGAN

Council Travel
Ann Arbor
Phone: (313) 998-0200
Fax: (313) 998-0741

GTI Travel Consolidators
Holland
Phone: (800) 829-8234
  or (616) 396-1234
Fax: (616) 396-7720

MINNESOTA

Campus Travel/Euroflights
Minneapolis
Phone: (800) 328-3359
  or (800) 292-4176 in MN
  or (612) 338-5616
Fax: (612) 338-6798

Council Travel
Minneapolis
Phone: (612) 379-2323
Fax: (612) 379-1754

Plymouth Travel
Minneapolis
Phone: (800) 736-8747
Fax: (612) 541-9115

MISSOURI

Group & Leisure Travel
Blue Springs
Phone: (800) 874-6608
  or (816) 224-3717
Fax: (816) 228-2650

UniTravel
St. Louis
Phone: (800) 325-2222
  or (314) 569-2501
Fax: (314) 569-2503

NEW JERSEY

**North American Travel &
  Tours**
Parlin
Phone: (800) 764-2687
  or (908) 727-3400
Fax: (908) 727-3422

Paul Laifer Tours
Parsippany
Phone: (800) 346-6314

or (201) 887-1188
Fax: (201) 887-6118

Rupa Travel
Edison
Phone: (800) 206-8869
   or (908) 572-5000
Fax: (908) 572-3456

Worldvision Travel Services
West Orange
Phone: (800) 545-7118
   or (201) 736-8210
Fax: (201) 736-9659

NEW YORK

Air Travel & Tours
New York
Phone: (800) 938-4625
   or (212) 714-1100
Fax: (212) 714-2180

Air Travel Discounts
New York
Phone: (800) 888-2621
   or (212) 922-1326
Fax: (212) 922-1547

All Continents Travel
New York
Phone: (800) 525-3632
   or (212) 751-9051
Fax: (212) 751-9053

Balkan Holidays
New York
Phone: (212) 573-5530
Fax: (212) 573-5538

Cedok Central European Tours
New York
Phone: (800) 800-8891
   or (212) 689-9720
Fax: (212) 481-0597

Consumer Wholesale Travel
New York
Phone: (800) 223-6862

or (212) 695-8435
Fax: (212) 695-8627

Council Travel
New York (Columbia)
Phone: (212) 666-4177
Fax: (212) 666-5012
New York (E 42nd Street)
Phone: (212) 661-1450
Fax: (212) 972-3231
New York (NYU)
Phone: (212) 254-2525
Fax: (212) 477-5643

Favored Holidays
Sheepshead Bay
Phone: (718) 934-8881
Fax: (718) 934-4115

Flytime Tours & Travel
New York
Phone: (212) 760-3737
Fax: (212) 594-1082

French Experience
New York
Phone: (212) 986-3800
Fax: (212) 986-3808

Globe Travel Specialists
New York
Phone: (800) 969-4562
Fax: (212) 843-9889

Magical Holidays
New York
Phone: (800) 228-2208
   or (212) 486-9600
Fax: (212) 486-9751

Payless Travel
New York
Phone: (212) 573-8986
Fax: (212) 573-8878

STA Travel
New York (Columbia)
Phone: (212) 854-2224
Fax: (212) 316-0523

NYC (NYU)
Phone: (212) 627-3111
Fax: (212) 627-3387

Student Travel Association
New York
Phone: (800) 777-0112
Fax: (602) 922-0793

TFI Tours International
New York
Phone: (800) 745-8000
    or (212) 736-1140
Fax: (212) 564-4081

Travac
New York
Phone: (800) 872-8800
    or (212) 563-3303
Fax: (212) 563-3631

Travel Center
New York
Phone: (800) 419-0960
    or (212) 545-7474
Fax: (212) 545-7698

2M International Travel
New York
Phone: (800) 938-4625
    or (212) 714-2121
Fax: (212) 714-2180

Tulips Travel
New York
Phone: (800) 882-3383
    or (212) 490-3388
Fax: (212) 490-3580

Up and Away Travel
New York
Phone: (800) 276-8001
    or (212) 889-2345
Fax: (212) 889-2350

Zig Zag Travel
Forest Hills
Phone: (800) 726-0249
    or (718) 575-3434

Fax: (718) 575-5135
Lynbrook
Phone: (800) 726-0249
    or (516) 887-0776
Fax: (516) 887-3682

NORTH CAROLINA

Council Travel
Chapel Hill
Phone: (919) 942-2334
Fax: (919) 942-1715

OHIO

American Travel
Cleveland
Phone: (216) 781-7181
Fax: (216) 781-7214

Council Travel
Columbus
Phone: (614) 294-8696
Fax: (614) 294-8775

OREGON

Azumano Travel
Portland
Phone: (800) 777-2018
Fax: (503) 221-6349

Council Travel
Portland
Phone: (503) 228-1900
Fax: (503) 273-8450

Emmett Travel
Portland
Phone: (800) 333-5190
Fax: (503) 293-0021

Unique Travel
Portland
Phone: (800) 397-1719
Fax: (503) 221-9522

PENNSYLVANIA

Council Travel
Philadelphia
Phone: (215) 382-0343

Fax: (215) 382-3010
Pittsburgh
Phone: (412) 683-1881
Fax: (412) 683-7242

Holiday Travel International
North Huntington
Phone: (800) 775-7111
　　or (412) 863-7500
Fax: (412) 863-7590

Pennsylvania Travel
Paoli
Phone: (800) 331-0947
　　or (610) 251-9944
Fax: (610) 644-2150

STA Travel
Philadelphia
Phone: (215) 382-2928
Fax: (215) 382-4716

RHODE ISLAND

Council Travel
Providence
Phone: (401) 331-5810
Fax: (401) 331-5821

TEXAS

Airfare Busters
Houston
Phone: (800) 232-8783
　　or (713) 961-5109
Fax: (713) 961-3385

Aries Tours & Travel
Dallas
Phone: (214) 638-7008
Fax: (214) 638-1907

Carefree Getaway Travel
Roanoke
Phone: (800) 969-8687
　　or (817) 430-1128
Fax: (817) 430-0522

Council Travel
Austin
Phone: (512) 472-4931

Fax: (512) 479-0803
Dallas
Phone: (214) 363-9941
Fax: (214) 363-7538

Embassy Tours
Dallas
Phone: (800) 299-5284
　　or (214) 956-9600
Fax: (214) 357-2580

EST International Travel
Houston
Phone: (713) 974-0521
Fax: (713) 974-0192

Katy Van Tours
Houston
Phone: (800) 808-8747
　　or (713) 492-7032
Fax: (713) 492-0586

New World Travel
Houston
Phone: (713) 779-9562
Fax: (713) 779-3656

Royal Lane Travel
Dallas
Phone: (800) 329-2030
　　or (214) 340-2030
Fax: (214) 340-2082

Skypass Travel
Dallas
Phone: (800) 381-8687
　　or (214) 634-8687
Fax: (214) 634-0559
Austin
Phone: (512) 467-8687
Fax: (512) 467-9353

TCI-Access Travel
Dallas
Phone: (800) 272-7359
　　or (214) 630-3344
Fax: (214) 630-3477

UTAH

Council Travel
Salt Lake City
Phone: (801) 582-5840
Fax: (801) 582-6025

Panorama Tours
Salt Lake City
Phone: (800) 527-4888
  or (801) 328-5390
Fax: (801) 524-8405

VIRGINIA

Fellowship Travel International
Richmond
Phone: (800) 235-9384
  or (804) 264-0121
Fax: (804) 329-4384

Hans World Travel
Annandale
Phone: (800) 963-4267
  or (703) 658-1717
Fax: (703) 658-1752

Landmark Travel Services
Alexandria
Phone: (800) 556-7902
  or (703) 750-3411
Fax: (703) 941-7535

Suburban Travel
Fairfax
Phone: (703) 273-7000

Travel Network
Burke
Phone: (703) 644-7866
Fax: (703) 644-3058

WASHINGTON

Americas Tours
Seattle
Phone: (800) 553-2513
  or (206) 623-8850
Fax: (206) 467-0454

C & G Travel
Seattle
Phone: (206) 363-9948
Fax: (206) 365-8559

Cathay Express Travel
Seattle
Phone: (206) 622-9988
Fax: (206) 621-9213

Council Travel
Seattle (Capitol Hill)
Phone: (206) 329-4567
Fax: (206) 329-1982
Seattle (University of Washington)
Phone: (206) 632-2448
Fax: (206) 632-6770

EZ Travel
Seattle
Phone: (206) 524-1977
Fax: (206) 524-1982

New Wave Travel
Seattle
Phone: (800) 220-9283
  or (206) 527-3579
Fax: (206) 527-3241

STA Travel
Seattle
Phone: (206) 633-5000
Fax: (206) 633-5027

Travel Network
Bellevue
Phone: (800) 933-5963
  or (206) 643-1600
Fax: (206) 649-9756

Travel Team
Seattle
Phone: (800) 788-0829
  or (206) 632-0520
Fax: (206) 632-2721

WASHINGTON, DC

Council Travel
Washington
Phone: (202) 337-6464
Fax: (202) 337-9068

Democracy Travel
Washington
Phone: (800) 536-8728
    or (202) 965-7200
Fax: (202) 342-0471

Euram Tours
Washington
Phone: (800) 848-6789
Fax: (202) 842-0608

STA Travel
Washington
Phone: (202) 887-0912
Fax: (202) 887-0031

Up and Away Travel
Washington
Phone: (202) 466-8900
Fax: (202) 296-4433

WISCONSIN

Council Travel
Milwaukee
Phone: (800) 226-8624

Value Holidays
Mequon
Phone: (800) 558-6850
    or (414) 241-6373
Fax: (414) 241-6379

West Allis Travel Service
West Allis
Phone: (414) 771-0818
Fax: (414) 771-0343

Canada

Travel CUTS
Vancouver, BC
Canada
Phone: (604) 681-9136

Vacances Escomptes
Montreal, PQ
Canada
Phone: (514) 861-9090
Fax: (514) 861-6271

Other Services

Services such as Airhitch and Air-Tech, which hesitate to call themselves travel agents, discount agencies, or stand-by services, offer an inexpensive way to travel to Europe. One-way fares usually cost less than US$200 regardless of whether you travel from the East or West Coast. There is a catch, though. These services get you there cheaply, but they rarely allow you to plan in advance. Here's how it works:

- You give them a window of three to five days when you want to travel.
- You provide them with your top three desired destinations. You might, for example, select Frankfurt, Amsterdam, and London in order of your personal preference.
- They get you a ticket according to availability. You won't know which destination you'll get until a few days before your departure date.
- Air-Tech also offers courier flights and regular confirmed/reserved seats on all major airlines to destinations throughout the world.

For more information, contact:

Airhitch
401-9362 Cameron Street
Burnaby, BC V3J 7N3
Canada
Phone: (800) 668-HITCH or (604) 294-5116

Air-Tech Ltd.
584 Broadway, Suite 1007
New York, NY 10012
Phone: (800) 575-TECH or (212) 219-7000
Email: info@aerotech.com

ARRANGING A LONG-TERM ABSENCE

Even if you plan to wait until your arrival in Eastern Europe to look for work, leaving home for an extended period requires more than just a passport and a plane ticket. Try to tie up as many loose ends as possible. Student loans and credit card debts don't disappear just because you do.

Forward your mail to a friend or relative until you have an address overseas, cancel or let your memberships and subscriptions run out, and either pay off your debts or set up a system for making payments while away.

Take your checkbook with you. Having access to your account will allow you to keep up with your banking and write checks for cash against your account at the nearest American Express office (assuming you're a cardholder). This can be very handy, particularly in case of an emergency or unforeseen event.

You can also entrust your financial matters to a responsible friend or relative at home. It is possible to set up an account with another person's name so they can sign checks as well. This would enable you to get cash advances and make credit card purchases, knowing they would be paid off promptly by whomever is managing your affairs.

Remember that credit card and finance companies are huge, bureaucratic operations that rely heavily on computers for their billing services. If you have debts that cannot be paid in full prior to your departure, it is well worth calling or writing to your credit or finance companies and explaining to a live human being that you will be living overseas. Ask them to make note of your situation so that if any problems should arise, they will be able to contact you. Keep copies of all written correspondence and take down the names of those you speak to on the telephone. If a problem does come up, you will have proof that you attempted to address the issue as a precaution against any misunderstandings or missed payments.

It is wise to take a list of your credit card and bank account numbers as well as the addresses and phone numbers of the respective financial institutions. If you should lose any credit cards, you will be able to cancel them immediately. In the event that something goes amiss with your arrangements at home, you will be able to take care of any necessary payments or inquiries from overseas.

As an American working abroad, you will be exempt from United States income taxes as long as you make less than US$70,000 annually. Remember, though, that you will still be required to file a tax return with the Internal Revenue Service. Even though you may not owe any money, not filing can result in huge hassles years down the line when you have long forgotten your failure to file. The burden will be yours to prove to the IRS that you were actually overseas at the time and that you didn't make enough money to require any tax payment.

WHAT TO PACK

When you pack your bags keep in mind that you will be setting up house in a foreign country. Not only do you need to pack clothes for four seasons, you also need to include items that you normally might take for granted. Certain essentials aren't readily available in Eastern Europe. Some of the things that you are used to at home will only have approximate equivalents abroad. You will likely find yourself wishing you had had the foresight to take a more careful inventory prior to your departure.

Make sure to bring a sufficient stock of personal necessities, especially items like birth control, contact lens solutions, tampons, and anti-perspirant or deodorant (not in heavy use in Eastern Europe). Bring a copy of your lens prescription in case you lose or damage your glasses or contacts. Also bring plenty of any medication you require, and have your doctor write out your prescription in generic terms so that a pharmacist in Eastern Europe can identify your medication should you require another prescription.

Other items to consider are those that can help make the transition easier. Photos of family and friends will not only make you feel more at home, they will assist you in breaking the ice with your newfound acquaintances abroad. There is something about a funny picture of your friends or family, especially if it includes you, that almost instantly induces laughter, endearing you to other folks, despite formidable language barriers. Small souvenirs from back home make great gifts for your new friends. Also think about bringing along materials

Lush, rolling forests, castles, and farmland surround Eastern Europe's major cities.

that will assist you in the classroom. Picture books, maps, children's stories and sing-along tapes all can help you entertain and educate at the same time.

If you are staying longer than six months, you might want to consider sending yourself a box of clothes to replenish your wardrobe. Winters in Eastern Europe can be blustery and bitter cold, while summers range from warm and pleasantly sunny to downright hot. You will need enough clothing to cover the range. Unless money is of little concern, sending a larger package air mail would be prohibitively expensive. You might as well buy new clothes abroad. But if you send packages via surface mail, and don't mind them taking a long time (around three months), you won't be set back nearly as much. You can also arrange for friends to send you occasional packets of teaching materials, such as current magazines and newspaper clippings. Though there is a fair amount of English-language reading material available in the larger cities of Eastern Europe, you might soon tire of the often limited selection.

Packing list

- Valid passport with a minimum of six months beyond your planned date of return remaining before expiration
- Visas or working papers, if you've managed to obtain them prior to departure

- Photocopy of your passport, birth certificate, and other important documents
- Traveler's checks
- Resumes and letters of recommendation from past employers, teachers, and even students
- Copies of your diplomas and certificates
- Guidebooks, dictionaries, phrase books
- Teaching materials (including an English grammar guide)
- Postcards or photos of your home city and travel brochures from your local chamber of commerce
- Passport photos (at least ten, black-and-white or color)
- Nice work clothes and shoes
- Light, casual clothing
- A coat and several articles of warm clothing, depending on your destination and the season
- Thermal underwear to wear under lighter clothes during the winter
- Comfortable walking shoes with thick soles
- Backpack, if you intend to travel
- Rain gear
- Toiletries and personal items (e.g., anti-perspirant, skin moisturizer, make-up)
- This book (of course!)

Optional

- Contact lens solution; definitely bring a pair of glasses if you normally wear contacts
- Small gifts
- Camera
- Music (an instrument, radio, cassette player)
- Athletic equipment (running shoes, soccer ball, tennis racket)
- Women's tights; pantyhose are plentiful, but real tights can be more difficult to come by
- Birth control (condoms, in particular, are of poor quality and difficult to find)
- A few good books (on audio cassette tape?)
- Some special treats (your favorite sweets, supplies for your hobby)
- Adaptors for any electrical devices that require 110 watts (Europe is 220 watts)

What to leave at home

- Drugs. Do not jeopardize your travel plans and your future. Jail is no place to find gainful employment.

- Weapons. We strongly discourage carrying weapons into Eastern Europe. If you feel strongly about doing so, we advise that you check the laws of the countries you will be visiting.
- Attitudes and abrasive modes of expression. Remember that you are a guest in another country. Tread lightly until you know what you're walking on.

CLEARING CUSTOMS

Provided that you use common sense and observe the above suggestions on what to leave at home, you shouldn't have any trouble gaining entry into any of the countries of Eastern Europe. Beyond getting your passport checked at the border or at the point of your arrival, you might not come in contact with any customs agents at all, much less have your baggage searched. Compared to their Western counterparts, most Eastern European countries don't have the resources to support large staffs of customs agents or border patrols.

If, by chance, you do encounter a customs official just be courteous and patient. You might get asked what your purpose is in entering the country or how long you plan to stay. Just say that you are traveling around and that you might stay for a month or two. More than likely, you won't have to say much at all.

OTHER DETAILS

Calling Eastern Europe

The telephone systems in most areas of Eastern Europe are badly in need of overhauls and upgrades. Many people still do not have telephone service, and there are long waiting lists for those who want phone service installed at home. It often is necessary to seek out public telephone centers at the local post office or telephone company building to get reliable service, especially for overseas calls. But if phones are in place, calling Eastern Europe from the United States is relatively easy. Just follow these steps:

1. Dial "011" to get an international operator.
2. Dial the "International Country Code":
   Czech Republic 42
   Slovakia 42
   Hungary. 36
   Poland. 48
3. Dial the "City Code." (This is the number within the parentheses.) Remember to omit the "0" when calling from overseas. For example, from the United States to Prague, dial 011-42-2-, then
4. Dial the telephone number.

Time difference

Don't forget the time difference when calling Eastern Europe (or vice versa). Eastern Europe is six hours behind the East Coast of the United States and nine hours behind the West Coast. So when it's 9PM in Prague, it's noon in San Francisco on the same day. When it's 9AM in Warsaw, it's 3AM the same day in New York.

Travel insurance

Because most United States insurance policies don't cover you when you are overseas, it's best to arrange coverage specifically for your trip. Your travel agent can provide you with a list of travel insurance carriers offering health insurance, lost baggage protection, and the like. Many credit companies offer some form of travel insurance and protection against cancellation of trips purchased using their credit cards. Insurance policies sold through such student travel organizations as Council Travel offer a comprehensive package of health and trip coverage. Special comprehensive coverage for educators is available at a cost of US$50 or more per month from such organizations as John Hancock (800) 767-0169, Hinchcliff International (607) 257-0100, or Seabury & Smith (800) 331-3047.

You might consider obtaining an International Teacher's ID for US$17 from CIEE, (800) GET-AN-ID. These cards entitle you to student-rate airfares and include a minimal health insurance policy.

Recommended reading

It's important to make sure you're well informed, so read up before you go. *Now Hiring! Jobs in Eastern Europe* covers employment opportunities and provides other kinds of information on getting along well during your stay abroad. There are other books out there that will provide you with useful information. Perusing a few different travel guides will help you make informed practical and logistical decisions regarding your trip, so you'll begin to get a feel for what lies ahead.

In order to get the most out of your trip to Eastern Europe, you might consider reading some history books and even some other, more literary works such as novels or essays. After all, travel books can get a little boring and repetitive after a while. Once you know the facts, you can concentrate on the thoughts and feelings associated with living in countries with rich cultural heritages. All of the countries under discussion here are home to world-renowned writers, poets, and philosophers.

Browse through your best local bookstore and select a few different books. When it comes time to pack your bags, you can tear out the most useful chapters from each travel book and bind them together with a sturdy rubber band, or take them to a local copy shop for inexpensive custom binding. You'll end up with a specialized travel guide that won't consume much room in your luggage. And if you select a few literary works to take with you, you can always barter with your fellow travelers down the line or sell/trade them at a local used bookstore, that way you won't have to worry about accumulating unwanted heft in your luggage.

Here's a very selective list of books and authors:

Eastern Europe
Travel guides

Berkeley's Guide to Eastern Europe: On the Loose. Berkeley Students in cooperation with the Associated Students of the University of California. Fodor's Travel Publications, 1994. 642 p.

Birnbaum's Eastern Europe. Harper Perennial, 1992. 549 p.

Central Europe: A Lonely Planet Shoestring Guide. Lonely Planet, 1995. 839 p.

Eastern Europe. Rowlinson Carter. Insight Guides. APA Publications, 1993. 390 p.

Eastern Europe on a Shoestring. David Stanley. Lonely Planet Publications, 1991. 928 p.

Fodor's Eastern Europe '95: Hungary, Poland, Slovakia, the Czech Republic and Bulgaria. Fodor's Modern Guides, distributed by D. McKay, 1994.

Let's Go: Eastern Europe. St. Martin's Press, 1995. 766 p.

History and contemporary events

Crisis and Reform in Eastern Europe. Ferenc Feher and Andrew Arato, eds. Transaction Publishers, 1991. 531 p.

Eastern Europe in Revolution. Ivo Banac, ed. Cornell University Press, 1992. 255 p. Partial proceedings of a conference held at Yale on Nov. 5, 1990.

God's Playground, a History of Poland. Norman Davies. Columbia University Press, 1982. Two volumes: v. 1. The Origins to 1795, v. 2. 1795 to Present.

Heart of Europe: A Short History of Poland. Norman Davies. Clarendon Press; Oxford University Press, 1984. 511 p.

The Other Europe: A Complete Guide to Business Opportunities in Eastern Europe. Christopher Engholm. McGraw-Hill, 1994. 361 p.

The Other Europe. Jacques Rupnik. Pantheon Books, 1989. 291 p.

The Rebirth of History: Eastern Europe in the Age of Democracy. Misha Glenny. Penguin, 1990. 244 p.

Surge to Freedom: The End of Communist Rule in Eastern Europe. J. F. (James F.) Brown. Duke University Press. 338 p.

We the People: The Revolution of '89 Witnessed in Warsaw, Budapest, Berlin and Prague. Timothy Garton Ash. Penguin Books, 1990. 156 p.

Without Force or Lies: Voices from the Revolution of Central Europe in 1989-90: Essays, Speeches, and Eyewitness Accounts. Mercury House, 1990. 315 p.

Literature and essays

Disturbing the Peace: A Conversation with Karel Hvizdala. Vaclav Havel. Knopf, distributed by Random House, 1990. 228 p.

Summer Meditations. Vaclav Havel. A.A. Knopf, 1992. 151 p.

Vaclav Havel; Or, Living In Truth: Twenty-Two Essays Published on the Occasion of the Award of the Erasmus Prize to Vaclav Havel. Vaclav Havel. Faber and Faber, 1987. 315 p.

Czech Republic and Slovakia

Travel guides

Czech & Slovak Republics: A Lonely Planet Travel Survival Kit. John King. Lonely Planet Publications, 1995. 497 p.

Czech and Slovak Republics. Alfred Horn, ed. Insight Guides, APA Publications (HK), distributed in the United States by Houghton Mifflin, 1993. 373 p.

Czech and Slovak Republics: The Rough Guide. Rob Humphreys. Rough Guides, distributed by Penguin, 1993. 459 p.

Essential Czech Republic (With Excursions into Slovakia). Michael Ivory. Passport Books, 1994. 128 p.

Fodor's Exploring Prague. Michael Ivory. Fodor's Travel Publications, 1995. 288 p.

Prague. Horst Becker. Insight Guides. APA Publications (HK); distributed in the United States by Houghton Mifflin, 1995. 102 p.

Prague Time Out Guide. Peter Fiennes, ed. Time Out Group/Penguin, 1995. 282 p.

Czech and Slovak authors

Vaclav Havel, Milan Kundera, Bohumil Hrabel, Ivan Klima, Carel Capek

Hungary

Travel guides

Essential Hungary. Michael Ivory. Passport Books, 1994. 128 p.

Hungary. Berlitz Publications Company, Inc., 1988. 192 p.

Hungary. Bob Dent. W.W. Norton, 1990. 366 p.

Hungary. Marton Radkai. APA Publishers, 1994. 93 p.

Hungary. Michael's Guides, distributed by Inbal Travel Information Ltd., 1991. 205 p.

Hungary. Robertson McCarta and Nelles Verlag. Nelles Guides, 1991. 256 p.

Hungary: A Travel Survival Kit. Steve Fallon. Lonely Planet, 1994. 443 p.

Hungary: The Rough Guide. Dan Richardson. Rough Guides, distributed by Penguin Books USA, 1995. 374 p.

Hungarian authors

Arany Janos, Jozsef Attila

Poland

Travel guides

Poland. APA Publications, distributed in the United States by Houghton Mifflin, 1995.

Poland. Jill Stephenson. Hippocrene Books, 1993. 179 p.

Poland: A Travel Survival Kit. Krzysztof Dydynski. Lonely Planet Publications, 1993. 528 p.

Poland: The Rough Guide. Mark Salter. Rough Guides, distributed by Penguin Books, USA, 1993. 571 p.

Polish Authors

Henryk Sienkiewicz, Jerzy Kosinski, Czeslaw Milosz, Witold Gombrowicz, Tadeusz Konwicki

Language tapes

Good bookstores sell foreign-language books and tutorial tapes. Though learning Czech, Slovak, Hungarian, or Polish is not essential to your success in these countries, mastering a few simple phrases will make life easier for you. Besides, learning the language that enables you to converse with the locals, however rudimentary your knowledge, can only enrich your experience in Eastern Europe.

Mental preparation

WHAT HAPPENS THE DAY I ARRIVE?

Because arranging accommodations in advance is virtually impossible unless you have family and friends abroad, your first task will be to find inexpensive, short-term housing. Youth hostels are one option, inexpensive hotels are another. And if you arrive at the main train or bus station of any of the larger cities during the busier travel times, you will likely be greeted by people who will offer you accommodation in a room in their home. Though this can be a very convenient method of finding immediate accommodations, make sure that you find out where they live in relation to both the downtown area and public transportation lines. Don't worry, this is not an uncommon practice, but be wary of those who are more interested in your money than in your enjoyment of their country.

Unless you're no mere mortal, some degree of travel exhaustion will likely set in, even as you are bombarded with new and exciting sights, sounds, and smells. You may feel a dreamlike sensation frequently associated with international travel. Remember, only hours ago you were sitting at home contemplating your upcoming new experience—a much different reality than actually living it out. And beware of jet lag! Adjusting to the time difference puts your body through a veritable time warp. Rest, relax, and get used to your new surroundings. Finding a comfortable place to regroup will help minimize culture shock.

After you get situated, our advice is to take things as they come. Study a map of the area and locate the nearest bus, train, and subway stations. Find out where tickets are sold and how much they cost. If you haven't already, familiarize yourself with the different currency and coin denominations. Walk around the area and note important landmarks and the local stores and restaurants. Stop and browse or buy something from a local vendor, just so you can begin to feel at ease. Search out the cafes and bars where other expats and English-speaking people hang out. These venues and those who frequent them will be your best resources when it comes to finding work, locating accommodations, and having a little fun in the process.

Settle in and absorb the strangeness. Don't expect to make great strides toward finding work or feeling at home for the first few days. The novelty will soon wear off, and there will be plenty of time to concentrate on more important matters after a few days.

CULTURE SHOCK

You will be joining thousands of North American travelers who venture each year into Eastern Europe. Although many travel for several weeks, few actually have the courage or desire to live in a foreign country for an extended period of time. It takes bravery and confidence, not to mention time, to immerse yourself in a foreign culture and adopt a whole new way of life. If you've gotten as far as reading this book, you may be ready to take the plunge!

Living and working in Eastern Europe will be the experience of a lifetime, full of new challenges and learning experiences. You will be exposed to new lifestyles, values, customs, politics, and languages. If you can come away with a better understanding of any of these things, your trip can be considered at least a partial success. An American expat accustomed to big city life in Eastern Europe remarked:

❝ *There are thousands of opportunities here. Some of them end up being false. You just have to figure out what is actually possible, usually through trial and error. And if you take the time to get to know people—get over all the hang-ups about foreigners—things get done here. There is a certain beauty to it all."*

Immersion in a foreign culture can be overwhelming. Discomfort can be minimized if you know what to expect before you leave. Culture shock is no small consideration. A bad reaction to staying in a completely new place without the aid of cultural instincts and a familiar social structure can make you want to return home very quickly, without reaping any of the benefits associated with living abroad. Symptoms of culture shock may range from mild uneasiness, homesickness, and outright unhappiness to panic, irritability, and hostility. The process of settling into a new place abroad can cause feelings of isolation and vulnerability, especially when a language barrier prevents you from communicating your most basic needs. Several interviewees expressed similar feelings, but one young American English teacher said it best:

❝ *Your heart can sink here—the pollution, the rudeness of the service, the dismal winters....All of a sudden you realize that you don't have someone around you can call and chat with. Yeah, you make friends, but it takes a while to establish the kinds of close relationships you have back home."*

To minimize the effects of culture shock, learn as much as possible about the place you are going to before you get there. If you can, try to hook up with someone who is either a native or has spent a lot of time in your country of choice. The closer you can get to immersing yourself in the culture before you go, the better off you'll be once you get there. She continued:

❝ *Get to know someone who is from the country you will be visiting. Talk to them and ask lots of questions. Maybe even get a few short language lessons. If you can connect the experience you have once you get there with something you have already heard, your depth of understanding will be much greater and more rewarding in the long run."*

A WORD TO WOMEN

Women who travel to Eastern Europe should expect to be treated more like women were treated fifty or one hundred years ago in the United States. Male chauvinism is rampant, especially among the older generations. Traditional gender roles that keep women at home and men at work still hold true in most households, even if appearances to the contrary seem common. Many women are forced to work out of economic necessity, not because they have achieved equal status and respect on a societal level. One sign of this lingering traditionalism is the common practice among older men of kissing the backs of women's hands instead of shaking them western-style. If you wish to avoid this, always offer your hand at hip level. If you offer it higher and somewhat more limply, it may signal that you expect the man to kiss your hand while giving his respects.

Though it is true that more Eastern European women, especially younger ones, are pursuing an education and a career rather than choosing to marry young and start a family, women traveling in Eastern Europe are still often subject to sexual prejudice or harassment. Although this type of behavior is usually relatively harmless, obvious stares or catcalls when walking down the sidewalk are not uncommon. The same type of common sense should be exercised on the streets of Eastern Europe as in any other part of the world. If you look like you know where you're going and make an effort to avoid risky or unpredictable situations, you shouldn't have any problem. Alone on a stroll around Old Town Square in Prague, a late twenty-something American woman traveler explained:

❝ *I have been traveling alone from the very beginning. I enjoy not having to compromise with someone else all the time. But it has its downsides, too. I don't go out at night by myself very often, and when I do, I make damn sure I look like I know where I'm going. Most of my paranoia probably comes from living in the States, though. It seems pretty safe here, maybe just an occasional stare, and I don't ever go into pubs by myself if they look like they're full of drunk Czech men.❞*

Feminism in Eastern Europe is a dirty word, not that it isn't on this side of the pond! But in Eastern Europe, calling yourself "feminist" carries a rather different ideological load. Feminism is closely associated with communism, and calling yourself feminist is, for most Eastern Europeans, tantamount to voicing support for the rather repressive political regimes of the past. If you can discuss the ideas of feminism without using That Word, it would probably be a good idea. In fact, it's a good idea in most of what you do to not be antagonistic! Try to brush off any indiscretions and know that you are doing your part to change those acts by ignoring their source. If you're adept linguistically, you might try learning a few choice phrases in order to express your displeasure at any unwanted attention.

ENCOUNTERING PREJUDICE

You should be aware that racism in Eastern Europe is also part of the culture. Similar to Eastern Germany, since 1993 there has been a notable increase in "racial attacks" against Romany groups, non-whites, Jewish people, and homosexuals. As with women, our advice is to try and avoid risky situations and quietly remove yourself if you get into one.

BEFORE ACCEPTING A POSITION

Don't necessarily accept the first job offer you receive. It will be worth your while to shop around, particularly if you are expected to sign a contract for longer than three months. You can prepare for the decision-making process before you even begin your job search, perhaps even before you leave. If you can, track down and talk to someone who has taught in your country of choice, or write ahead to a few schools to inquire about their hiring practices. Find out about work schedules and compensation terms. Inquire about how much preparation time is necessary or expected outside the classroom. When you begin your job search, set up a checklist for every school you get information on or apply to. Include pay, size of classes, level of students, expected time commitment, and any benefits. Find out whether the school will help you get a work permit or find accommodations. If you are well organized in the early stages, you will be able to better assess your options before you make a final decision. Some of the most important questions to ask are:

- How long has the school been in existence, and how many students does it have? (You want to make certain that you're not wasting your time with some fly-by-night, take-the-money-and-run business.)
- How many hours per week do most teachers work? What are the normal teaching hours? Are outside duties such as administrative tasks expected of you as a teacher? (You need to be able to plan you work time and know in advance if you'll have enough time to pursue other activities.)
- How much and how often are teachers paid? Are there any other forms of compensation or assistance, such as subsidized accommodations, etc. (Most schools in Eastern Europe will only offer pay as compensation, but it's worth asking about anyway.)
- What sort of assistance and materials are provided for teachers? (This will give you some indication of how committed the school is to teaching. Some are just in it for the money. You will appreciate working for someone who sincerely supports your effort.) Are teachers' books provided? Does the school own class sets of any books? Does the school have an audio cassette tape player or VCR?

Words of warning

In order to avoid any undue hassles, take note of the following precautions:

- Employers have no legal reason to hold onto your passport. Do not, under any circumstances, surrender your passport to anyone but the appropriate immigration authorities. It should be sufficient for someone to record your passport number, not to take it into their possession.
- Do not sign any contract or written agreement with an employer until you fully understand what will be required of you and what your compensation will be. Signing a contract is the final step in any negotiation. Beware of anyone who wants to rush you into signing a contract.
- Whether oral or written, be sure to clarify any part of an agreement that is vague or unclear to you. Don't let someone make promises they can't keep. And remember, any good business agreement can be (and should be) committed to paper.

MONEY MATTERS

No matter where you go in Eastern Europe, you undoubtedly will be surprised by the disparity between the cost of living you are accustomed to in North America and the remarkably low cost of living in the four countries under discussion here. For example, dinner at a bustling pizza joint in the heart of Prague will only set you back the equivalent of a few dollars. A trip to the grocery store almost anywhere in Eastern Europe will cost you a fraction of what you would pay back home. And traveling across the Czech Republic or Slovakia by train might cost you ten or fifteen dollars, roughly equivalent to a taxi fare across town in a mid-sized American city.

Because you don't have to worry so much about making as much money as possible to cover a high cost of living—as you would if you chose to teach English in Japan, for example—you can focus on the positive aspects of living in Eastern Europe, such as getting to know new people, learning about the culture and history, or tackling a new language. Don't be surprised if low-cost living spoils you. After getting acclimated to life in Eastern Europe, you likely will cringe at the prospect of paying North American prices for a drink in a fancy hard-currency hotel in Warsaw, Prague, or Budapest. And returning home to North America will bring a whole new meaning to the words "sticker shock."

Whether you end up teaching English or pursuing some other line of work, it is not hard to live well in Eastern Europe on a rate of pay that would have you waiting in line at the nearest soup kitchen in the United States or Canada. You will not have to work long hours as a teacher to be able to go out on the town in the evenings or take a few weeks' vacation in a different part of the region. Be aware, though, that your ability to live well while you reside in any of the four countries discussed herein does not mean that you will be able to amass a sizable savings account. Eastern European currencies (except the Czech crown) remain only internally convertible, which means you cannot easily exchange your Slovak crowns, zloty, or forints back into dollars when you leave these countries. And if you stay longer than six months or a year, inflation could work against you. Eastern European economies are struggling to catch up with the West. Instability within these economies can cause currencies to lose value, which often translates into rising prices.

For most people, a long stay in Eastern Europe is meant to be an enriching learning experience, not a means of filling the coffers. Those who aim to amass wealth should consider other options.

Even though Eastern Europe is so cheap when compared to the West, it's still wise to keep track of your spending habits. There will likely come a time when you will make the transition from living off of the money that you brought with you to the money that you make from your employment. Though you can live quite comfortably if you work as a teacher, you will still need to make sure that your spending doesn't exceed your earning capabilities. It's especially easy to fall into the trap of assuming that since everything seems so cheap that you couldn't possibly live beyond your means. Be particularly careful about keeping enough money around to pay your rent. Long-term accommodations don't come as cheaply as you might imagine when you begin to look at what percentage of your monthly income they can consume.

Wages for English teachers

Country	School	Private Tutoring
The Czech Republic and Slovakia	$2.50–$6.50/hr.	$2.50–$10.00/hr.
Poland	$2.00–$8.50/hr.	$4.00–$10.50/hr.
Hungary	$4.00–$7.00/hr.	$4.50–$11.00/hr.

Cost comparisons

Item	Czech/Slovakia	Poland	Hungary
Opera/theater ticket	$5.00–$8.00	$5.00–$6.00	$4.50–$6.50
Average lunch	$1.50–$3.00	$2.00-$4.00	$2.50–$4.50
Mailing a letter to the U.S.	$.33	$.25	$.30
Music cassette tape	$3.00–$5.00	$1.50–$4.50	$4.00–$8.00
Bottle of beer	$.50–$1.00	$.60–$1.25	$.70–$1.50
English-language newspaper	$1.05	$.95	$.80

● ●

BUDGETING TIPS

The following suggestions can help you manage your money and generally get along better financially during your stay in Eastern Europe:

- Get to know what things cost early on in your trip so that you don't get taken advantage of. If you get mistaken for a free-spending tourist, chances are you'll end up putting more money into the local vendors' pocket than you should.
- Find out if there is a different price structure for locals and residents than there is for tourists and travelers. If you have a work permit and a resident's card, you often won't have to pay the higher prices that foreigners are usually subject to.
- When you order from a restaurant menu, take note of the name and price for each item that you order so that you can match them with the tab you receive at the end of your meal. Stories abound about unsuspecting foreigners being taken advantage of by unscrupulous waiters.
- Make sure that you know the different currency denominations and count your change.

Exchange rates

Country	Per U.S.$	U.S. Equivalent
Czech Republic	25.10 crowns	.0398
Slovakia	28.10 crowns	.0355
Poland	2.45 zloty	.4081
Hungary	139 forints	.0071

Current as of January 1996

● ●

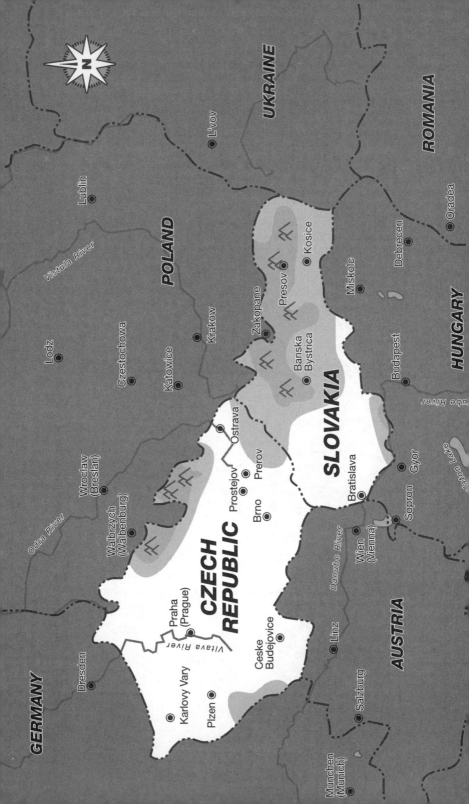

The lay of the land

A PROFILE OF THE CZECH REPUBLIC AND SLOVAKIA

Czechoslovakia formally separated into the Czech and Slovak Republics (also known as Slovakia) on January 1, 1993. Though they are in fact independent countries, their shared history and proximity as neighbors puts them in a unique position with respect to the purposes of this book. These newly independent countries still share much of the infrastructure that was built up over the years since the Republic of Czechoslovakia formed in 1918. Consequently, this section will cover both countries, though they will be treated as separate entities.

Population

The Czech Republic has a population of nearly 10.5 million people. Though many ethnic groups, including Czechs, Slovaks, Germans, Poles, and Romanies (also known as Gypsies), populate this small Eastern-European county, well over eighty percent are of Czech ethnicity.

Slovakia, on the other hand, can count roughly 5.4 million inhabitants with greater ethnic diversity than its neighbor. Ethnic Slovaks, Hungarians, Poles, Ukrainians, Russians, and Romanies all make their homes there.

Geography

Located in the land-locked heart of Europe, the Czech and Slovak Republics together comprise a relatively narrow territory that stretches lengthwise from west to east-southeast. The Czech lands border Germany to the west while Slovakia reaches to the southwestern edge of the Ukraine on its eastern border. Poland borders both republics in the north, while Austria dominates the southern border of the Czech lands and part of Slovakia's western frontier. Hungary shares the majority of Slovakia's southern border.

To put these two Eastern-European countries into geographical perspective, Prague, the capital of the Czech Republic, lies west and north of Vienna, putting it in the geographic center of the European continent. Slovakia's capital, Bratislava, is bisected by the Danube River, which also flows through Vienna and Budapest, putting Bratislava on an important and historical trading route.

Of the Czech and Slovak lands, the Czech topography is the gentler of the two, with predominantly rolling hills and a few flat areas.

Slovakia boasts more rugged terrain. The spectacular Tatra and Carpathian mountain ranges provide many outdoor recreation opportunities for skiers and hikers.

Climate

The climate in both republics is temperate, though Slovakia's tends to be more extreme during the winter months. The region experiences four seasons. Summers are generally mild, warmer in late July and August, but rarely hot. Temperatures average in the high sixties and low seventies in most areas. Winters, however, can be bitter cold. Expect snow and ice from November through February. Winter temperatures generally reach the lowest in January and February.

Unfortunately, skies don't always look so friendly over Eastern Europe. Because brown coal is still burned as a common source of heat and modern pollution controls are lacking, air pollution is rampant in Eastern Europe, especially during the winter months when cold air settles over the land. The Czech and Slovak Republics offer little reprieve from these pollutants, particularly in the larger cities and industrial regions. People who are susceptible to bronchitis and other respiratory problems should consult a medical professional before deciding to spend the winter in certain areas of the two republics, or pack a small pharmacy of over-the-counter cure-alls.

Politics

The breakup of Czechoslovakia into two independent republics was due in large part to long-standing political imbalances between Czechs and Slovaks. Historically, Czechs have exercised greater political and economic power than the Slovaks. After all, the seat of the government of Czechoslovakia rested in Prague, and the Czechs have long garnered greater international recognition. Czech President Vaclav Havel is a world-famous dissident and playwright. The people of Slovakia had for many years felt slighted by the more visible and powerful Czechs. In their country's former incarnation, many Slovaks felt that they were not getting a fair shake. Certain cultural issues also exacerbated the disagreements between the two federations prior to their separation. Czechs tend to be more urbane and agnostic, while Slovaks are considered more provincial and religious. One thing is certain, though: the division occurred peacefully. After the revolution of 1989, the Czechs and Slovaks chose different paths of political and economic reform. The Czech leadership advocated a fast transformation to a market economy, while the Slovak government wanted more gradual change.

Dotted with ski villages on both sides of the border, the Tatras mark the Polish/Slovakian divide.

Both countries are governed via parliamentary democracy. A president acts as head of state with a prime minister and a cabinet. Both parliaments are bicameral, each with an upper and lower house.

The Czech Republic has enjoyed greater political stability since the breakup of the two countries. Vaclav Havel was elected president in 1990 and held office until 1992, when he made it clear that he would not continue to directly oversee the breakup of the former Czechoslovakia. The Czech parliament then re-elected him after the split was completed. Vladimir Klaus, an economist by training, was appointed Prime Minister. Put in charge of restoring the economy, he was instrumental in implementing the "shock therapy" version of economic transformation. The Czech's adherence to economic conservatism has yielded positive effects. Unemployment remains low, especially when compared to Slovakia and other neighboring countries, and the accumulation of foreign debt has been severely curtailed.

Slovakia cannot match the economic successes of the Czech Republic. Since the beginning of 1993, the government has struggled to maintain both economic and political stability. The Slovak Prime Minister, Vladimir Meciar, has demonstrated little proficiency for either stimulating the economy or keeping his foot out of his mouth. He is a proponent of the slow course to economic reform, which means that the Slovaks have seen little sign of the better lives that they were promised after the conversion to a market-driven economy.

Religion

For the most part Czechs are not a very religious people, especially when compared to their Slovak neighbors. Over forty percent of Czechs do not practice any religious faith. Many are agnostic. The majority of those who do practice religion are Roman Catholic. As in Slovakia, Lutheran denominations attract a small percentage of the population.

Slovakia is predominantly Roman Catholic. Over sixty percent of Slovaks are members of the Roman Catholic Church, while a good portion of the remainder belong to other Christian faiths. Roughly ten percent of the population claims no religious affiliation.

History

Czechoslovakia's history as an independent republic only goes back to 1918, just after the end of World War I. The history of the Czech and Slovak people, however, extends much further back. The seventh century brought the most significant early settling of Slavic peoples in the territory that came to be known as Czechoslovakia. They came from the East, and supplanted several tribes who previously had settled in the area .

Not much is known about these Slavs during the two centuries that followed, until the formation of the Great Moravian Empire in the early part of the ninth century. This empire encompassed a region that extended beyond the present-day boundaries of the Czech and Slovak Republics. The end of the Moravian reign of power in the region witnessed two crucial events that changed the course of history of these two peoples: the rise of the Roman Catholic Church and the division of the Czech and Slovak peoples into two separate camps. The Czechs sided with Western powers, while the Slovaks came under domination of the early Hungarian peoples, the Magyars.

From the tenth and eleventh centuries well into the fourteenth century, the rulers of Bohemia (now the Czech lands) garnered great political influence in Eastern Europe and the region became the Holy Roman Empire. Charles IV came to power during the latter part of the fourteenth century and made the greatest early contributions to Czech culture. As the King of Bohemia, he founded Charles University in Prague (which still exists today), declared Czech one of the official languages of his country, and devoted much of his time to art and architecture. Prague's present-day beauty owes much to Charles IV.

The influence of the Roman Empire in Bohemia came under attack in the early years of the fifteenth century when a Protestant named Jan Hus led a rebellion inspired by what he saw as rampant corruption in the Catholic Church hierarchy. Hus's actions on behalf of the Bohemian lower classes sparked a widespread uprising that resulted in civil war. The Hussite Wars lasted from 1419 to 1434.

From the fifteenth century until the end of the eighteenth century, the Czech lands came under the spell of what is now known as the Dark Ages. The Austrian Habsburgs brutally ruled much of Europe during these years. So much so, in fact, that the enforced Germanization of the region nearly eradicated the Czech language. It wasn't until Maria Theresa, and later her son, Joseph II, came to power during the middle of the 1700s that things began to improve for the Czech people. Their tolerance eventually brought freedom of worship and greater freedom of expression.

The Slovaks were not so lucky. They suffered much longer under Austro-Hungarian domination. Their lands were relegated to an area then known as Upper Hungary. The Hungarian language dominated until the end of the nineteenth century, so much so that it nearly wiped out the Slovak tongue all together.

The events surrounding World War I brought about the call for an independent Czechoslovak state. Neither the Czechs nor the Slovaks were keen to side against their fellow Slavs, the Russians and the Serbs. Nor were they willing to fight along side Austrians and Hungarians, whom they hated. It was at this time that the Czechs and Slovaks decided to join together after centuries of separation. The new state was formed in 1918, and in 1920, under the Treaty of Trianon, the border that separated Slovak lands from Hungary was drawn. In the process, nearly three quarters of a million Hungarians were stranded on the Slovak side.

The first Republic of Czechoslovakia attained an economic position that ranked in the top ten of the world's industrialized nations. Perhaps more importantly, though, the country achieved the enviable position of becoming the only functioning democracy in the region, not to mention one of the few in the world at the time.

Democracy and economic prosperity brought a level of content that had never before been witnessed, but it was momentary. The seeds of disaster were sown long before World War I, and the Treaty of Trianon only exacerbated the situation in a way that displaced ethnic minorities. The nationalist sentiments of the various ethnic groups from the Hungarians who lived on the Slovak side of the border to the Germans of the Sudetenland would aggravate the region for decades to come. Even the Czechs and Slovaks couldn't refrain from expressing resentment and disdain for one another.

With the onslaught of worldwide economic depression in the thirties and the simultaneous rise to power of the Nazi party in Germany, the First Czechoslovak Republic was doomed. Hitler's aggression was

Despite the dramatic changes of recent years, images and ideas of communism linger throughout Eastern Europe.

too much for the Czechs and Slovaks. In October 1938, Hitler's troops marched into the Sudetenland, and by the following spring they occupied all of what was left of Czech territory. With Nazi backing, the Slovaks declared independence under the leadership of Jozef Tiso.

The Second World War brought the wrath of Hitler and the Nazis down upon the Jewish population of both the Czech and Slovak regions. Most of these Jewish people were deported to concentration and death camps in Poland. Few survived. The Nazis reigned over the area until the end of the war in 1945, when the Soviets liberated the region. As an occupied, protectorate state of the Nazis from the beginning of the German occupation in 1939 until 1945, the country did not experience the physical decimation endured by many of the surrounding cities as a result of Nazi bombs.

In 1948, after the liberation of Czechoslovakia, nearly four decades of domination by Soviet-backed communist rulers began. The formation of the Czechoslovak Socialist Republic was declared in 1960. In

1968, after a period of slow transformation, Alexander Dubcek, the Czech leader, instituted reforms in an attempt to liberalize hard-line communist policy. Czechs were allowed greater freedoms of expression, assembly, and travel. The Soviets, however, did not approve, especially when Czech citizens began to demand even more freedom, including the right to form political opposition parties. In August of the same year, Soviet tanks and Warsaw pact forces rolled into Prague and crushed the Prague Spring rebellion. A Soviet-backed, puppet government was put in Dubcek's place. The following years brought severe political repression and widespread environmental devastation, stemming from poor industrial practices. It was a grim period for Czechoslovakia, one that remains seared into the memory of many Czechs today.

With growing economic difficulties in the Eastern bloc and the U.S.S.R. during the late 1970s and early 1980s came the possibility that the Soviets could no longer maintain their stranglehold on Eastern Europe. The Russians had a hard enough time playing one-upsmanship games against the United States, and their centralized economic policies had long shown signs of weakness and decay. The people of East Germany, Poland, Hungary, and Czechoslovakia (among others) seized the day by rising up against the flimsy communist leaderships in their respective countries. In Czechoslovakia, it was called the Velvet Revolution. The streets of Prague filled with Czech citizens who demanded an end to repression. They succeeded, and a former dissident named Vaclav Havel was swept into power. He became the first elected President of the newly democratic Republic of Czechoslovakia.

Though the Czech and Slovak people had managed to wrest power from the communists in a peaceful manner, they could not remain unified on how they should govern themselves. The threads of this disagreement are deeply sewn into the patchwork-like fabric of the region's history. Czechs and Slovaks have been suspicious of one another for a thousand years, and despite the best intentions of leaders like Havel, there seemed to be no chance of reconciling the people's divergent social and political views. On January 1, 1993, Czechoslovakia ceased to exist. Two new republics were formed along the boundaries of an ancient ethnic divide. Once again, all was settled peacefully, a grand accomplishment given the situation in several other areas of Central and Eastern Europe.

Expat life in today's Czech Republic and Slovakia

There is no doubt that the countries of Eastern Europe have much in common. Years under Soviet control created a sort of lowest common denominator. And nearly all Eastern European people who lived at the time could share a few similar stories of the effects of Soviet-style government on their lives. Perhaps more to the point, however, are the differences between the Czech Republic and Poland or Hungary, and what effect these differences have on expatriate life.

One thing is certain. More expats choose to stay in the Czech Republic than probably in all of the other Eastern European countries combined. There are several likely reasons for this: the Czechs are affable and usually welcoming to foreigners, the Czech economy has not suffered as greatly as other Eastern European countries during the economic transition from the Soviet system, the country wants all the international exposure and assistance it can get, and Prague is one of the great cities of the world for anyone who appreciates culture, history, beauty, and plain old inexpensive fun. Simply stated, the Czech Republic is by and large a cooperative and friendly place.

Especially in Prague, the Czechs have made it possible for foreigners to come in and set up small businesses, particularly if this involves partnerships with Czech companies or individuals. You will find all sorts of expats involved in various business endeavors such as bookstores, cafes, import-export, consulting, and advertising. This doesn't mean it's easy to set up shop there, but at least the Czech government doesn't interfere all the time. In fact, most expats involved in business in the Czech Republic can tell you nightmare stories of all the bureaucratic red tape they had to go through just to get started. Some will tell stories of having to pay bribes. In some cases, persistence pays off and people stay for the long haul. Others give up after a year or two.

Though Slovakia benefits to a certain extent from its former association with the Czech Republic, it does not attract as many foreigners. In general, Slovaks don't go out of their way to stimulate interest in their country. Outside of teaching English, there simply aren't as many avenues for ambitious expats to explore as in the Czech Republic. Having played second fiddle to the Czechs for so long, the Slovaks seemed determined to make their own way the world. Unfortunately, they don't appear to be as savvy as the Czechs in the pursuit of economic revitalization. Perhaps the repressive pall cast down by Soviets during their tenure has had greater long-term effects on the Slovaks. Whatever the explanation, the fact remains that when compared to the Czechs, the Slovaks create more obstacles for the average expat who wants to settle down for a while to teach English and sop up the local culture.

Introducing: An expat in Prague

Taken from an interview with William Corley, a former English teacher, who is presently a self-employed consultant in Prague.

Most Americans come here to teach, at least in the beginning. Then they discover that teaching may not be the best use of their time. Teaching is a skill, so after you do it for a while, you discover what your natural abilities are. Not everyone is cut out to teach, though some find it very enjoyable.

There are basically two kinds of expats in the Czech Republic. There's the coat-and-tie bunch, who work for Czech or foreign concerns. They make good money and are usually paid in hard currency. The second group is comprised of the creative-artist types who end up turning into entrepreneurs. The starving-artist thing seems to be falling by the wayside, especially for those who are living solely on the local economy. Unless you find really cheap housing, you might have to work three jobs to support yourself well.

When I came here, I found a teaching job and hung out a lot. But I was living on Czech crowns, while most students were having money wired to them. I spent most of my time with Czechs and not Americans, so I haven't really met anyone with the same experiences I've had.

After a while, I moved on to a press agency where I spent my time proofreading and correcting English. It was there that I began to learn Czech. Eventually, I looked into the want ads in *Annonce*. I ended up finding a job in an import/export company. And I think the key to staying here long term is to get beyond teaching English.

The Czech Republic is an interesting place. During the old regime, people couldn't do anything beyond what they were told to do. Everyone wanted their own cubicle, their own little niche. Even now, you can rub people the wrong way if you fail to understand this. People have always had only one thing to do, though it's changing now of course.

TRAVELING TO THE CZECH REPUBLIC AND SLOVAKIA

The Czech Republic attracts thousands of visitors each year. Many of these travelers, especially the younger set, decide to hang out for several months or more. Of course, the length of their stay depends upon their means of support and their motive for coming in the first place. Most are drawn by the charm of the capital city, Prague. Others come to escape the boredom they feel they face in their lives at home. Regardless of their specific destination, travelers to the Czech and Slovak Republics quickly discover how cheap it can be to stay and live pretty well at the same time.

Getting to Prague or Bratislava is generally inexpensive, depending on your mode of travel.

Via airplane

Flying directly to the Czech Republic or Slovakia from the United States or Western Europe is by far the fastest and most expensive way of traveling to either country. Most international flights land at Prague's Ruzyne Airport (roughly twelve miles northwest of the city) before continuing on to points further east, including Bratislava and other destinations in Slovakia. Several international airlines fly directly to Vienna (only 50 kilometers from Bratislava) and then continue to Bratislava by train or bus. This is usually not the cheapest way to get to Slovakia, however.

If the Czech Republic is your final destination, your best bet is to fly directly to Prague. From the centrally located capital city, you can reach your intended stop by train or bus. Prague is accessible from most major cities in Western Europe or by flights that originate in the United States. You can fly direct to Prague from New York City on CSA, the national Czech-Slovak airline. This same flight connects to Bratislava at no extra charge. Western airlines (Air France, British Airways, KLM, Lufthansa, SAS, Sabena) also have service to Prague from points in Western Europe or the United States. Consult a travel agent for current flight information.

Airlines with service to Prague and Bratislava

Prague

Air France .... (02) 422-7164
Czechoslovak Airlines (CSA) .... (02) 421-0132
or (02) 481-5110
British Airways .... (02) 32 90 20 or (02) 32 90 40
KLM .... (02) 422-8678
Lufthansa .... (02) 481-1007 or (02) 33 44 56
SAS .... (02) 421-4749 or (02) 36 78 09
Sabena .... (02) 36 78 13 or (02) 334-4323

Bratislava

Czechoslovak Airlines .... (07) 33 07 88, (07) 31 12 17,
or (07) 33 07 90
Tatra Air* .... (07) 22 77 15
*for flights between Bratislava and Prague, Brno, Poprad, and Kosice

● ●

Via train or bus

As with other destinations in Central and Eastern Europe, travelers often choose to fly into an airport in a major Western European city, then continue by train or bus to their final destination in the Czech Republic or Slovakia. This method of combining air and overland travel is popular among those who have few time constraints because it affords an opportunity to see more of Europe as a whole. Certain train and bus fares allow a traveler to stop along the way, provided that travel continues in the same direction as the train or bus route.

International train and bus routes that originate in Western Europe are not cheap, so you should calculate the cost of your combined air and overland fares in order to compare them with the airfare that will take you directly to your destination. Of course, your final choice will depend upon your priorities. Trains and buses generally give you greater flexibility, while allowing you to sightsee along the way.

Because train and bus travel is usually less expensive than flying, more budget-conscious young people, both expats and Europeans, opt for the tracks and the highways, so you'll have a better chance of meeting young people who are perhaps of a similar bent.

WHEN YOU ARRIVE

Ruzyne airport outside of Prague will likely be your first stop if you choose to fly directly to the Czech Republic. Those who are traveling to Slovakia may consider flying into Vienna instead of Prague. It's only thirty miles from Bratislava.

Airport

Ruzyne is small, relatively clean, and easy to navigate. Only twelve or so miles from central Prague, it is easily and quickly reached by taxi or bus.

Traveling by taxi from Ruzyne into Prague is often a greater challenge. The taxi stands at the airport are controlled by a syndicate of sorts, which means that you may have to pay a premium to get into the city. Buses, on the other hand, are remarkably cheap. CSA offers a shuttle from the airport to downtown Prague for just a few crowns. You can also take a city bus to the nearest Metro stop (Dejvicka), and then continue on the subway to your final destination.

If you should choose to fly to Vienna in order to travel overland to Bratislava, you will have to contend with both Austrian currency (in order to purchase your ticket) and a connecting train or bus ride. Vienna is a great city, though, so the added expense and inconvenience may be worthwhile.

Train stations

If your final destination lies somewhere in Slovakia, then you will probably have to travel to Bratislava first. It is the main hub for all domestic train travel in the Slovak Republic. Because it also lies close to both Vienna and Budapest, it can be a pivot point for international travelers in Central and Eastern Europe. Its main train station lies outside the center of the city, but is connected to downtown Bratislava by several tram lines. Don't expect much from this train station because it doesn't offer much besides luggage storage and shelter for a few drunks.

When you take the train to Prague, you will likely arrive at Hlavni Nadrazi, the main train station which also houses a centrally located metro stop. Some international trains terminate their service to Prague at Holesovice, another of Prague's larger train stations (and also a metro stop on the same line as the main station). With the steady influx of tourists since the early 1990s, the incidence of theft on trains and at the stations has also risen significantly, so be careful.

Because all of the train stations that handle international trains are located on metro lines, it's both inexpensive and convenient to reach your final destination. You probably won't even have to bother with a taxi, unless you prefer to be driven directly to a particular doorstep.

LOCAL TRANSPORTATION

Of the four countries covered in this book, the Czech Republic boasts the best local transportation systems. Prague's Soviet-built metro is clean, efficient, and well-planned (a rare testament to the success of the old regime). Combined with an extensive bus and tram system, it's very easy to get around Prague without an automobile. Be aware, though, that this ease and efficiency brings considerable crowding, especially during rush hours.

None of the other major cities of the Czech Republic or Slovakia, including Bratislava, have metro systems. There are, however, extensive bus, tram, and trolley lines to help you get across town.

If you plan to use public transportation regularly, you should check into getting a monthly pass. You will save money and time, and you won't have to worry about getting "controlled" by a transit officer without the proper pass or ticket.

Metro

Prague's three metro lines crisscross the city and divide it into roughly equal parts. If you combine a metro ride with either tram or bus travel, it's cheap and easy to get to almost any part of the city. Metro trains run from five in the morning until midnight, so don't stay out late unless you don't mind getting home by night tram, bus, or taxi.

Metro tickets can be purchased individually or in booklets from vending machines or ticket windows located in every station. Unless you carry a monthly pass, make sure you validate your ticket in the orange machines before you enter the platform areas. If you're caught without a valid ticket by a controller you will be fined the equivalent of about six dollars (not really worth the hassle considering a ticket costs a small fraction of the fine).

Trams

Trams help make commuting easy while lending charm to the cities of Europe. Both Prague and Bratislava have extensive tram networks that compliment their other forms of public transportation. As with metros and buses, trams require a valid ticket for each ride. Ticket validators on trams are usually located just inside the tram doors, on the posts that support the hand rails.

Most of the cities in Slovakia and the Czech Republic that offer tram service utilize the same tickets for all modes of public transportation. Trams usually run twenty-four hours in the larger cities, though their night runs may be less frequent and less extensive.

Buses

Buses are the backbone of all public transportation systems in the smaller towns and cities of both republics. In the larger cities, they complement subway and tram lines by radiating outward from the tram and Metro stops to smaller and more obscure destinations in the outlying areas.

Depending on where you are, buses may run twenty-four hours a day. Like trams, they usually run at a reduced frequency after 11PM or midnight. Be sure to confirm which bus lines operate at night. The nocturnal routes will usually bear different numbers than the same daytime lines. Some night buses operate on a smaller segment of the route than during daytime.

Unlike trams, buses provide service from the transportation hubs in the larger cities to smaller towns and rural areas. The further you get from the more heavily populated areas, the more you will need to rely on buses. You won't be alone. Intercity or otherwise, buses are often cramped and crowded so make sure to make reservations whenever possible.

In general, intercity and other domestic bus fares are either comparable or somewhat more expensive than rail fares. It's generally a toss-up whether buses are more comfortable than trains or vice versa. Trains give you the option of getting up and moving around whenever you want, while buses usually make stops on longer trips so you can stretch, use the restroom, smoke a cigarette, or gobble a snack.

Taxis

All over Central and Eastern Europe, taxi drivers are notorious for overcharging unsuspecting foreigners. The larger cities of the Czech Republic are no exception, particularly in Prague. As a general rule, settle on a price before you get into a cab. If the driver tries to ream you, you can turn him down with a polite "no thank you." Once you board the cab, the ball is in the driver's court. So make sure the meter is in operation. If you can, chat with the driver a bit and try a little Czech on him if you know any. Show him that you know where you're going. Act as though you've been through it before so he'll be less inclined to try to bilk you for more money.

Domestic trains

Prague, Plzen, and Brno are the main rail hubs in the Czech Republic. In Slovakia, Bratislava and Kosice are the primary rail crossroads. CSD is the name of the national railroad. It is still shared by both countries.

CSD offers two types of trains: *rychlík* (express train) or *osobny vlak* (local train). Local trains are notoriously slow, so avoid them whenever possible unless you want to stop at every podunk station in the Czech or Slovak countryside.

SHORT-TERM ACCOMMODATIONS

Youth hostels, hotels, and private rooms are the most common types of short-term accommodations in the Czech and Slovak Republics. Though not necessarily plentiful, short-term accommodations are generally easier to find than long-term rentals. If you are looking for longer-term accommodations, *Annonce*, a Czech triweekly publication, has apartment listings (in Czech). Also, many real estate agencies, for a fee, will assist foreigners in finding apartments.

By far the most convenient way to locate a place to stay is to contact an accommodation agency. When searching for short-term accommodations, both the language barrier and your unfamiliarity with the area can prolong your search to the point where you become frustrated enough to settle for something you might regret.

Accommodations agencies

Prague

Accommodation Service
Hastalske namesti, Stare Mesto
Phone: (02) 31 02 02
Fax: (02) 481-0603

American Express
Vaclavske namesti 56 (near
　Muzeum metro station)
Phone: (02) 421-5397
Fax: (02) 422-7786

AVE LTD. Travel Agency
Hlavni Nadrazi
(main train station)
Phone: (02) 422-3226
　or (02) 422-3218
Reservations (02) 461-7133
　or (02) 54 97 44
Fax: (02) 54 22 39
　or (02) 54 97 33

AVE LTD. Travel Agency
Holesovice train station

AVE LTD. Travel Agency
Ruzyne Airport
Phone: (02) 334-3106

Cedok
Panska 5
Phone: (02) 421-3495
　or (02) 421-4192

Cedok at Ruzyne Airport
Phone: (02) 36 78 02
　or (02) 36 78 03

Hello Ltd. Travel Agency
Senovazne 3 (Goreko namesti)
Phone: (02) 421-2741
Phone/fax: (02) 421-2647

Prague Suites
Melantrichova 8 (near Mustek
　metro station)
Phone: (02) 422-9961
　or (02) 422-0467
Fax: (02) 422-9363

Toptour
Rybna 3
Phone: (02) 232-1077
Fax: (02) 3481 4100

CK Prague International
Senovazna 23
Prague 1
Phone: (02) 414-2751
　or (02) 414-2432

Cristal Tour
Reznicka 5

Prague 1
Phone: (02) 29 98 70

Rhia Tours
Skolska 1, Prague 1
Phone: (02) 29 48 43

Bratislava

Bratislava Information Service (BIS)
Panska 18
Phone: (07) 33 43 25

CKM
Hviezoslavovo namestie 16
Phone: (07) 33 16 07
   or (07) 33 41 14

Satur
Jesenskeho 3
Phone: (07) 36 76 13
   or (07) 36 84 06

Tatratour
Frantiskanske namesti 3
Phone: (07) 33 36 47

Tourist information offices

Prague

American Hospitality Center
Melantrichova 7
Phone: (02) 423-9062
   or (02) 423-3067

American Hospitality Center
Male namesti 14
Phone: (02) 422-5502

Cedok
Na prikope 18 (main office)
Phone: (02) 419-7350
   or (02) 419-7642

CKM Student Centre
Jindrisska 28
Phone: (02) 26 85 32
   or (02) 423-0218

Prague Information Service (PIS)
Old Town Square 22
Phone: (02) 421-2844
   or (02) 421-2845 (information in English)

Prague Information Service (PIS)
Na prikope 20
Phone: (02) 22 43 11 for city tours

Prague Information Service (PIS)
Panska 4
Phone: (02) 421-3703
Fax: (02) 421-2750

Prague Information Service (PIS)
At the main train station

Prague Information Service (PIS)
Info-by-phone (02) 54 44 44

Bratislava

Bratislava Information Service (BIS)
Panska 18
Phone: (07) 33 37 15
   or (07) 33 43 70

CKM
Hviezdoslavovo namestie 16
Phone: (07) 33 16 07
   or (07) 33 41 14

Satur
Jesenskeho 3
Phone: (07) 36 76 13
   or (07) 36 84 06

Slovakoturist
Panska 13
Phone: (07) 33 35 11
Fax: (07) 33 36 15

Youth hostels

Not all youth hostels and junior hotels (operated by the National Youth Travel Organization) are open year-round in the Czech and Slovak Republics. The closer you are to the center of a larger city, the more likely they are to stay open in the off-season (meaning the late fall and winter months). Hostels and junior hotels are inexpensive and therefore crowded. Don't expect to find peace and quiet or privacy in a hostel. And plan to abide by certain rules, such as curfews and wake-up calls, that you wouldn't encounter in a hotel or private room.

If, on the other hand, you want to meet droves of rowdy and often beer-soaked young travelers, then hostels might be just the thing for you. They can be ridiculously cheap, often just a few dollars per night.

Prague

Hostel Petrska
Petrska 3
Phone: (02) 31 51 89
    or (02) 31 64 30

Hostel Sokol
Holeckova 1
Phone: (02) 997-1691

Hotel ESTEC
Strahov
Vanickova 5/1
Prague 6
Phone: (02) 52 12 50, (02) 52
    73 43, or (02) 52 73 44

Youth Hostel B&B
Jankovcova 163/A
Phone: (02) 80 48 91

Universitas Tour
Kolej JEDNOTA
Opletalova 38
Prague 1
Phone: (02) 26 04 26

Bratislava

Bernolak (SD)
Bernolakova 1
Phone: (07) 49 77 21
(June–Aug.)

Mlada Garda
Racianska 103
Phone: (07) 25 31 36
(mid-July to mid-Aug.)

Nesporak
Svoradova 13
Phone: (07) 31 15 40

Sputnik Junior Hotel (HI)
Drienova 14
Phone: (07) 29 41 67

YMCA na Slovenska
Karpatska 2
Phone: (07) 49 80 05
(mid-July to mid-Aug.)

**Ustav Vzdelavania v
    Stavebnictve**
Bardosova 33
Phone: (07) 37 52 12

Hotels

Because of the ever-increasing popularity of tourism in the Czech Republic, and to a lesser degree Slovakia, inexpensive hotels can be hard to find. Whereas in Krakow you might find a room for the equivalent of ten to twelve dollars, Prague's equivalent hotel accommodations will run five to six times that much. Though this may not seem like much relative to the price of accommodations in the West, it's a fair amount to spend given the remarkably low cost of living in these two countries. Unfortunately, there is a serious shortage of hotel accommodations in Prague, Bratislava, and the other popular tourist destinations, especially during the summer months.

Finding an inexpensive hotel room, or any available hotel room for that matter, takes time. Plan ahead by making reservations well in advance whenever possible, especially in Prague. If you plan to find a room on your own, start early in the day. You can also book hotel rooms through a travel agency or booking service. Try any Cedok office, or any other booking service. In Prague, check around Na Prikope, where most of these agencies are located. Because it might take you the better part of a day to find an appropriate room, any nominal fee you might pay will be worthwhile.

Locating a room through a travel agent or booking agency will take care of several potentially frustrating problems:

- Most travel and booking agents are bilingual, employing either English or German as their second language.

- The agency will possess a map to enable you to select an appropriate area of town.

- Perhaps most importantly, the agency will have a telephone available so they can determine room availability for you in advance. (This will save you the hassle of locating a public telephone that works.)

Prague

Hotel Opera
Tesnov 13
Prague 1
Phone: (02) 31 56 09
    or (02) 31 57 94

Pension Unitas
Bartolomejska 9 (near Narodni
    trida metro station)
Phone: (02) 32 77 00
    or (02) 32 77 09

Hotel Balkan
Svornosti 28
(near Andel metro station)
Phone: (02) 54 07 77

Hotel Garni
Zaviskova 30
Phone: (02) 692-5668

Pension Krokodyl
Belehradska 26
Phone: (02) 691-1061

Hotel MIRA
Vlastislavova 7
Prague 4

Garden Pension
Kratka 39
100 00 Prague 10-Strasnice
Phone/fax: (02) 77 33 84

Bratislava

American House
Kremnicka 7
Phone: (07) 83 88 90

Hotel Gracia
Razusovo nabrezie
Phone: (07) 33 21 32
Fax: (07) 33 21 31

Clubhotel
Odjojarov 3
Phone: (07) 25 63 69

Hotel Krym
Safarikovo namestie 7
Phone: (07) 32 54 71

Private rooms

Because thousands of tourists flock to the area each year, primarily during the summer months, there are literally thousands of private rooms offered for rent in Czech and Slovak homes. Booking agents who handle private room reservations can now be found all over Prague and in many of the other well-visited areas. You won't even have to search out a booking agent if you arrive on one of the more crowded international trains at Prague's main station. As soon as you step onto the platform, you will likely encounter people offering accommodations in their homes. Most of these folks are just trying to supplement their meager incomes with a little hard currency. You don't need to be suspicious unless a gut feeling tips you off that the person is more interested in your money than your general well-being. No matter whether you employ a booking agent or follow an ordinary citizen to their own doorstep, make sure that you are shown the location of your prospective lodging on a map. You will also want to know if it is located conveniently for taking public transportation and how long it takes to get to and from the center of town. Only intending to stay in Prague for five or six nights, a lucky traveler related his good fortune:

❝ *When I arrived in Prague at the main train station, I was approached by a cheery elderly lady who asked me in broken English if I needed a room for the night. She showed me pictures of the apartment where I could stay and proceeded to explain that I would meet a couple of Spaniards who were staying in the next room. She looked nice, and the price and location seemed good enough, so I rode the subway and bus back to her place. I ended up staying for almost two weeks."*

Find out what the daily rate is before you traipse off to have a look at the place. If it meets your needs, decide on a daily or weekly rate before you take the room. If you plan to stay longer than a week, see if you can get a deal. You shouldn't have to pay the same rate as you would on a daily basis because your host is assured occupancy without having to spend time recruiting new guests down at the station.

If your host doesn't speak English, sketch out your intentions on a piece of paper by writing down the dates you plan to stay and the amount you agree to pay. Keep the piece of paper. In case of any later confusion, you can refer to it.

Finding a teaching position

OVERVIEW

Under the Soviet-backed regime, Russian-language instruction was compulsory in all state-operated schools. Forced language learning was resented by the majority of Czechoslovakians primarily because it evidenced subjugation. After the revolution, Russian dropped by the wayside as the second language only to be replaced by English, which garnered popularity because it represented the freedom of the West. English-speaking ability was, and still is, seen as the foundation for economic salvation on a personal level. That is, if you learn to speak English, you're closer to understanding the mechanisms of a market economy. Five years beyond the momentous toppling of the Berlin Wall, English has become the foreign language of choice for people all over the Czech and Slovak Republics. English teaching jobs are advertised regularly in the classified sections of both Czech/Slovak and English-language newspapers. In the larger cities in places where young people congregate, help-wanted notices are posted on bulletin boards and the like. Visit the American Cultural Center in Prague, the Globe Bookstore and Cafe (Janovskeho 14, Prague 9), or the British Council library in Bratislava and you will find notices, and sometimes even lists, that prospective employers place to find native-speaking English teachers.

In the Czech and Slovak Republics most teaching jobs are found in the private sector. There are more small private language schools than there are larger public institutions. And private schools usually have more money available to pay native-speaking teachers. In terms of the demands made on teachers, however, public and private schools operate similarly. Broad curriculums are generally provided by the school. Individual teachers are responsible for making adaptations that fit the specific requirements of the class. Most school directors realize that a certain level of standardization is beneficial but that teachers have unique styles and skills that should be made available to students. Teachers may be expected to abide by rough guidelines or even specific lesson plans provided by the school. Regardless of a school's particular requirements, preparation can eat up a good deal of a teacher's time outside the classroom. Full-time teaching may require only twenty or so classroom hours per week, though most teachers will tell you that this is a deceptive number. No matter how experienced a teacher may be, improvising lessons on a daily basis when trying to juggle several different classes each day can sap the deepest stores of mental energy. Teaching English requires patience and adaptability. Preparation allows you to focus on the needs of your students without becoming preoccupied by the demands of extemporaneous language instruction.

Full-time teaching may require forty or more hours a week if you combine classroom and preparation time, but actual time spent in the classroom will rarely exceed eighteen to twenty hours per week, unless you make special arrangements to take on an abnormally large class load. Teaching jobs in the public sector usually demand a little less classroom instruction, while the number of hours of preparation time is left up to the individual teacher. In private schools, roughly twenty hours per week of classroom instruction are expected. Because private schools must meet the scheduling demands of a broader segment of the population in order to be viable, classes may be offered anytime throughout the day and early evening. You may even be asked to teach at a couple of different locations on any given day, though you will generally know in advance. Some schools even offer classes on Saturdays. The important thing to remember here is that, as a general rule, the better-established programs generally provide more structure for teachers both inside and outside the classroom. If you want to take a position in a smaller private school or recently established public school program, the burden of setting up a viable curriculum may rest on your shoulders. For example, if you choose to find a job in a public school in a small, out-of-the-way town that has never had an English language program, a good portion of your interview may be spent trying to convince the local school administrator that you have the necessary experience and formal knowledge that it takes to design a language instruction program from scratch. So it's obviously important to decide where you want to focus your energies so that you can determine what kinds of questions to ask during the interview, and for that matter, even before you formally apply for a job.

In the Czech Republic, the influx of expatriates has upped the ante in the field of English language instruction. In other words, employers are expecting more from prospective teachers than they were just a few years ago. The ability just to speak English is no longer sufficient qualification for most teaching jobs, especially in Prague. Beyond RSA or TEFL certification, you may need to further convince your interviewer of your tenacity and dedication. Be prepared to answer questions regarding why you came to the Czech Republic, how long you plan to stay, and what you want to achieve while you're there. Try to communicate that your are genuinely interested in teaching, that it's not simply the means to fund whatever you choose to do in your

Tourists are never in short supply in Prague, one of the most popular tourist destinations in the world.

spare time. It's important to set yourself apart from the average expat who has come to teach simply because they've heard that teaching jobs are easy to find.

For the last several years there has been much discussion in both the Czech and expatriate communities about why people come to the Czech Republic and what they have to offer. Some people, especially on the Czech side, feel that they are being taken advantage of because their country is at once attractive and inexpensive. And even among expats, discussion often centers on what can be actively done on their part to benefit the Czech people. Because English teaching is perhaps the most common form of employment among younger expats, questions often arise about the level of professionalism and dedication that many teachers bring to their jobs.

Though there may be many of these kinds of questions posed outside the classroom, the situation inside the classroom in both the Czech and Slovak Republics is a different subject altogether. Don't expect things to get too heated. Czech and Slovak students are generally a courteous bunch who understand and appreciate the rigors of learning. Whereas most Czechs and Slovaks despised being forced to speak German or to study Russian, many now welcome the opportunity to learn English. Needless to say, enthusiasm usually is not in short supply in the classroom, particularly with students who were subjected to compulsory Russian.

Outside of the fact that Czechs may strike you as slightly more urbane and Western in their orientation than Slovaks, in general, both Czech and Slovak students resemble something of a cross between Polish and Hungarian students. In general, they are more likely to be vocal in class than Hungarians and a little less gregarious and open than Poles. In many respects, though, the Czech and Slovak sensibility bears greater resemblance to that of the Polish because they share in the Slavic heritage. Hungarians are thought to be more hot-blooded and open, while the northern Slavic peoples may come across as a little more distant and reserved, especially in public. In this case, the public may include the classroom, particularly in the beginning of each term before you have ample time to impress your students with your teaching expertise and your sense of humor.

WHERE TO START

The majority of prospective language teachers who decide to settle in either the Czech Republic or Slovakia begin by looking for jobs in either Prague or Bratislava because these two capital cities have a well-established expat communities that provide a feeling of a home away from home. Deciding where to start depends upon your individual needs and expectations. The following sources of information will help you begin your search for a teaching position.

The classifieds

English-language and Czech/Slovak newspapers alike provide classified ad sections with help-wanted listings. Teaching positions often command large portions of the classified page(s). Given the size of the expat community in Prague, a general news-oriented English-language newspaper has sprung up in the last five years. The *Prague Post* can be found at most major newsstands across the country. You can get the *Prague Post* before you go by ordering a subscription via

Prague Post
Na Porici 12
Prague 1 110 00
Phone: (02) 487-5000
Fax: (02) 487-5050 or (02) 32 87 77
Email: PRGPOST@Traveller.CZ
    or 100120.361@compuserve.com

Annonce is a Czech newspaper specializing in classified ads. Though not necessarily as useful when conducting a job search for a teaching position, it is worth getting acquainted with because it may list other interesting positions. It is most popular among expats for its apartment and room-for-rent listings.

Follow up on every ad you find, even if you don't possess all the qualifications listed. Make a phone call to find out if you might be considered for the teaching position, or better yet, simply show up at the address listed to see if you might get an interview. If you meet some of the needs of the position and if there are not enough fully qualified or experienced teachers to fill the demand, you might just land your first teaching job. Besides, if you talk with an employer in person, you will be able to find out more about the idiosyncrasies of the present job market.

Advertising your services

Putting up fliers that advertise your services as a native-speaking tutor is a common and often effective way to attract private students. Bulletin boards that cater to prospective students, such as those found in English-language bookstores and libraries, student lounges, and businesses that serve the English-speaking community are generally good places to start. In Prague, try the library at the American Cultural Center, the Globe Cafe and Bookstore, or the bulletin board in the downstairs lobby of the British Council as a start. In Bratislava, check out the British Council English-Language Resource Center or the Slovak Academic Information Agency (SAIA). If you are truly ambitious, you could even advertise in the local newspapers' classifieds sections. Of course, you would need to be settled enough to have a steady address or phone number and either know how to draw up an ad in Czech or Slovak or be able to find someone to help you.

The British Council English Teaching Centers, which are located in most major cities in Central and Eastern Europe, are good resources for all prospective teachers. They were set up to further the cause of English-language instruction in general and are not necessarily reserved only for British teachers. The British Council often will furnish bulletin boards, lists of local language schools that hire native speakers, and other English-language-oriented resources.

British Council in Prague
14 Vorsilska
Prague 1, Czech Republic

British Council in Bratislava
Panska 17
Bratislava 811 01, Slovakia

The British Council has an American counterpart called the American Cultural Center. Though not necessarily as geared toward furthering the causes of English-language instruction, the American Cultural Centers in Central and Eastern Europe usually provide libraries and other resources that may benefit the expat job hunter.

American Cultural Center—Czech Republic
Hybernska 7a
Prague 1 117 16, Czech Republic

American Cultural Center—Slovak Republic
Hviezdoslavovo Namesti 4
Bratislava 811 01, Slovakia

Word of mouth

Let everyone you bump into know that you're looking for a teaching job or for students to teach privately. Hang out in places where you will find other expats or Czechs and Slovaks who are interested in learning English. Local pubs, bookstores, coffee houses, and even laundromats are good places. If you get to know people, you will undoubtedly cross paths with people who can point you in the right direction.

EMPLOYMENT OPTIONS

You only need to glance at the *Prague Post* to see that teachers are still in high demand around the two republics. There are enough schools, both public and private, looking for teachers that you should be able to find a good position in a place suited to your needs, whether you're seeking the environs of a city like Prague or an out-of-the-way town in Eastern Slovakia. The competition is greater in Prague and Bratislava, but these are attractive places because they offer lifestyles well matched to restless and rambunctious expat types. If you lack formal teaching credentials and teaching experience, your chances of finding a teaching position are better the further you get from Prague, and to a lesser degree from Bratislava. Nonetheless, a higher level of competition has not stopped many inexperienced teachers from finding work. So, if Prague is the place for you, you'll just have to be more persistent and tenacious.

According to a teacher at one of the larger private schools in Prague, when asked what he saw as the future of English teaching:

❝ *The demand itself will not change over the next several years. It will remain high. However, the mode of offering classes will evolve. More small private schools will pop up, and there will be a greater need for private teachers. Studying English has already lost much of its novelty among Czech students, but that doesn't mean* *that the demand will fall. In fact, our teachers are being hired out to private companies in increasing numbers. Some have even been hired out as translators and proofreaders for television stations."*

As in the other countries of Central and Eastern Europe, English-teaching positions are found under the following general situations:

Private schools

Private-sector English teaching jobs are the most common type of employment for expat teachers in the Czech and Slovak Republics. Private schools operate mainly in the mid- to larger-sized cities where the populations of prospective students are large enough and wealthy enough to support them. Teaching jobs in private schools are generally more lucrative and less structured than those found in the public sector. Private schools usually pay their teachers on a cash-only basis, and rarely provide other forms of compensation such as subsidized accommodations or paid vacations. In the Czech Republic and Slovakia, you can expect to make the equivalent of US$6 to $8 per hour, or from 150 to 200 crowns. Given the slight difference in currency rates between the Czech and Slovak crowns, you might make slightly less per hour in Slovakia, but the lower cost of living in Slovakia should make up the difference.

Private schools are businesses that profit from the tuition they collect from their students. Whether or not the school really looks after the best interest of its students and its teachers depends upon the integrity of the school owner or director. If profit is their only motive, you undoubtedly will find disgruntled students and teachers. These kinds of schools are obviously the ones to avoid because they generally don't stay in business too long; or at very least, they don't attract the kinds of teachers and students you will want to spend your time with. Don't let this dissuade you from pursuing work in private schools, just be aware of the realities. Try to find a school that balances its priorities so that your aims are compatible with the school's overall goals. Before you accept a position, talk to the school's teachers and students in order to find out whether or not you might want to work there. There are plenty of good schools that offer classes set up to benefit students. Find out what kinds of support they offer their teachers, too. It's important to know that your employer values both your position and the benefit you bring the school.

The following schools hire native speakers, though their requirements vary:

Czech Republic
Prague
Agentura Euro Contact
Janovskeho 52
Prague 7 170 00
Czech Republic
Phone: (02) 80 15 27
Fax: Same as phone
Hiring requirements: Varies according to school
Hourly wage: 150 Czech crowns
Length of contract: Varies
Classes taught: Varies according to school
To apply: Apply in person, or send a resume and cover letter with a
photo.
Comments: This is a placement agency for teachers, not a school.
There is no fee for placement.

The American English School of Prague (AESOP)
Ul. M. Horakove–Prasny Most
P.O. Box 181
Prague 6 160 00
Czech Republic
Phone: (02) 320 144
Fax: (02) 322 765
North American staff: 1
Total staff: 5
Students per class: 8
Hiring requirements: Applicants should have a college degree in TEFL.
Hourly wage: Varies, depending on type of course; 105 Czech crowns
is average
Length of contract: One year minimum
Classes taught: TOEFL
To apply: Send a resume, a copy of your passport, and a copy of your
TEFL certificate. The school will then send an application.
Comments: Health security and work permit are provided, though
there is no help with accommodations. The school calendar runs
from September through January and from February through June.

Anglictina Express
Vodickova 39 (passage Svetozor)
Prague 1 110 00
Czech Republic
Phone: (02) 26 15 26

Fax: (02) 25 68 33
North American staff: 12
Total staff: 15
Students per class: 15 max.
Hiring requirements: Applicants should have a college degree in education.
Hourly wage: 115–120 Czech crowns
Length of contract: One year minimum
Classes taught: Conversational English
To apply: Send or fax a resume and cover letter.
Comments: This school uses audio cassettes for teaching Conversational English. They help find accommodations, offer health security, and provide a work permit. The school year runs from September through June with eight weeks summer vacation.

The Bell School
Nedvezska 29
Prague 10 100 00
Czech Republic
Phone: (02) 781 5342
Fax: (02) 782 2961
North American staff: 5
Total staff: 65
Students per class: 12 in regular class; 8 in business class
Hiring requirements: Applicants must have a college degree, TESL certificate, and teaching experience.
Hourly wage: 160 Czech crowns
Length of contract: One year
Classes taught: Cambridge English, Cambridge Advanced English, Cambridge Proficient English (TOEFL equivalents)
To apply: Send a resume, cover letter, and two references.
Comments: The school provides help finding accommodations. Applicants must take care of obtaining work and resident permits. (It takes about three months to get a permit.) Teachers pay part of their health insurance. The school year runs from September through June. Summer classes are available. Applications for The Bell School Annex must be processed through this office.

The Bell School Annex
Ortenovo Namesti 37
Prague 7 170 00
Czech Republic
Phone: (02) 667 121 53 or (02) 667 21 25

To apply: Send a resume and cover letter with a photo to the main office (Nedvezska 29, Prague 10; see above).

Comments: Information is the same as for The Bell School main office, above. This school is an extension of The Bell School. All applications must be processed through the main office.

Berlitz
Jecna 12
Prague 2 120 00
Czech Republic
Phone: (02) 299 958
Fax: Same as phone
North American staff: 4
Total staff: 110
Students per class: 1–5, depending on lesson being taught
Hourly wage: 210 Czech crowns
Monthly wage: Varies according to work load
Length of contract: Varies
Classes taught: Conversational English, TOEFL, GMAT/GRE
To apply: Apply in person and fill out an application, or send a resume and cover letter with a photo.
Comments: Work schedules are flexible. Group and individual lessons are taught, as well as intensive courses.

Berlitz
Na Porici 12
Prague 1 110 00
Czech Republic
Phone: (02) 2487 2052
Fax: (02) 2487 2080
North American staff: 10
Total staff: 20
Students per class: One-on-one instruction
Hiring requirements: Applicants must have a college degree, though not necessarily in teaching. Training is provided by the school.
Hourly wage: 110 Czech crowns
Length of contract: One year minimum
Classes taught: Conversational English
To apply: Send or fax a resume and cover letter.
Comments: Health security and a work permit are provided, but no help is given finding accommodations. There is non-stop teaching year-round with 20 holidays per year.

Berlitz
v. Jame 8
Prague 1 110 00
Czech Republic
Phone: (02) 2421 3185
North American staff: 6
Total staff: 20
Students per class: 2–3 average; 6 max.
Hiring requirements: Applicants must have a college degree, though not necessarily in teaching. Training in Berlitz method is provided by the school. An interview is required.
Hourly wage: 110 Czech crowns
Length of contract: One year minimum
Classes taught: Conversational English and special courses for businesses and companies. Graduates receive a Berlitz diploma.
To apply: Send resume and cover letter. The school will then send an application.
Comments: Health security and a work permit are provided. They provide no help finding accommodations. There is non-stop teaching year round, based on demand. This is a new Berlitz school, opened in September 1995.

Berlitz
Vlkova 12
Prague 3 130 00
Czech Republic
Phone: (02) 277 101
Fax: Same as phone
North American staff: 6
Total staff: 20
Students per class: 2–3 average; 6 max.
Hiring requirements: Applicants must have a college degree, though not necessarily in teaching. Training in Berlitz method is provided by the school. An interview is required.
Hourly wage: 110 Czech crowns
Length of contract: One year minimum
Classes taught: Conversational English and special courses for businesses and companies. Graduates receive a Berlitz diploma.
To apply: Send a resume and cover letter. The school will then send an application.
Comments: Health security and a work permit are provided. They provide no help finding accommodations. There is non-stop teaching year round, based on demand.

California Sun School (main office)
Na bojicti 2
120 00 Prague 2, Czech Republic
Phone: (02) 294 817 or (02) 295 681

California Sun School
Gotthardska 8
Prague 6 160 00
Czech Republic
Phone: (02) 32 44 44 or (02) 32 33 33
Fax: (02) 32 26 67
North American staff: Varies
Total staff: 30 average
Students per class: 5–8 average; 15 max.
Hiring requirements: A TEFL certificate is highly preferred. Particular preference is given to experienced teachers.
Hourly wage: Provided upon application
Monthly wage: Provided upon application
Length of contract: Minimum six months; bonus given after 10 months
Classes taught: Conversational English, one-month intensive course; drop-in classes; individual lessons; special programs for children
To apply: Send a resume and cover letter.
Comments: Health security, a work permit, and housing are provided. Two-thirds of the cost of a bus pass is reimbursed. A copy allowance is also provided. There is non-stop teaching year-round with 14 days vacation at Christmas. The school's main office is located at Na Bojicti #2, Prague 2 120 00. Call (02) 2914 817 or (02) 295 681 for information.

English Link
Kolodejska 8
Prague 10 100 00
Czech Republic
Phone: (02) 360 3515, ext. 229 or (02) 781 7625
Fax: (02) 360 3515
North American staff: 2
Total staff: 25
Students per class: Varies
Hiring requirements: Applicants must have an ESL degree.
Monthly wage: 9,000–12,000 Czech crowns
Length of contract: Six months to one year
Classes taught: Preparation for the Cambridge exam (TOEFL equivalent)

To apply: Send a resume with a cover letter and photo.

Comments: Teachers are provided with a work permit and help finding accommodations. Teachers receive a two-week Christmas vacation and a three-week paid vacation after completing their contract. If telephoning this school, make sure it is during business hours, otherwise the switchboard will not connect you.

Language School of Prague
Narodni 20
Prague 1 116 72
Czech Republic
Phone: (02) 2491 4114 or (02) 2491 2236
Fax: (02) 2491 4114
North American staff: 6
Total staff: 150
Students per class: 20 max.
Hiring requirements: Applicants should have a college degree in education.
Monthly wage: 9,000 Czech crowns average; 7,300–7,500 Czech crowns at entry level
Length of contract: One year minimum
To apply: Send a resume with a cover letter and photo.
Comments: This school uses a particular Czech method for teaching Conversational English. The school calendar runs from September through June with eight weeks of summer vacation.

Linga Pro
Vinohradska 28
Prague 2 120 00
Czech Republic
Phone: (02) 252 610
Fax: (02) 733 520
North American staff: 4
Total staff: 45
Students per class: 8–10
Hiring requirements: Applicants must have a college degree, preferably in education or humanities. Priority is given to experienced teachers.
Hourly wage: 150 Czech crowns
Monthly wage: 12,000 Czech crowns
Length of contract: One year
Classes taught: One-on-one TOEFL, weekend English language camp in recreational areas, and the Cambridge course (TOEFL equivalent)

To apply: Send a resume and cover letter. Include age.
Comments: The school provides help finding a work permit and accommodations. The school calendar runs from September 10 through June 30.

London School of Modern Languages
Belgicke 25
Prague 3 130 00
Czech Republic
Phone: (02) 25 68 59
Fax: (02) 2424 7025
North American staff: 4
Total staff: 40
Students per class: 6–10
Hiring requirements: Applicants must have a bachelor's degree with certification in TESL.
Monthly wage: 6,000–8,500 Czech crowns
Length of contract: One year
Classes taught: Classes vary according to student needs. Programs include preparation for the Cambridge exam (TOEFL equivalent) and courses for business people.
To apply: Send a resume and cover letter.
Comments: Accommodations and a work permit are provided. The school calendar runs from September through June. There are two weeks of vacation around Christmas and one week of spring vacation.

Brno
Berlitz
Dominikanske namesti
Brno
Czech Republic
Phone: (05) 4221 3302

Brno English Center
Kravy Hora
Brno 616 00
Czech Republic
Phone: (05) 4121 2262
Comments: This school formerly served as the language center for Travel 2002 in Brno.

ILC

Sokolska 1
Brno 611 00
Czech Republic
Phone: (05) 4124 0494 or (05) 4121 0723
North American staff: 0
Total staff: 10. Currently, all staff is from Great Britain, but they are interested in hiring North Americans.
Students per class: 16 max.
Hiring requirements: Applicants should have teaching certification.
Monthly wage: 3,000–4,000 Czech crowns
Length of contract: By semester or for one year.
Classes taught: All levels, including Cambridge (TOEFL equivalent)
To apply: Send a resume and cover letter with a photo.

Universum

Korenskeho 23a
Brno 621 00
Czech Republic
Phone: (05) 4122 5173
Fax: Same as phone
North American staff: 2
Total staff: 15
Students per class: Approx.15
Hiring requirements: Applicants should be native English speakers.
Hourly wage: 90 Czech crowns
Length of contract: One school year (9 months, September–June).
Classes taught: Cambridge exam (TOEFL equivalent)
To apply: Send a resume with a cover letter and photo.
Comments: The school provides assistance with work and residency permits.

Slovakia
Bratislava

The English Club

Pri Suchom Mylne 36
Bratislava 811 04
Slovakia
Phone: (07) 372 106
Fax: (07) 372 411
North American staff: 2
Total staff: 5
Students per class: 12–15

Hiring requirements: Applicants should have a degree in education and TEFL certification.
Hourly wage: 80 Slovak crowns
Length of contract: One year, minimum 30 hours per week
Classes taught: Conversational English
To apply: Send a resume and cover letter with a photo.
Comments: This school provides assistance finding accommodations (usually with families) and obtaining working permits.

ENLAP Language School
Lazaretska 3, Room 67
Bratislava 845 105
Slovakia
Phone: (07) 231 300, ext. 234
North American staff: 2
Total staff: 10
Students per class: 8–16
Hiring requirements: Applicants should be native speakers of English.
Hourly wage: Varies
Monthly wage: Varies
Length of contract: Indefinite
Classes taught: All levels, including Conversational English and Cambridge (TOEFL equivalent)
To apply: Applicants should apply in person, or send a resume and cover letter with a photo.

Divina
Zakladna skola Divina
Divina 013 31
Slovakia
Phone: (089) 846 82
Fax: Same as phone
Email: zsdivina@uvt.utc.sk
North American staff: 0
Total staff: 16
Students per class: 22
Hiring requirements: Applicants should have a teaching degree.
Hourly wage: 30 Slovak crowns
Monthly wage: 5,000–6,000 Slovak crowns
Length of contract: One full school year (10 months)
Classes taught: Conversational English, TOEFL
To apply: Send a resume and cover letter with a photo.

Martin
Gymnazium Viliama Paulinhyo–Totha
Mala Hora 3
Martin 036 01
Slovakia
Phone: (0842) 331 91
Fax: (0842) 310 26
Email: alica@sco.gymmt.sk
Classes taught: Conversational English
To apply: Send a resume and cover letter with a photo.

Spisska Nova
Gymnazium Spisska Nova Ves
Javorova 16
Spisska Nova Ves 052 01
Slovakia
Phone: (0965) 257 57
Email: vlasnv@auriga.ta3.sk
North American staff: 15
Total staff: Approx. 45
Students per class: 16
Length of contract: One year minimum
Classes taught: Conversational English
To apply: Send a resume and cover letter with a photo.

Zilina
Skolska sprava Zilina
Komenskeho 35
Zilina 010 93
Slovakia
Phone: (089) 318 06
Email: zsdivina@uvt.utc.sk
North American staff: 0
Hiring requirements: Applicants should have a college degree.
To apply: Send a resume and cover letter with a photo.
Comments: This is an elementary school. If they are not hiring or if your qualifications are not quite right, they may forward your resume to the nearby secondary school in Banska Bystrica.

Public schools

For teachers with formal credentials and experience, public schools in the Czech Republic and Slovakia are great places to find rewarding teaching positions. And though they would like to attract teachers who are credentialed and experienced, not all public schools have this luxury. When they need to fill a vacancy quickly, they may hire someone with a lot of enthusiasm, but without much experience or even formal qualifications.

In general, public schools do not pay as well as private schools, although the benefits they provide may help compensate for the differences in salary. Public schools often help their expat teachers locate accommodations, and in some cases they may actually provide room and board free of charge. Another advantage: public schools must operate within the bounds of the law. Consequently, they help you arrange all necessary work visas and residency permits. In addition, public schools deduct all of your social security taxes from your salary so that you will qualify for all public health care benefits. Salaries in the public schools typically range from US$200 to $280, or roughly 5,000 to 7,000 crowns per month. Yes, these seem like paltry sums, but it's amazing how little you can live off of in either country, particularly if your accommodations are covered and you avoid trying to set records for successive nights of partying. And remember, there are different ways to supplement your income if you organize your time efficiently.

Teaching positions in public schools may differ significantly from private sector jobs in other ways, too. Because schools contribute to the foundation of a community, you will have the opportunity to get more deeply involved in Czech or Slovak society. Public schools exist in places where you won't be able to find a private school for miles. If rural or small-town living appeals to you, you will have a better chance of finding your niche in the public school sector.

An American woman who was director of a local teacher volunteer organization in Bratislava said:

❝ *In smaller communities, foreigners are more often respected and well liked."*

If you are interested in applying for a position in a public school in the Czech or Slovak Republic, contact the organizations below:

Ministry of National Education-Czech Republic
Ministerstvo Skolstvi
Mladeze a telovychovy CR
Karmelitska 8
Prague 1, Czech Republic
Phone: (02) 519-3111 (switchboard), (02) 519-3604 (foreign relations), (02) 519-3796 or (02) 519-3471 (general information)

If you write, you can request a list of schools and towns that are in need of English teachers. It's almost impossible to find information over the phone, and it's difficult to find someone who speaks English.

Czech Academic Information Agency
Senorazne namesti 26
Prague 1 111 21, Czech Republic
Phone: (02) 422-9714

Education for Democracy
P.O. Box 40514
Mobile, AL 36640
Phone: (334) 434-3889
Fax: (334) 434-3731

Education for Democracy (EFD) recruits teachers for Slovakia and Russia. However, at the time of this printing (December 1995), EFD is restructuring its organization and refocusing its direction. While they are not currently accepting applications, they are certainly worth contacting for more information. Generally, transportation to and from Slovakia and teacher training is paid for by the volunteer in exchange for a salary and paid accommodations. Volunteers must agree to a minimum commitment of one semester. Some ESL experience may be required.

Slovak Academic Information Agency (SAIA)
P.O. Box 108
Hviezslavovo namestie 14
Bratislava 810 00, Slovakia

Matej Bel University, SAIA
Komenskeho 20
Banska Bystrica 974 01, Slovakia

Technical University, SAIA
Letna 9
Kosice 042 00, Slovakia

The Slovak Academic Information Agency is an independent, non-profit organization that was set up to further the cause of "international cooperation in education and research." Aside from distributing all sorts of educational materials, SAIA conducts workshops, organizes conferences and seminars, and helps to place volunteer native speakers in Slovak schools to assist in language education.

Freelance private tutoring

Private tutoring is fairly common among established teachers in the Czech Republic and Slovakia. Because private lessons command the highest hourly pay of the various types of teaching jobs, it's a great way to supplement your regular salary. It will be up to you to negotiate your pay rate with each individual student. Though you may wish to set a standard hourly rate, it may be to your advantage to remain flexible so that you can attract students of varying means. Of course, you will need to be sensitive or discreet if your students know one another. You might think of it in terms of a sliding scale. With individual students, consider charging in the range of 100 to 200 crowns per hour, which converts to US$5 to $8 per hour. If you work with groups of two or more, figure on lowering your hourly rates accordingly. After all, you can't expect your group study students to pay the same rates as those who receive individual attention.

Finding private students, though, takes time and a little finesse. Unless you have an unusually effective marketing strategy, it's difficult to attract students without some kind of personal introduction by a mutual friend or acquaintance.

Undoubtedly the best place to find private students is through your regular teaching job. Ask your students if they know anyone who would like to study privately—perhaps another family member or close friend. Though it may take a while to get a response, you're sure to find a student or two. Once you prove your effectiveness to someone else, the word will spread.

Though freelancing on a private basis may seem attractive because of the freedom you have to schedule teaching appointments, conducting your own lessons your own way may not turn out to be as appealing as it first sounds. Students are bound to cancel lessons at the last minute on occasion. And because telephones are unreliable, it is often difficult for students to cancel in advance or reschedule their lessons. There will be times when you show up for a lesson only to find that your student is nowhere to be found.

One way to alleviate the kinds of problems inherent in private tutoring is to offer group lessons, where you teach two or more people in the same session. Small groups of four to five students are probably best because they are large enough to take care of the attendance problem yet not so large as to be unmanageable. If one person in the group doesn't show up for a lesson or two, it neither inconveniences you nor dents your pocketbook. Getting a group together in the first place is no small task, though. You must multiply the persistence and energy required to recruit one private student, and then manage the group once it forms by coordinating meeting times and places. Group lessons have advantages for your students as well. The social element built into group lessons can be used as an effective teaching tool by you, while your students don't have to feel the same kind of pressure they might in a one-on-one situation, where the burden to perform well rests solely on their shoulders. And since you probably wouldn't charge as much as you would for a strictly private lesson, your students won't have to cough up as much cash per lesson, while you still make more than you would with a single student.

Rural towns offer a sense of community to those willing to take the path less traveled and shy away from the major cities.

If you are truly ambitious, you might even team up with another native speaker, or perhaps an English-speaking Czech or Slovak person. Establishing a teaching duo might take some of the burden off of you, while enabling you to teach more people at the same time.

In-company instruction

As the economic transformation of these economies continues, more and more Czechs and Slovaks will need to learn to speak English in order to get by in the international business world. By the same token, Czech and Slovak companies must stay competitive, which means they must maintain well-trained and knowledgeable staffs. Consequently, more and more companies are requiring their management teams to study English. And as more foreign and international concerns invest in the two republics, the demand for employees who can speak English is increasing even more. Many companies are responding to this trend by offering English-language instruction to their employees. Some contract with language schools, who provide both the instructors and the teaching materials. Others hire teachers independently.

The amount of money you can make depends on whether you find the position yourself or get it through a contract arrangement with your school. In the former case, you will have to rely on your negotiating skills to create a well-paying teaching position. A little research into what private schools charge their students combined with an understanding of general wage and salary ranges for private teaching should prove to be instructive. A quick glance at the pay ranges quoted above should get you started. Settling on reasonable compensation for in-company teaching will depend on what exactly is expected of you by the company. Your wage or salary should be commensurate to both industry standards and your specific job description. Know what the company expects before you accept a position.

On the other hand, if you work for a language school and not for the company directly, then you will likely be paid your normal hourly wage. In this case, you won't have to worry about negotiating anything.

In-company teaching jobs are hard to come by if you seek them out on your own. Chances are you will need some kind of connection to land an in-company teaching job. Nevertheless, it's worth a try if you're up for the challenge.

Full-time vs. freelance

In the Czech and Slovak Republics, freelance tutoring is a great way to add some variety to your teaching schedule. Freelancing also provides some financial incentive to teach a few hours per week in addition to your full-time position. It is rare, however, for expats to teach exclusively on a freelance basis because it's more appealing in theory than in practice. Coordinating your lessons so you don't have to run all over town while staying abreast of each student's progress is no easy feat. The structure inherent in an in-school job frees you to concentrate on teaching. It's the school's job to manage the students and coordinate classes.

ADVANCE PLANNING

It's not necessary to find a job before you leave for the Czech Republic or Slovakia. If fact, it's not even recommended, particularly if you don't possess formal qualifications and want to find a job with a private school. As with the other countries in Central and Eastern Europe, travel is inexpensive enough so that you should be able to visit different areas to determine where you might like to live for awhile.

The following organizations should provide you with the kinds of information you need in order to decide whether or not to begin your job search in advance:

East European Partnership
15 Princeton Court
53-55 Felsham Road
London SW15 1AZ
United Kingdom
Phone: (441-81) 780 2841

Academy for Inter-Cultural Training
Georgetown University
P.O. Box 2298
Washington, DC 20057
Phone: (202) 687-7032

Language for Eastern European Development (LEED)
41 Sutter Street, Suite 510
San Francisco, CA 94104
Phone: (415) 982-5333

OTHER OPPORTUNITIES

Of all the countries in Central and Eastern Europe, the Czech Republic holds the most promise for foreigners who want to seek employment opportunities outside of language instruction. Given a relatively high tolerance for foreign involvement in the establishment of a market economy, many young Americans have traveled to the Czech Republic in search of a new and novel way of life. Though most younger expats begin their adventure teaching English by day and taking advantage of the low cost of living by night, after a while the initial allure of teaching may wear off. And partying every night can bring its own set of complications. When the glamour of teaching by day and carousing by night wears off, there is usually a choice to be made: stay and find some other kind of employment or leave and go somewhere else. Not surprisingly, a lot of people choose to pursue other kinds of work. Some network with friends or colleagues in order to find jobs which will simply enable them to get by. Others strike out on their own and start up small businesses or find positions in international companies which require more responsibility and longer time commitments. Regardless of the particular paths they choose, what generally sets these people apart from other expats is that they discover something truly inviting about the country and its people which gives meaning to their expatriate lifestyle. Most commonly, they learn to speak Czech or Slovak so that they can both socialize and work effectively with the locals. In fact, they may actually spend more time with their Czech and Slovak friends than they do with other expats. After all, most of them want to make the most of their experiences.

One American expat interviewee contributed:

**" *Now that I've begun working primarily with Czech people, I rarely speak English during my time in the office. And since my girlfriend is Czech, we speak* **

Czech together at home. In fact, now that I'm no longer teaching English, I rarely see other native English speakers anymore."

For the most part, the people who stay and work in the Czech and Slovak Republics make certain compromises with respect to both their careers and their personal lives. Staying overseas for a long period of time means carrying on long distance relationships with friends and family back home. The difference between living and working in the states and in Eastern Europe are significant. Time itself almost seems to have a different character when you live outside the context of the time and place that you are accustomed to. And when it comes to your career or work life, this warping of context often becomes even more pronounced. You might begin to ask yourself questions such as:

- Do I want my job experience in Eastern Europe to be directly relevant to my future career plans back home? Or, am I staying and working because it's a valuable life experience and I might not have such an opportunity later on?
- How long will I need to stay in order to feel that I have accomplished enough to return home with the kind of experience that will look good on my resume?
- Though I am making enough money to live well while I am staying in Eastern Europe, am I willing to forgo making what I could back home if I really applied myself to a job?

Though these questions apply no matter where you decide to stay and work, there are distinct differences between the Czech and Slovak Republics. Just across a recently formed border with the Czech lands, Slovakia has not welcomed as many expatriates nor attracted much foreign investment.

Slovaks seem naturally more suspicious of foreigners than do Czechs. This doesn't mean that you can't teach English or create other opportunities in Slovakia. There are quite a few expats who have stayed for a time in Slovakia and enjoyed their work there immensely. It's just more likely that you will attract certain kinds of unwanted attention or have to deal with more red tape. You must be both resilient and patient to find work other than teaching English in Slovakia.

Referring to many Slovaks' sentiments toward foreigners, an American who lives there said:

❝ *No one is paying any attention to Slovakia, so people here often look up to those who come here to try* *to help. But there is something of a 'foreigner-go-home sentiment.' And with the bureaucracy the way it is, you're subject to the whim of the day. Sometimes it seems that all along the way people are able to make decisions which get in your way. Even so, the expat community here is small but relatively decent. You find people who have heads on their shoulders. They're not trying to escape from something, which often seems to be the case in places like Prague."*

It's worth repeating here that Slovakia is not as far along on the road to economic recovery as the Czech Republic. There isn't as much to go around for either the Slovaks or expatriates in search of opportunity: the Slovak crown isn't worth as much as the Czech crown, Slovakia's infrastructure isn't as well developed as the Czech Republic's, and perhaps most importantly, Bratislava is not the thriving business center and vibrant tourist attraction that Prague is.

A Czech-speaking American who has traveled extensively in the Czech Republic commented:

❝ Whereas the Czech Republic has virtually completed the privatization process, Slovakia has slowed its drive toward privatization. I think about 30 percent of Slovak industry is now in private hands compared to 80 percent in the Czech Republic. There isn't a feeling of entrepreneurial drive in Slovakia, and the Slovaks are more wrapped up in nationalistic sentiment. I was in Bratislava on a Monday morning and it was difficult to find a good place to get a pastry and a cup of coffee. There were a lot of places boarded up, even in the center of town."

The following is a list of the kinds of fields in which American expatriates have pursued employment in the Czech Republic, and to a lesser degree, in Slovakia. It is intended to give you a general idea of what goes on outside of the English-teaching field.

- Service industry: restaurants, bars, hostels, and hotels
- Computer software: engineering and consulting

- Law: international law, business and contract law
- Graphic design and architecture
- Book and magazine publishing
- Marketing and advertising
- Translation and interpreting
- Retail: bookstores and T-shirt shops
- Import-export industry
- General business consulting
- Food catering
- Various entrepreneurial and small business endeavors
- Freelancing in any of the above fields

Unless you want to apply for a job with an international company that does business in either the Czech Republic or Slovakia, your chances of creating opportunities without first venturing across the Atlantic are pretty slim. Most of the people who end up living and working in the republics begin by teaching English and then moving on from there. After all, no matter whether you are relocating to another city in North America or across the Atlantic, it takes time to get situated and to make the kinds of contacts that can lead to new job opportunities. Few who succeed at finding work outside of the English teaching field do so before they have established at least some range of local contacts.

If you're searching for a job that requires either technical knowledge or an advanced degree, or if your area of interest or expertise is fairly specialized, it may be to your advantage to begin your job search in the United States or Canada. Those hired in North America are more likely to be well-compensated (i.e., paid a hard currency salary on a Western pay scale). If you leave before you begin your search, contact the agencies listed below. But remember: no matter where you are, the best way for you to find work is to make as many contacts as possible. A Texan who came to Prague looking for non-teaching work stated:

❝ *I spent three weeks advertising in a classified ad in Annonce before I got an interview. The business sector here is a big market and the most important thing is knowing how to make contacts. If they don't teach English, most expats get started in the service industry."*

Send out resumes and cover letters to companies that do business overseas and arrange to meet with someone who has worked or lived in Slovakia or the Czech Republic. Make contact with a Czech or Slovak person who might maintain either business or family ties with the old country, or consult the director of a foreign exchange or study program in either country through your college or university.

The United States Department of Commerce in the Czech and Slovak Republics publishes a list of all American companies that do business in both countries. The list contains addresses and brief descriptions of each company's business. Contact:

The American Cultural Center
U.S. Department of Commerce
Hybernska 7
Prague 1 117 16
Czech Republic

Another reliable source of information for job seekers are the American Chambers of Commerce in the Czech and Slovak Republics. They keep up-to-date files of resumes of people who are seeking employment in the Czech Republic and Slovakia, so that their members have access to a database of prospective employees. Joining the Chamber of Commerce is expensive, so you should make an appointment to speak with someone about the benefits of joining. Individual memberships cost US$250. Contact:

The American Chamber of Commerce—Czech Republic
Karlovo namesti 24
Prague 1 110 00
Czech Republic
Phone: (02) 29 98 87
Fax: (02) 29 14 81

Settling in

A PLACE TO LIVE

The Czech Republic is the most popular destination for young North American expatriates, which means competition for inexpensive long-term accommodations is fierce. Finding an affordable apartment when you are working on Czech or Slovak wages is no small feat. You need either connections or good fortune.

Renting an apartment

By American standards, most apartments in the two republics seem incredibly cheap to rent; but given their relative lack of amenities, this shouldn't come as any surprise. It's rare to find an apartment with a telephone and most are drab and fairly cramped. Czech and Slovak landlords are well known for charging exorbitant amounts when renting to foreigners, especially North Americans or Western Europeans.

Though many foreigners experience few problems when renting long-term accommodations in either country, it is worth taking advice from those who have been less fortunate. Cultural differences tend to become most evident after relationships have been established, and the tenant-landlord pairing is no exception.

The manager of a language school in Prague, an English man in his early thirties, advised:

 ❝ *If you want to work here in Prague, the first thing you need to do is find a place to live. And the problem is that there is no protection for foreigners, no renters' rights. We need guarantees for both labor rights and tenant rights. Landlords seem to think that if you're from the West, you must be loaded. Privacy is understood differently here, too. Some landlords think that they can enter your apartment when you are not home without first notifying you.* ❞

If you don't know anyone who can help you find an apartment, peruse the classified section of your local paper. In Prague, try the English-language paper *Prague Post* for rental listings, but note that those listed usually involve an agency and therefore are more expensive. A Czech classified newspaper called *Annonce* is also a good place to look. Just make sure you find someone who can help you understand the listings.

Housing in Prague can range from 5,000 to 10,000 Czech crowns or more per month for a room in a house or a small apartment. Bratislava rents do not command as high a range, and apartments outside of the larger cities are considerably less expensive, but not necessarily more readily available.

Consider the following before you sign a rental agreement or lease:

- Renting "gray" or "black," which means your landlord does not pay taxes on rental income, tends to create certain problems for foreigners. For example, you may not be able to receive mail at government-owned properties, and there may be no binding contract that protects you from being cheated by your landlord. Beware of paying large rental deposits without a contract.
- Check out the electrical, plumbing, and heating systems to make sure they are in good working order before you make any commitment.
- If there is a telephone, make sure that you understand how you will be billed, especially if you are sharing it with another party. You may be asked to put down a security deposit for long-distance charges. Unfortunately, foreigners have given themselves a reputation for sticking their landlords with large sums on unpaid long-distance bills.
- Your landlord may have expectations regarding your housekeeping practices. If you can, have a Czech or Slovak speaker interpret any questions you might have for your prospective landlord before you hand over your money. Address all your concerns up front, and ask what is expected of you as a tenant.

CZECH AND SLOVAK LANGUAGES

Czech and Slovak are Slavic languages that are so closely related as to be mutually comprehensible. In fact, it's a matter of contention among linguists whether they are actually separate languages. Many Czechs argue that Slovak is merely a Czech dialect, or at least a distant cousin tongue. Slovaks, on the other hand, naturally regard their language as more than simply a derivative of Czech. Regardless of the argument, the similarities will prove useful if you plan to travel to both countries.

Though linguistic ability generally must be complimented by other skills, fluency in either Czech or Slovak will put you in a good position to find a job. According to an American expatriate who came to Prague to find work as an architect,

❝ *Knowing Czech is extremely valuable. You can do anything.* ❞

Gaining a useful level of proficiency in either language is no simple endeavor, however. There is a very high ratio of consonants to vowels, which makes pronunciation difficult. Grammar, too, is difficult to conquer. Unless you plan to spend a good deal of time studying, you can probably get by learning a few useful words and phrases. Expressing gratitude, giving directions, and offering greetings in the local tongue will earn you enough respect to get by in daily life.

Older people often speak German or Russian (though it is not recommended that you speak Russian in either the Czech or Slovak Republics), while the younger folks tend toward English. So if you can't twist a Slavic tongue, try a Germanic one.

Czech-language schools

For additional language schools that teach Czech and Slovak to foreigners, look in the Yellow Pages under "Jazykove skoly."

Anglictina Express
Vodickova 39
Prague 1 (passage Svetozor)
Phone: (02) 415-2525

Berlitz
Na Porici 12
Prague
Phone: (02) 487-2052

Berlitz
Kouritska 18

Prague
Phone: (02) 324-473

Berlitz
Vlakova 12
Prague
Phone: (02) 27 71 01

Language School of Prague
Narodni 20
Prague
Phone: (02) 491-2229

CZECH AND SLOVAK FOOD AND DRINK

The two republics have several cultural common denominators. Meat and alcohol consumption are among the greatest of these shared traits. If you are an indiscriminate carnivore who likes to wash down well-done cuts of meat with copious quantities of beer, follow your palate's desire right into the land-locked heart of Eastern Europe, where menus read all turf and little surf.

Taste is relative, though. If you come from a meat-and-potatoes background, you might not mind the food. A Czech fellow in his mid-forties—a former dissident who never signed on with the communist party—explained:

❝ *Because I am a translator and an interpreter, I had the opportunity to leave Czechoslovakia prior to the revolution. I could have gone to France or Sweden, but I would have missed Czech cooking, and that was one of the main reasons I stayed.*"

Meat and potatoes, or versions thereof, are the staples of the Czech and Slovak diets. Stewed meat served with dumplings is very common. Given the very conservative use of spices, most dishes are relatively bland. Vegetables are given short shrift in both countries, while dairy products are common ingredients in many dishes.

Vegetarians should familiarize themselves with Czech and Slovak food vocabularies in order to avoid tainting their diets with meat products. Vegans are advised to steer clear of the region, unless they are willing to spend a great deal of time learning the language, shopping for ingredients, and cooking for themselves. There simply are not many Czechs or Slovaks who will understand the absolute avoidance of all animal products in their diet.

On a positive note, food prices are affordable. Beer and wine is usually cheap, too, and especially in Prague, you can purchase almost any gourmet ingredient at the giant supermarkets. The K-Mart supermarket in Prague even has an "American Import Aisle" with taco mix, peanut butter, maple syrup, and pancake mix.

COMMON CUSTOMS

You probably won't find the Czech or Slovak way of life so foreign that you need to police your every action. And unless you speak Czech or Slovak, don't worry too much about tripping over your tongue. You should, however, remember that Slavic culture's rich history has produced certain customs and modes of politeness that are worth observing. Consider the following:

- Opt for formality when addressing someone, especially if you don't know them well. Use a person's title followed by their last name. Remember that women's last names end in -ova. For example, if a husband's last name is Havel, his wife's last name will be Havelova.
- Use the formal hello (*dobry den*) and good-bye (*nashledanou*)

Newer-style public telephones are definitely preferable. They take debit cards instead of coins and are more reliable than older phones.

when arriving and departing. *Ahoj*, the more colloquial term used for both greeting and bidding farewell, should be reserved for friends. Handshakes are the common gesture of greeting no matter how well you know someone.

- When you are invited into someone's home, you will likely be treated with great generosity and hospitality. If you can, bring some small gift with you (flowers or some wine) and be sure to offer thanks whenever you are presented with food or drink. You will also be offered a pair of slippers when you enter, so always take your shoes off.
- Czechs and Slovaks keep both hands above the table when eating. Follow suit (if you can break your parents' admonishing spell over you).
- Though not as prevalent in the Czech Republic and Slovakia as in the U.S., tipping is customary. In restaurants, simply round up the bill by about 10 percent. Tip taxi drivers 10 percent, as well.

- When you are riding a subway train, bus, or tram, always give up your seat to an elderly person or a disabled person. If you don't someone will surely point it out to you.

SHOPPING

Western-made goods are becoming increasingly available. In Prague, and to a lesser degree in Bratislava, you can satisfy most of your routine shopping needs. But the further you get from these metropolitan areas, the harder it is to find many of the everyday items that you take for granted at home. Even though the cost of living is much lower than in the West, expect to pay the U.S. dollar equivalent for items that come from Western Europe or North America.

Many of the stores still operate as they did prior to the revolution, which means that you may still have to wait in long lines. Under the Socialist regime, "service with a smile" was virtually non-existent. You would simply take what you could get, no matter how slow or surly the service. Though many stores have adopted the Western self-service method, there are still quite a few stores in which the person behind the counter gets you what you need. Unless you speak Czech or Slovak, this can make for time-consuming transactions.

Here are a few hints to make your trip a little more pleasant:

- Bring birth control from home. You'll be able to rest assured it's of reliable quality.
- If you have highly individualistic taste in music, make tapes or bring recorded music from home, especially if you don't like classical music. In general, however, mainstream and most alternative styles of music are available in either county.
- Medication, even if it's sold over the counter at home, may require a prescription overseas. Make sure that you know the generic name of your medication before you leave, so you can write it down for the Czech or Slovak pharmacist or doctor.
- To avoid being yelled at when entering a supermarket, always carry a basket provided by the store (yes, even if you only want a quart of milk).

FINANCES

If you work legally in the Czech Republic or Slovakia, taxes should be deducted automatically from your pay by your employer much in the same way that you would have taxes withheld from your paycheck in the United States In other words, if you possess a work permit, you are required to pay tax on the money you earn.

Be sure that you know what your employer is withholding from your pay and where it is going. It's not uncommon for some employers to shirk their fiscal responsibilities in order to keep a little more money for themselves.

Even though you reside outside of the U.S., you're still required to file a tax return with the IRS when you work overseas. Forgetting to do so can cause you untold trouble down the road when you have to explain where you were, what you were doing, and be able to prove that you didn't make enough money to pay United States income taxes. Since you don't have to pay tax until you make more than US$70,000, most younger expats who work in Eastern Europe won't have to worry about forking out any money to Uncle Sam.

Most Czech and Slovak banks will perform simple services such as foreign currency exchange, cash advances, and the like. You can also set up both crown and hard currency accounts.

Banks

Prague

American Express
Vaclavske namesti 56
Phone: (02) 421-5397
  or (02) 422-7786

American Express
Hybernska 38
Phone: (02) 421-9992
  or (02) 421-9978

Ceska obchodni banka
Na prikope 14
Phone: (02) 411-1111

Komercni banka
Na prikope 28

Thomas Cook
Vaclavske namesti 47
Phone: (02) 422-8658
  or (02) 422-9537

Vseobecna uverova banka
Celetna 31
Phone: (02) 422-0891

Zivnostenska banka
Na prikope 20
Phone: (02) 412-1111
  or (02) 112-1111
Fax: (02) 41 56 55

Bratislava

Vseobecna uverova banka
Danubeska 24

Useobecna uverova banka
Namestie SNP 19

Slovenska spritelna
Venturska 18

**Tatratour (local American
  Express agent)**
Frantiskanske namestie 3

Cash machines

For information on cash machine locations in Prague, call Cirrus/Mastercard (more common) at (800) 424-7787, or Plus Network (800) 843-7587.

TELEPHONES AND MAIL

At the time of publication, the telephone systems in both the Czech and Slovak republics were undergoing a conversion to digital technology. This has created havoc and frustration. Telephone numbers are changing to meet the requirements of the new system, which means that businesses have had to reprint their business cards and other important literature. Reaching a friend across town can take several tries, even with the right number. Long distance calls are even more difficult, especially when they require the services of a Czech or Slovak operator.

As an expat living in the republics, you will likely rely on public telephones. Be forewarned that public pay phones anywhere in either country are bound to cause you grief. There are simply no two ways about it. If you find a phone that works properly on a regular basis, befriend it and treat it gently. Be prepared, however. The relationship may not last long. And if you do find a phone in working order, you won't be alone—expect to wait in line. One American expatriate from Texas who did not have a phone in his apartment in Prague said:

❝ *It's truly amazing. You can wait in line for ten minutes or more and then get up to the phone to make your call, and all of a sudden it doesn't work any more. And you've just watched ten different people make calls on the same phone."*

Public telephones

- Newer public phones take phone debit cards rather than coins. Make sure to get a phone card soon after your arrival. They can be purchased at larger post offices, tobacco shops, magazine kiosks, airports, train stations, metro stations, larger department stores, and hotels. Look for a sticker in the window that depicts a credit card with a phone receiver on it.
- Newer-style telephones are definitely preferable. They are more likely to work properly. If you must use an older phone, make sure to carry several different coin denominations, as some public phones still take coins.
- As in the rest of Central and Eastern Europe, the main post office is a good source of reliable pay phones. Try the office nearest you.
- Don't break your hand in an attempt to punish an uncooperative public phone! For long-distance calls within the Czech and

Slovak republics dial 00, then dial the area code and number without pausing in between.

- Also available in Prague, if you don't have a phone, are voice-mail or message centrals. See the English-language classifieds for information.

If you make frequent international collect calls to North America, arrange for the person you're calling to call you back. It's much cheaper to place a direct call from the United States to the Czech Republic or Slovakia than it is to pay for collect calls in local currency. In fact, your best bet is to make plans for your friend or family member to call you at a prearranged time. Another way to accomplish the same thing is to call collect and have the person on the receiving end refuse the call, and then call you back directly. Obviously, this method calls for some minor tactical planning between you and the person on the other end. In Prague you will see listed in the *Prague Post* or on bulletin boards, advertisements for "call-back" long distance dialing, which can reduce your phone bill by 50 percent.

Calling home

These services allow travelers to call the United States easily and economically. They can be used from any phone in the Czech Republic and Slovakia.

AT&T operator (USA Direct)..............................00-420-00101
(for collect and direct calls)

MCI operator (WorldPhone) 00-420-00112

Sprint operator.. 00-420-87187

Bell Canada Operator 00-420-00151

When calling from a private home, dial 0133 to reach an international operator. To make a collect call from a public or private phone, without using USA Direct, dial 0132.

International calls can be made from the Main Post Offices in Prague and Bratislava. In Bratislava, calls can also be made from the Post Office Branch at ul. Kolarska 12 and at Hotel Forum, Mierove namestie 2.

Mail

The Czech and Slovak postal services are fairly efficient most of the time. Airmail letters and small packages take five days to two weeks to travel between the republics and North America, depending on where you send them from. As a general rule, the farther you are from a major city the longer it takes (both sending and receiving).

If you don't have a stable address, you can receive mail poste restante, or if you have an American Express card or American Express traveler's checks you can receive mail through the American Express offices in

Prague or Bratislava. (The services available through American Express can be invaluable, so get their checks or a card if you can.) Make sure to carry identification with you when you pick up your mail. A passport is your best bet.

Prague
Send or receive mail
Main Post Office
Jindrisska 14
Phone: (02) 26 41 93
24 hours a day
(You can receive faxes here at (02) 32 08 78, or telexes at 1211726VDSC.)

Post Office–Main Train Station Branch
Hlavni nadrazi
Wilsonova 80

American Express
Vaclavske Namesti 56
(Wenceslas Square)

American Express
near Muzeum Metro Station
Phone: (02) 26 75 28

American Hospitality Center
Na Mustku 7
(off Vaclavske namesti)
Phone: (02) 26 20 45

Poste restante
Main Post Office
Window 28
Address letters:
Poste Restante—your name
Posta 1 (Hlavni posta)

Jindrisska 14
Prague 110 00
Czech Republic

American Express
Address letters:
Your name
American Express
Client Letter Service
Vaclavske namesti 56
Prague 1 113 26
Czech Republic

Bratislava
Send or receive mail
Main Post Office 1
Namestie SNP 35

Post Office Branch
ul. Kolarska 12
(This branch has 24-hour telephone, telex, and telegram services.)

Poste restante
Main Post Office 1
Window 6
Address letters:
Your name
Main Post Office 1
Namestie SNP 35
Bratislava 810 00
Slovakia
Poste Restante

HEALTH CARE

Medical care in the Czech and Slovak republics is generally not on a par with Western Europe or the United States. Doctors may be knowledgeable and highly skilled, but the availability of up-to-date medical facilities lags behind the West. If you only require routine care, seeking treatment shouldn't cause you any worry. For more serious problems, you may want to seek treatment in Western Europe or at home, depending upon the immediate severity and the long-term consequences.

The accessibility to free public health care in the Czech and Slovak republics depends upon payment of social security taxes. If you have both work and residency permits and your employer deducts taxes from your pay, then you are eligible for free health care.

Because of the republics' transformations to market economies, it is becoming increasingly common for physicians to set up private practices. If you wish to see a doctor in private practice, you will need to pay for their services yourself. If you will be away for more than six months, it's a good idea to arrange private medical traveling insurance before you leave. Most of the health care facilities listed below have English-speaking personnel.

Medical facilities and assistance

Prague

Diplomatic Health Care for Foreigners
Na Holmoce 724
Prague 5
Phone: (02) 5292-2146
(7:30 AM to 4PM)
Phone: (02) 5292-1111
or (02) 5292-2191 (after hours)

First Aid
Prvni Pomoc
Palackeho 5
Prague 1
Phone: (02) 422-2521
or (02) 422-2520 (24 hours)

Facultni Polikinika
Karlovo namesti 32
Prague 2
Phone: (02) 490-4111
(switchboard)

First Medical Clinic of Prague
Vysehradska 35
Prague 2
Phone: (02) 29 89 78
Phone/fax: (02) 29 22 86
24-hour emergency phone (02)
0601 22 5050 (cellular)

Bratislava

Main Adult Outpatient Clinic
Mytna 5
Phone: (07) 49 65 80

Pharmacies

Prague

Lekarna
Na prikope 5
Prague 1
Phone: (02) 421-0229
24 hours

Konevova 150
Prague 3
Phone: (02) 644-1895
24 hours

Bratislava

Pharmacy
Spitalska 3
Phone: (07) 51 01 14
24 hours

Pharmacy
Mytna 9
Phone: (07) 4 65 15
24 hours

OTHER SERVICES

Embassies

Prague

United States Embassy
Trziste 15
Mala Strana
Prague 1
Phone: (02) 451-0847 (weekdays
    8AM–1PM and 2PM–4:30 PM)
Phone: (02) 451-0852
    (after hours)

Canadian Embassy
Mickiewiczova 6
Hradcany
Phone: (02) 431-1108

Bratislava

United States Embassy
Hviezdoslavovo namestie 4
Bratislava 811 02
Phone: (07) 33 08 61 or (07) 33
    33 38 (weekdays 8AM–11:30
    AM and 2PM–4PM)

Visa Office
Foreigners' Police
(Cudzinecka policia)
Svoradova 11
Phone: (07) 208-1111 (week-
    days 9AM–noon and 2PM–4PM)

Laundromats

Prague

Laundry Kings
Dejvicka 16
Prague 6
Phone: (02) 312-3743

Pradelna
Londynska 71
Prague 2
Phone: (02) 25 11 24

Prague Laundromat
Korunni 14
Prague 2
Phone: (02) 25 55 41

Important telephone numbers

Prague

Fire emergency 150
Ambulance 155
State police emergency 158
City police emergency (Prague) 156
Road accidents .... 154 or (02) 42 41 41
Directory assistance (for numbers
   in Prague) 120
Directory assistance (for numbers
   elsewhere in Czech
   and Slovak Republics) 121
Prague credit card hotline (for
   reporting lost or stolen cards) .... (02) 236-6688

Bratislava

Police emergency (main police station
   is at Sasinkova 23) 158
Ambulance .... 155 or (07) 4 44 44

LANGUAGE TIPS

Czech and Slovak are both Slavic languages. Because Czech and Slovak are mutually comprehensible, only Czech words and phrases will be included in the following list. If you plan to stay in either country for more than a few months, you will definitely need to expand your vocabulary beyond this cursory list. Slovaks will definitely appreciate any attempts to speak Slovak rather than Czech. Likewise, most Czechs prefer to hear Czech.

Regardless of the linguistic rivalry between the Czechs and Slovaks, both languages are grammatically difficult. So, do your best. And good luck!

Numbers

one	*jeden/jedna/jedno*
two	*dva/dve*
three	*tri*

four	*ctyri*
five	*pet*
six	*sest*
seven	*sedm*
eight	*osm*
nine	*devet*
ten	*deset*

Important words and phrases

Yes	*Ano*
No	*Ne*
Good morning	*Dobré ráno*
Good afternoon	*Dobry den*
Good evening	*Dobry vecer*
Good bye	*Nashledanou*
Thank you	*Dekuji vám*
Please	*Prosím*
Where is the bus station?	*Kde je autobusové nádrazí?*
Where is the train station?	*Kde je zeleznicní stanice?*
Where is the toilet?	*Kde je toaleta?*
Nice to meet you.	Tesí me.
I don't understand.	Nerozumín.
I don't speak Czech.	Nemluvím cesky.
My name is _____.	Jmenuji se _____.

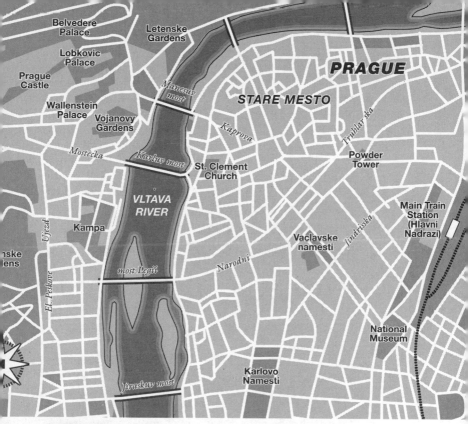

City Profiles

PRAGUE

For visitors, expatriates and the people who live there, not a day goes by in Prague where some glimpse of its magnificence doesn't grab you. Without question, Prague stands as one of the most beautiful cities in all of Europe. Centered in the western half of the Czech Republic known as Bohemia, with a population of 1.4 million and an unemployment rate in the negative, Prague attracts more tourists and expatriates than any other city in Eastern Europe.

Tourism

Since 1989, Prague can account for as many as 77 million tourists annually. In the peak of the tourist season, May through August, it may seem that in the middle of the city you hear people speaking more English or German than Czech. But persevere a little off the beaten track and you will always find the quiet cafe, a square, or a neighborhood pub where the tourists following their guide books never dare to venture.

Expat life

Prague's popularity is a result of several factors: its architectural gran-
deur, natural beauty, rich history, and location in the geographical
center of the European continent. The fact that it survived World War
II and that it serves as the capital of the Czech Republic are also important considerations. Expatriates flock to Prague for all of these reasons and a few more. The cost of living, especially when compared to
the West, is definitely lower, but keep in mind that as the country
opens up to the world market, prices respond accordingly, especially
where rents are concerned.

The Czechs are usually tolerant of expatriates who come to live
and play in their capital city, especially if those foreigners show an
effort at the language and an interest in the local culture. Westerners,
usually Americans or Canadians, have opened bars, restaurants, and
night clubs in the city which cater to both Czechs and foreigners,
although most Czechs find these places prohibitively expensive to
patronize on a regular basis.

Due to the high concentration of expatriates in the city, your chances
of finding your niche through contacts are much greater than in less-
developed centers. All year long, Prague hosts both local and international festivals of film, music, and the arts. More and more, any European cultural exhibition or tour inevitably finds its way to Prague.

Weather

Prague's climate is moderate. Winters are worse for their constant grey-
ness than for their cold temperatures. Spring and summer are inspira-
tional to say the least, and even though Prague is no exception to the
general rule that the air in Central Europe is polluted, on a positive
note, it's at its worst in the winter because of the burning coal, but the
red sunsets and golden glow of the city at night almost make up for it.

Places of interest

With the Vlatva river twisting its way through the middle of the city,
Prague Castle presiding above it on a hill, and the old town square
just a ten minute jaunt away, Prague strikes an uncanny storybook
pose. Stare mesto (Old Town), Nove mesto (New Town), Mala Strana,
and Hradcany are all fascinating, labyrinthine neighborhoods best seen
on foot. Starting from Old Town, head across the Charles Bridge (built
in the 14th century) to Mala Strana, and up the hill to the Prague
Castle. Here you will find museums and the 14th-century St. Vitus
Cathedral, as well as President Havel's offices. Vaclavske namesti
(Wenceslas Square) is located in Nove mesto. This enormous city square
was the site of political demonstrations during both the Prague Spring
of 1968 and the Velvet Revolution of 1989. Josefov is Prague's Jewish

neighborhood. The area contains five synagogues, including the Old-New Synagogue (built in 1270), and the Old Jewish Cemetery. Vysehrad is an ancient fortress that predates the Prague Castle as the seat of Czech government. Worth seeing are the Slavin Cemetery (where many famous Czechs, including Capek, Dvorak, and Smetana are buried), and the Rotunda of St. Martin. This is also a good vantage point from which to look out over the beautiful city.

All in all, Prague is a magical place, and nearly everyone who has lived or visited there will vouch for its alluring qualities.

English schools

Number of staff	Number of students per class	Entry pay (Czech crowns)	Send resume/cover letter	
n/a	n/a	150/hr	✔	**Agentura Euro Contact** Janovskeho 52 Prague 7 Czech Republic (02) 80 15 27
15	15 max	115–120/hr	✔	**Anglictina Express** Vodickova 39 (passage Svetozor) Prague Czech Republic (02) 26 15 26
110	1–5	210/hr	✔	**Berlitz** Jecna 12 Prague 2 Czech Republic (02) 299 958
20	1	110/hr	✔	**Berlitz** Na Porici 12 Prague 1 Czech Republic (02) 2487 2052

Number of staff	Number of students per class	Entry pay (Czech crowns)	Send resume/cover letter	
n/a	n/a	n/a	✔	**Berlitz** v jame 8 Prague 1 Czech Republic (02) 2421 3185
20	2-6	110/hr	✔	**Berlitz** Vlkova 12 Prague 3 Czech Republic (02) 277 101
30	5-15	n/a	✔	**California Sun School** Gotthardska 8 Prague 6 Czech Republic (02) 32 44 44 or (02) 32 33 33
n/a	n/a	n/a		**California Sun School** [main office] Na bojicti 2 Prague 2 Czech Republic (02) 294 817 or 295 681
25	varies	9,000–12,000/mo	✔	**English Link** Kolodejska 8 Prague 10 Czech Republic (02) 360 3515, ext. 229 or (02) 781 7625

Number of staff	Number of students per class	Entry pay ((Czech crowns)	Send resume/cover letter	
150	20 max	7,000–9,000/mo	✔	**Language School of Prague** Narodni 20 Prague 1 Czech Republic (02) 2491 4114 or (02) 2491 2236
45	8–10	150/hr	✔	**Linga Pro** Vinohradska 28 Prague 2 Czech Republic (02) 252 610
40	6–10	6,500–8,500/mo	✔	**London School of Modern Languages** Belgicke 25 Prague 3 Czech Republic (02) 25 68 59
5	8	105/hr	✔	**The American English School of Prague** (AESOP) Ul. M. Horakove-Prasny Most P.O. Box 181 Prague 6 Czech Republic (02) 320 144
65	8–12	160/hr	✔	**The Bell School** Nedvezska 29 Prague 10 Czech Republic (02) 781 5342

Number of staff	Number of students per class	Entry pay (Czech crowns)	Send resume/cover letter	
n/a	n/a	n/a	✔	**The Bell School Annex** Ortenovo Namesti 37 Prague 7 Czech Republic (02) 667 121 53 or (2) 667 21 25

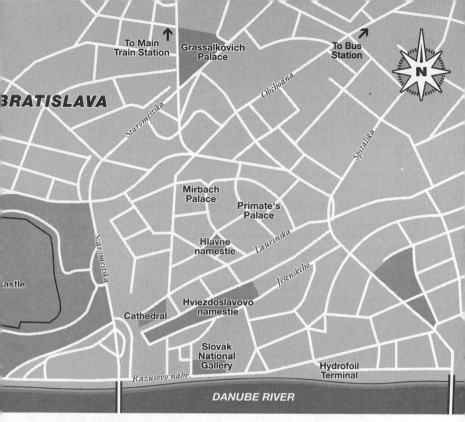

To Main Train Station

Grassalkovich Palace

To Bus Station

N

BRATISLAVA

Staromestska

Obchodna

Spitalska

Mirbach Palace

Primate's Palace

Hlavne namestie

Laurinska

Staromestska

Jesenskeho

Castle

Hviezdoslavovo namestie

Cathedral

Slovak National Gallery

Hydrofoil Terminal

Razusovo nabr.

DANUBE RIVER

BRATISLAVA

Often overshadowed by their Czech neighbors, the Slovaks have been known to say that there are advantages to being number two—no false image of competence to maintain, no irrationally inflated ego to burst, and no chance of slipping from number one.

History

Bratislava hosts a population of nearly half a million people, combining to create a distinct and fascinating culture. Historical mentions of the city go all the way back to the year 907 in the Salzburg annals. It's part historical Eastern Europe, with beautiful old buildings and meandering cobbled streets, and part Stalin and Brezhnev, with its grey, uninspiring Soviet-realist architecture.

The Bratislava Castle dominates the city center and its four towers have become a symbol of the city. Since its reconstruction, the castle now shelters the historical part of the Slovak National Museum.

Like Vienna and Budapest, Bratislava lies on the shore of the River Danube. Bratislava's Old Town offers smaller shops and restaurants, but unlike the other Eastern European capitals, Bratislava can strike an unsuspecting visitor as sleepy. There doesn't seem to be as much vitality—an unfortunate economic reality. But that is not to say entertainment is not to be found. As the economy changes, new gathering places open.

City character

There are definitely fewer expatriates to compete with for teaching jobs or apartments in Bratislava. And those who do decide to live in Bratislava usually find the smaller community of foreigners to be more cozy, and perhaps more genuine in their desire to take in Eastern European culture.

Since Bratislava doesn't have as many bars and restaurants that cater to Western expatriates, those who do live there generally feel compelled to look harder for interesting things to do. For an adventurous expatriate, Bratislava's greatest attraction may be its proximity to other Eastern Europe capital cities—Prague, Budapest, and Vienna, Austria's biggest city, which is only an hour away by car or by train. And if your tastes cater to the outdoors, the High Tatra mountains offer some of the best skiing, climbing, and hiking available, without the expensive lift tickets and equipment and accommodation costs you find in the West.

Places of interest

Bratislava Castle, having been restored to its 15th-century appearance, now houses Municipal Museum collections, as well as the Slovak National Assembly. Old Town, which is centered around Hlavne namestie, is well-suited for walking tours. Stops along your walk might include the Bratislava Municipal Museum and Hviezdoslavovo namestie, which is adorned with classic 19th-century Slavic architecture. Devin Castle sits on a hill near Bratislava. The castle commands an impressive view of the confluence of the Morava and Danube Rivers.

Weather

The climate is Continental, with hot summers and cold winters, the coldest month is January, and the snow lasts on average 130 days of the year.

Whether or not you reside permanently in Bratislava, it is definitely a worthwhile Eastern Europe destination.

English schools

Number of staff	Number of students per class	Entry pay (Slovak crowns)	Send resume/cover letter	
10	8–16	varies	✔	**ENLAP Language School** Lazaretska 3, Room 67 Bratislava Slovakia (07) 231 300, ext. 234
5	12–15	80	✔	**The English Club** Pri Suchom Mylne 36 Bratislava Slovakia (07) 372 106

BRNO

Located about two and a half hours southeast of Prague by bus (an hour north of Vienna, Austria), Brno is the second largest city in the Czech Republic with a population of over 400,000. Historically, an important center of arts and trade, Brno became the capital of Moravia in the 1300s. With the import of the textile industry from Germany, Holland, and Belgium during the 18th century, the city functioned as the industrial heart of the Austrian empire. Today, Brno remains the urban hub of the Czech Republic's Moravian region.

Changing its image

Slowly overcoming its image as an ugly industrial town, Brno actually has a lot to offer visitors without the crowds of Prague. Medieval and Baroque architecture adorn the city, trade fairs are held almost every other week, and the city hosts the world-championship Motorcycle Grand Prix at the end of August. In fact, because Brno is absorbing much of the overflow of expatriates from Prague (and their money and labor), the city is undergoing somewhat of a renaissance with renovation of the city center and development of a lively nightlife, including classical music concerts, live theater, rock and jazz clubs, and pubs that serve their own micobrewed beer.

Places of interest

Most of Brno's historic sites reside within the city center and are in easy walking distance of each other. Spilberk Castle was built during the early 13th century. Located at the top of Spilberk Hill, the castle affords an excellent view of Brno below. Magnificent churches, cathedrals, and monasteries, many dating from the 13th century, populate Brno's urban landscape. Some of the more magnificent structures include the Cathedral of Saints Peter and Paul, the Church of the Holy Cross, and the Church of the Assumption of the Virgin. The Church of the Holy Cross was built in 1651 and is home to some 150 mummies in its crypt, including rooms with clothed skeletons of monks and aristocrats. The Church of the Assumption of the Virgin is a fine late-Gothic building that houses the oldest painting on wood in the Czech Republic: the Black Madonna, dating from late 13th century.

Other places to check out are the Cabbage Market, Brno's marketplace since the 13th century. This is still a daily market with fruits, vegetables, and flowers. Reduta is one of the oldest theaters in Eastern Europe, dating back to the 17th century. In 1767, Mozart conducted his own works here.

Food and drink

The restaurants of Brno tend to favor Moravian food, which leans toward Hungarian. Cheap buffets can be found all around town. They provide mounds of food served precapitalist-style: in line, standing up.

Around Brno

Moravia is a beautiful region of fertile wine country, and Brno is a good place from which to venture out into this less-touristy part of the Czech Republic. The Moravian Karst is a scenic, heavily wooded, and hilly area north of Brno. The countryside is carved with canyons and honey-combed with some 400 limestone caves, four of which are open to the public. The area is great for hiking and walking and is located about an hour from Brno by bus.

English schools

Number of staff	Number of students per class	Entry pay (Czech crowns)	Send resume/cover letter	
n/a	n/a	n/a		**Berlitz** Dominikanske namesti Brno Czech Republic (05) 4221 3302
n/a	n/a	n/a		**Brno English Center** Kravy Hora Brno Czech Republic (05) 4121 2262
10	16 max	3,000–4,000/mo	✔	**ILC** Sokolska 1 Brno Czech Republic (05) 4124 0494 or 4121 0723

Number of staff	Number of students per class	Entry pay (Czech crowns)	Send resume/cover letter	
15	15	90	✔	**Universum** Korenskeho 23a Brno Czech Republic (05) 4122 5173

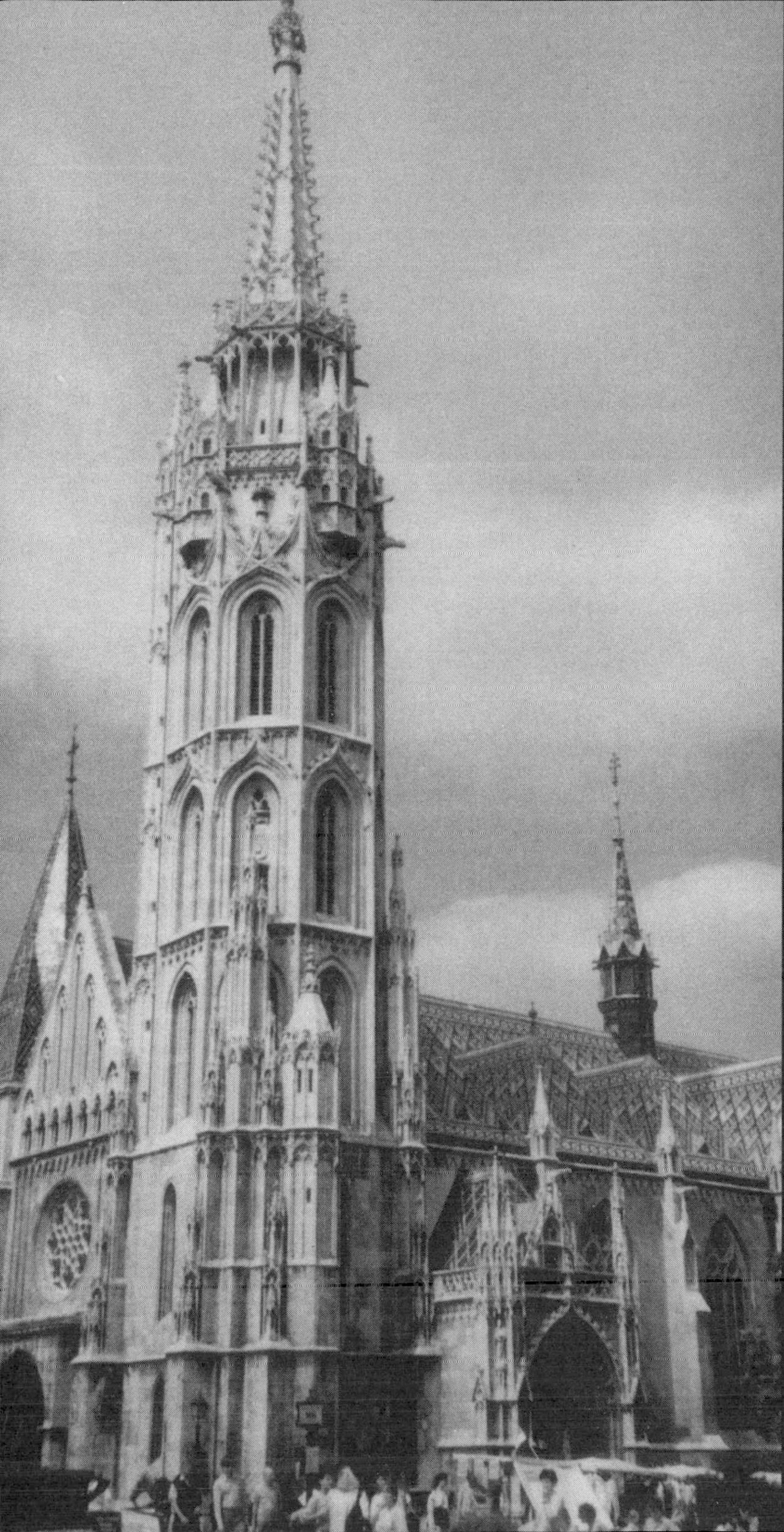

HUNGARY 4

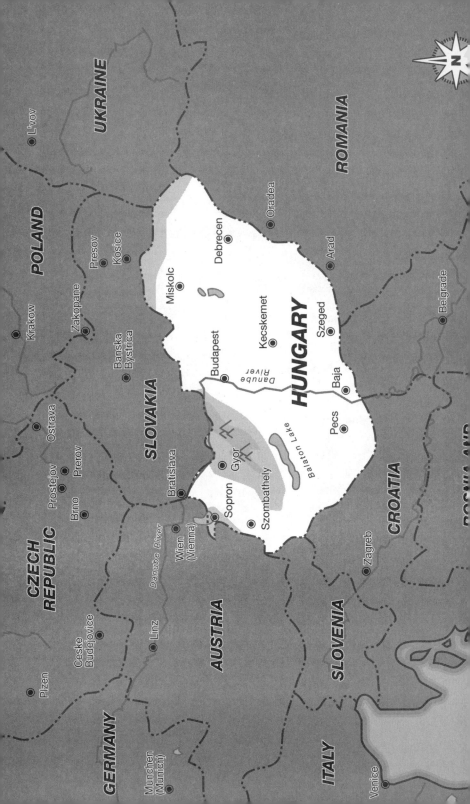

The lay of the land

A PROFILE OF HUNGARY

Population

Hungary is home to over 10.5 million people, the vast majority of whom are ethnic Hungarians, or Magyars. Minorities—only three percent of the entire population—include Germans, Romanians, and Slovaks. Hungary is also home to many Romanies and Jewish peoples. The Magyars are Central Asian in origin, and their language is unrelated to the language of Slavic peoples, who dominate Eastern Europe. (Poles, Czechs, Slovaks, Serbs, Croats, and Russians are all Slavic peoples.) Twenty percent of the entire population lives in Budapest, the capital, while the next largest city has a population almost ten times less.

Geography

Hungary is a country of just under 36,000 square miles, situated between Austria, Slovakia, the Ukraine, Romania, and the trio of formerly Yugoslavian territories: Slovenia, Serbia, and Croatia. The Danube River, running north-south, partitions the country roughly into two distinct regions. The western portion of the county, called Transdanubia (or Dunatul in Hungarian), has a varied topography of smaller mountains and numerous hills mixed with flat, open ranges. To the east is a flat area known as the Great Plain, which stretches to the east and south of Budapest. At the top of the eastern portion of the county, stretching toward the border with the Ukraine, are the mountain ranges of northern Hungary.

Climate

Hungary's climate is temperate, with little variation throughout the country. July and August are the hottest months, when temperatures may average in the low eighties. The coldest months of winter are usually January and February when temperatures may dip into the mid-twenties. Snow is not uncommon during the winter months.

Politics

Presently, Hungary is governed by a multi-party parliamentary democracy, composed of a parliament, a state president, and a prime minister. The president acts as the head of state and holds the power to veto laws that are deemed unconstitutional. The prime minister leads the government and chairs meetings of cabinet ministers.

Because of economic instability since the revolution of 1989, the parties that govern Hungary have changed frequently. The voting populace seems uncertain of where to place the power, not knowing which party will live up to its promises to better the standard of living and curtail the rapid rates of inflation and unemployment.

Prior to 1989, the Hungarian government's brand of communism differed markedly from the rest of the region's regimes. The government allowed limited private enterprise, so Western products have been available in Hungary for decades. Hungarians were also allowed to travel outside the country, so Western influence has been evident since the 1960s.

Religion

Hungary is predominantly Christian, with Roman Catholics making up the majority, followed by Calvinists and Lutherans. There is a small Jewish population.

History

Hungary boasts a rich and varied history, one that stands apart from those of its neighboring countries. The Magyar people came to Hungary from Central Asia late in the ninth century. Though they quickly established ties with their Slavic neighbors, their language and culture remain distinct to the present day. Hungarian is a Finno-Ugric language, which holds no resemblance to the Slavic language family.

Prior to World War I, Hungary joined with Austria to form the Austro-Hungarian Empire. The outcome of the war brought an end to this union in 1918, devastated the population, and resulted in the loss of much of Hungary's territory. When World War II began less than thirty years later, Hungary joined with the Germans and Italians, hoping to reclaim the lands lost in the previous world war. Early in 1945, the German forces in Hungary were defeated by the Soviets. The Soviet victory foreshadowed the onslaught of the communist regime which was to rule Hungary for the next four decades.

In 1956, an uprising against the Soviet-backed government, which included student rallies in Budapest, forced the Soviets to bring in their tanks. The secret police opened fire on demonstrators, students attempted to take over the radio station, and rebel units of the Hungarian army fought against the incoming Soviet tanks. After nearly a week of fighting and general unrest, the Soviets agreed to withdraw. Later in the year, however, the Soviet army returned to Budapest in even greater force to crack down on the unrest. The tanks showed no mercy by destroying buildings, while Soviet troops sprayed machine gun fire at Hungarian civilians. Thousands died and an even greater number left the country.

Budapest, like many cities in Eastern Europe, is filled with historic architecture and monuments.

Though the Soviet tanks were effective in their mission to quell the popular uprising, the relatively quiet period that followed could not be construed as tacit acceptance of Soviet policy in the region. The Hungarians continued to express their disenchantment in more subtle ways. In the late 1960s, the government introduced several economic reforms that resulted in greater decentralization of control and management of the larger production facilities. Though these reforms helped to increase the standard of living among the general population, they did not put the larger factories and production entities into private hands. At this point, Hungarians may have been further along than their Central and Eastern European neighbors in terms of economic productivity and individual freedom, but they still lagged far behind Western Europeans.

The reforms and subsequent increases in productivity during the 1970s did not create enough momentum to carry Hungary on the same track during the 1980s. Among other things, obsolescence in the industrial sector dragged the economy into a period of decline. Rampant pollution further exacerbated Hungary's problems. And with the Soviets going bankrupt, the whole region slid into a state of disarray.

Centralized socialist economies simply could not keep up with the burgeoning markets of the rest of the developed world. In 1989, the ruling communist party in Hungary fell from power after the Soviets could no longer provide economic assistance. The Hungarian people replaced the single party system with a multi-party parliamentary democracy in 1990 and held free elections.

The fall of the Berlin Wall in 1989, which so poignantly symbolized the collapse of the communist regimes in Central and Eastern Europe, did not bring immediate relief to the people of the region. For many, it further complicated their lives. The personal freedoms that resulted brought sighs of relief from many people, but the challenges that lay ahead seemed bewildering, even frightening, to the many people who had only dim recollections of the period before 1945. Without the widespread government subsidies and full-employment policies of the old regime, many would be left to fend for themselves in the unfamiliar environs of an open market.

It will take years, if not decades, for the Hungarian economy to function smoothly enough to compete with the well-established market economies of the West. Hopefully, Hungary's experience with the gentler brand of communism that allowed some free enterprise, combined with a willingness to improve upon their situation will bring economic prosperity in the not-so-distant future.

Today's Hungary and expat life

Hungary is unique. Of the countries under discussion, it possesses most strongly a character all its own. Like other Eastern European countries, Hungary suffered under Soviet rule, but it's easy to see what sets Hungary apart from either Poland or the Czech and Slovak Republics in terms of expatriate life. Hungary got a head start on these countries in many ways, not all of which ended up being beneficial.

A lot of expatriates have chosen to stay in Hungary, primarily to teach English. Though other opportunities can be created, it is certainly not as easy to start a business or even teach as it can be in the Czech Republic, for example. Hungarians are protective of their economy. While it's true that they want to raise their quality of life up to a level that would put them more in line with the countries of the EEC, they want to do it themselves.

For those expats who do stay in Hungary, there are probably more hoops to jump through both before you go and once you get there. If you want to teach English, then you should have some kind of qualification. And if you want to pursue other opportunities, then you have to do a good job of convincing the authorities that you're uniquely suited to your profession.

This is not to say that you will encounter insurmountable obstacles in Hungary, just don't expect things to be a breeze. And you should know that some of these obstacles are not necessarily unique to Hungary, or to any particular country. One city or town might welcome your planned endeavors more than another. Some areas are more in need of English teachers than others. And what it really amounts to is that your determination will pay off if you let it. For example, if you want to grow a business in Hungary, you may be required to find a Hungarian partner. If you are really determined, you should start networking to find someone who shares common interests. And maybe that requires that you learn to speak some Hungarian. In this case, you will definitely have your work cut out for you.

All of that aside, if you want to feel a little closer to Western culture than you might in any of the Slavic countries, Hungary is probably your best bet. Budapest looks and feels more like a sophisticated Western city than does Prague or even Warsaw. Prague feels very magical and yet very foreign, while Warsaw will remind you more of Russia than of the West. And the Hungarian people possess more sophistication and international awareness than do people from the other countries, particularly in and around Budapest and the northwestern portion of the country.

___

Introducing: An English teacher in Hungary

Peter Dibuz, who speaks Hungarian, taught English privately.

Though I was born in the U.S., my parents grew up in Hungary. I learned to speak Hungarian before I learned English. And I still speak Hungarian with my parents and their friends, most of whom are Hungarian. Consequently, when I go to Hungary, I can be both Hungarian and American, so my perspective is a little strange.

I guess that I can point out how living in Hungary is different from living in North America. I'm not really sure where to begin. If you're not sure where you want to go in Hungary, I can offer a few helpful generalizations about the different regions. Northwestern Hungary, which extends north and west of Budapest, tends to be more cosmopolitan and sophisticated. Historically, the Austro-Hungarian Empire made the greatest impact on this part of the country. It's evident in the architecture, and in the people, too. You will find that people here are more cultured and better educated. Northeastern Hungary, on the other hand, tends to be less interesting for visitors because it's more industrial and the people are generally not as well-educated. Both southeast and southwest Hungary are fairly rural. There are a lot of small towns that are populated by farmers. Most of these people have not been exposed to big city life, so you have to contend with more rigid attitudes.

No matter where you go, you should always use common sense, just as you would at home. Be suspicious of anyone who flaunts wealth. You'll recognize the tell-tale signs. If someone is wearing a lot of gold jewelry or driving an expensive new car, it's likely that they came upon their wealth dishonestly. Bureaucracy used to be the biggest problem in Hungary, now it's organized crime and bribery. It seems like you have to pay bribes to accomplish anything important, whether it's seeking medical treatment or getting a telephone installed in your apartment. By the way, don't seek medical treatment in Hungary if you can help it. Go to Austria. My uncle was mistreated when he needed a small skin graft. And I've heard lots of other horror stories.

Hungarians are well-known for their hospitality. If you're invited over to someone's home or out to dinner, you can expect to be offered great quantities of food and drink. So it's important to learn how to politely decline an offer of another helping or another drink. Be especially careful of how much alcohol you consume, because Hungarians are known for putting down copious quantities. When someone offers a toast, make sure that you look them in the eye when you clink your glasses and don't take a drink until the person who gives the toast lifts the glass to their mouth. Also, make sure that you take a drink before you set down your glass, otherwise you'll look like you're rejecting the toast. Another thing, never toast with glasses of beer. If you go out to dinner with someone, make sure that you put up an argument when it comes time to pay the bill. It's impolite to just let someone else pay without putting up a fight. Of course, what goes around comes around. After you get to know people, you'll be expected to pay now and again. Make sure that you don't overspend when it's your turn. And be wary of freeloaders. Anyone who doesn't pay every once in a while is probably along for a free ride.

If you go to Hungary to teach English, remember that Hungarians are taught to be quiet and respectful in the classroom. For the first few weeks, you probably won't get many responses from your students when you ask questions or try to stimulate dialogue. Be patient. It takes time for them to get used to speaking up in class.

● ●

TRAVELING TO HUNGARY

The chances are good that your first stop in Hungary will be Budapest. Being Hungary's only truly international city and the main hub for all domestic transportation, it is a great place to start your stay. From there, you can easily make your way to any other city or town throughout the country.

Via airplane

Though not necessarily the cheapest way to get to Hungary, flying directly from the United States or Western Europe into Budapest's Ferihegy airport is very convenient. There are non-stop flights from New York to Budapest four days per week. It's also easy to fly to Budapest directly from most of the major European cities. London and Frankfurt are usually the best bets because they frequently are the least expensive ports of entry into Europe when flying from the U.S.

Airlines with service to Budapest

Aeroflot .... (01) 118-5955
British Airways .... (01) 118-3299
Delta .... (01) 118-7922
Lufthansa .... (01) 118-4511
LOT .... (01) 117-2444
SAS .... (01) 118-5377
Swissair .... (01) 117-2500
Malev .... (800) 262-5380
                                                        or (800) 223-6884
Al Italia .... (800) 223-5730

● ●

Via train or bus

Many travelers to Hungary choose to fly from the United States to a major city in Western Europe, then travel the rest of the way by train or bus. Though considerably slower than flying, traveling overland has several advantages. Depending upon the time of year and the pre-

Budapest is a vibrant city filled with expatriate opportunities and world-class views.

vailing whims of the airline industry, it can be cheaper to fly into, let's say, Frankfurt (or another major Western European airport), and then jump on a train or bus going to Budapest. Intercity trains travel from Vienna in less than three hours. You are more likely to meet other prospective teachers or job hunters on the trains and buses. Some travelers also enjoy the slow and easy introduction to a new country that train or bus travel affords them. And there are some decent budget train passes, if you plan to do some serious traveling. For example, the European East Flexipass provides unlimited train travel on the national railways of Austria, Hungary, the Czech Republic, Slovakia, and Poland for five days for US$185.

Should you travel by train or bus? For many North Americans, trains are a big part of the allure of traveling in Europe. Trains figure prominently in many of the spy novels and other works of literature set in Europe, conjuring up notions of romance and intrigue in the minds of readers. Buses (also known as motor coaches), on the other hand, suffer a less lofty reputation. Though your personal preference may or may not be molded by your reading habits, the following considerations may come in to play when deciding between bus or train travel:

- In Europe, train fares are almost always more expensive than bus fares.
- Trains generally run more frequently than buses between large cities in Europe, but buses are a better bet for getting to out-of-the-way places.

- In terms of theft and the like, buses are generally safer than trains because there are fewer people traveling together, there is less room for people to move around, and the people who start the journey together usually finish together. On a train, a thief could be four cars away or even off the train before you realize something is missing.
- Buses are more cramped than trains, though buses usually stop every three or four hours so passengers can stretch, find a restroom, or grab a bite to eat.
- Trains offer more choices (e.g., sleeper cars, couchets, first and second class compartments, etc.).

WHEN YOU ARRIVE

If you fly to Hungary, you will likely land at Budapest's Ferihegy airport. If you travel to Budapest by train, you will arrive at one of three train stations: Keleti palyaudvar (east station), Nyugati palyaudvar (west station), or Deli palyaudvar (south station). Those who arrive via bus will first come to the Erzsebet ter bus station, located in the heart of downtown Budapest.

Airport

Ferihegy airport has two terminals which are situated several miles apart. The Hungarian airline, Malev, uses the newer Ferihegy-2 terminal while most other flights arrive and depart from the much older Ferihegy-1 terminal. Ferihegy airport lies roughly 14 miles southeast of Budapest.

Taking a taxi into Budapest from the airport might end up costing you a lot more than it should because—as in other cities in Eastern Europe—a syndicate controls the taxi stands. Unless you are lucky and find an honest cabby, the fares will be several times higher than normal.

Airport Minibusz is a reliable shuttle express service that runs to and from the airport. It is relatively inexpensive, runs frequently, and you can find out the schedule at any airport information desk. If you are calling from outside the airport, the phone number is (01) 157-6283 or (01) 157-8993. You can also catch the number 93 bus from both airport terminals to take you downtown.

Train stations

All three of the main trains stations in Budapest are situated near metro (subway) stops of the same name, which makes them very convenient to most destinations within the city. Most trains coming in from the West stop at Keleti palyaudvar, as do trains from Bucharest, Warsaw, and Sophia. Trains that serve Prague, Berlin, and points in eastern Hungary use Nyugati palyaudvar. Deli palyaudvar services trains going to points south in the former Yugoslavia and also Austria. The Eurocity express train to Vienna arrives and departs from Deli palyaudvar. Nyugati palyaudvar and Keleti palyaudvar are located in downtown Budapest, on the Pest side of the Danube. Deli palyaudvar lies on the Buda side of the river, over Castle Hill from downtown.

LOCAL TRANSPORTATION

Hungary has a surprisingly efficient transportation system, including international, domestic, and commuter trains, buses, trams, and subways. Regardless of the mode of transport, fares are remarkably affordable, if not downright cheap.

For frequent commuters, monthly passes that cover all modes of public transportation are available at all major metro ticket booths and other main transit stations. If you are a student or younger than twenty-six, be sure to ask for the discounted student pass or youth fare. A cheaper tram-and-metro-only pass is offered for those who don't need to rely on the bus system. The Hungarian Flexipass allows travel throughout Hungary for 10 days in a month for US$69.

Metro

Budapest is the only city in Hungary with an extensive public transportation system that includes a combination of metro, tram, and commuter bus lines.

Budapest's metro is both efficient and inexpensive. It's composed of three color-coded lines that intersect in the center of town and radiate outward. Each station is marked with an "M" enclosed in a circle. The Pest side of town is far better served by metro lines than the older Buda half of the city. Unless you live near the one metro line that crosses under the Danube into Buda, you will need to become familiar with both the tram and bus lines.

Though the Budapest metro is easy to figure out, you can buy a metro map at any of the stations from the same window that sells tickets. Tickets also are available from coin-operated dispensers that demand exact change and from some tobacco shops. Before you enter the main part of the metro platform, you must validate your ticket in one of the little orange machines standing in the passageway to each platform. If you're caught riding the metro without a valid ticket, you will likely be scolded and issued a small fine. (It's not worth the embarrassment just to save a few *forints*.) Also, remember to validate a new ticket every time you switch lines. The metro only runs from 4:30 AM to 11PM, so you will need to catch a taxi, a bus, or a night tram if you stay out too late.

Trams

Tram lines snake through many of the main streets in Budapest, but they aren't as extensive as the bus routes. In the heart of the city, the trams are often jam-packed, but they are quick. Remember to punch your ticket in one of the validators located near the doors, if you can muscle through the crowd.

Buses

Buses are the best bet for reaching the more out-of-the-way places in Budapest. Though they run frequently, they often are crowded.

If you travel outside of Budapest, domestic bus fares in Hungary are comparable to train fares, though the trains are generally more comfortable. Because buses travel to some of the more out-of-the-way places where trains don't venture, you will need to familiarize yourself with bus routes and schedules if you settle in a remote small town.

Though it's usually possible to buy your ticket when you board, we recommend getting a reservation in advance. You never know when the bus will be crowded.

Taxis

Taxi cabs are great if you want to get where you're going fast. Taxi drivers, on the other hand, can cause you a lot of grief if you're not careful. No matter where you are in Eastern Europe, taxi drivers are notorious for overcharging foreigners, especially those who obviously are fresh over the border. Try to avoid expensive-looking taxis such as Mercedes or other fancy makes, and make sure the meter works. Fares should be posted on the dashboard. If the driver tries to put one over on you by taking a circuitous route or by not using his meter, make him aware (politely) that you know his game.

Domestic trains

Most train lines in Hungary employ Budapest as their hub and radiate outward from there. Though the train network does have lines that connect cities and towns in the outlying areas, sometimes it is faster to go back through Budapest to reach your final destination.

Local trains are very slow when compared to express trains, so it's wise to differentiate between them if your final destination lies on an express train line. You will find yourself pondering many a pasture or field if you make the mistake of riding a local train when an express is available.

All train reservations must be made in person at one of the main stations in Budapest, at Ibusz (the national travel agency), or at the central office of either MAV (Hungarian rail agency) or Malev (Air Hungary).

SHORT-TERM ACCOMMODATIONS

Since you may not be certain of where you'll end up, your first step should be finding temporary accommodations. If you take the time to find a place that is both reasonably priced and convenient, you'll appreciate the effort later on when you need to focus on getting work and arranging long-term accommodations. Buy a map and get to know your local area, so you can make the right decisions from the very start.

You might check out some of the agencies in Budapest listed below. Accommodation agencies and tourist information offices are good resources for finding a place to stay.

Accommodation agencies

Ibusz
Ferenciek ter 10
Phone: (01) 137-0939

Ibusz
V. Petofi ter 3
Phone: (01) 118-5707
    or (01) 118-4842
Fax: (01) 117-9099
24 hours

Budapest Tourist
V. Roosevelt ter 5
Phone: (01) 117-3555

Cooptourist
VI. Bajcsy-Zsilinszky utca 17
Phone: (01) 156-9567

Duna Tours
(next to Cooptourist)
Phone: (01) 131-4533

To-Ma Tour
V. Oktober 6 utca
Phone: (01) 153-0819

Tourist information offices

Tourinform
V. Suto utca 2 (off Deak ter)
Phone: (01) 117-9800

Ibusz
Ferenciek ter 10
Phone: (01) 137-0939 .

Ibusz
V. Petofi ter 3
Phone: (01) 118-5707
    or (01) 118-4842
Fax: (01) 117-9099
24 hours

Budapest Tourist
V. Roosevelt ter 5

Phone: (01) 138-3594
    or (01) 118-1658

Budapest Tourist
VI. Rozsa ut 111
Phone: (01) 112-9210

Express
V. Semmelweis utca 4
Phone: (01) 117-8600

Express
V. Zoltan utca 10
Phone: (01) 111-6418

Express
XI. Bartok Bela ut 34
Phone: (01) 185-3173

Express
V. Szabadsag ter 16
Phone: (01) 131-7777

Cooptourist
XI. Bartok Bela ut 4 (on the
Buda side of Szabadsag
bridge)
Phone: (01) 166-5349

Cooptourist
Nyugati ter
Phone/fax: (01) 132-7126

Cooptourist
Kossuth Lajos ter
Phone: (01) 132-4144
or (01) 111-6839
Fax: (01) 111-6683

Cooptourist
I. Derek ut 2
Phone: (01) 156-8122

Youth hostels

Most youth hostels in Budapest—particularly in the summer, and especially in Budapest—are packed with rambunctious young folks from around the world who spend much of their time drinking and otherwise carousing. Consequently, these hostels often are noisy and cramped. If cleanliness and peace and quiet are important to you, you might want to consider another option. Frequently, youth hostels are only open during the late spring, summer, and early fall, so make your plans accordingly. Express, the national, youth-oriented tourist agency (see the list of tourist information offices above), can make hostel reservations for you. Expect to pay US$5 to $10 per person per night for a bed in a hostel in Budapest.

Schonherz
XI. Irinyi Jozsef utca 42
Phone: (01) 166-5422

Universitas
XI. Irinyi Jozsef utca 9-11
Phone: (01) 186-8144

Bridge
IX. Soroksari ut 12
Phone: (01) 113-7604

Flora Martos College
XI. Sztoczek Jozsef utca 5-7
Phone: (01) 181-7171

Komjat
XI. Rimaszombati ut 2-4
Phone: (01) 166-5355

More Than Ways
Phone: (01) 266-6107

More Than Ways
Donatil Donati utca 6
Phone: (01) 201-1971

More Than Ways
Diaksport
XIII. Dozsa Gyorgy ut 152
Phone: (01) 140-8585

Felvinci
II. Felvinci ut 6
Phone: (01) 135-0668

Strawberry Youth Hostels
Raday utca 43-45
Phone: (01) 138-4766

Strawberry Youth Hostels
Kinizsi utca 2-6
Phone: (01) 117-3033

Baross
XI. Bartok Bela ut 17
Phone: (01) 185-1444

Vasarhelyi
XI. Drusper utca 2-4
Phone: (01) 185-3794

Martos
XI. Stoczek utca 5-7
Phone: (01) 181-1118

Bakfark Hostel
I. Bakfark utca 1-3
Phone: (01) 201-5419

Bercsenyi
XI. Bercsenyi utca 28-30
Phone: (01) 166-6677

KEK
XI. Szuret utca 2-18
Phone: (01) 185-2369

Hotels

Unless money is no object or unless there are no reasonable alternatives, you probably don't want to stay in a hotel in Budapest. Cheap hotels in Budapest generally cost upward of US$25 or $30 per night for a single room. It is possible to find inexpensive hotel lodging in other towns and cities for the equivalent of US$15 to $25 per night. In Hungary, hotels are rated on a five-star system, with one being the least expensive and least luxurious.

When you make reservations or check in, be sure to communicate how many nights you plan to stay. If you are vague, you might find yourself getting kicked out, so that the hotel can make room for an incoming group with definite reservations. The national travel and tourist agency Ibusz has locations in Budapest (see the tourist information offices listings above) that can provide information and make reservations for you in most hotels 24 hours a day.

Ulloi
VIII. Ulloi ut 94-98
Phone: (01) 133-7932

Ventura
Fehervari ut 179
Phone: (01) 181-0758

Flandria
XIII. Szegedi ut 27
Phone: (01) 129-6689

Goliat
XIII. Kerekes ut 12-20
Phone: (01) 149-0321

Lido Hotel
III. Nanasi ut 67
Phone: (01) 250-4549
Fax: (01) 250-4576

Aquincum Panzio
III. Szentendrei ut 105
Phone: (01) 168-6426
Fax: (01) 250-2394

Unikum Panzio
XI. Bod Peter ut 13
Phone: (01) 186-1280

Private rooms

For prospective job seekers, taking a room in a private residence may be the best option. When you arrive at the train or bus station, you will probably notice people who are jockeying for position in an attempt to corner the next foreigner off the train. More than likely they are just offering rooms for rent. Though some of these small-scale entrepreneurs may be more interested in your money than in offering you reasonable accommodations, most of them are just trying to supplement their incomes by renting out extra rooms in their homes.

You usually can find comfortable, convenient, and inexpensive rooms with minimum hassle if you exercise a little common sense. Size up the person who is offering you accommodation by asking a few questions. Find out where they live, and get them to show you on a map. Agree on a rate in advance. Most importantly, ask to see the room before you agree to anything. If they seem receptive to your inquiries, you just might have found yourself a good place to stay.

One more thing: if you like what you see and plan to stay a week or more, make an offer that is 10 to 20 percent less than the normal daily rate. The less time your host has to spend recruiting newcomers at the train station, the more likely she will be to compromise on the cost of your room.

❝ *We stayed with a woman in downtown Budapest who charged us around 10 dollars per night for a double room, and we ended up staying for almost two weeks. Much to our chagrin, we later found out that she was charging about six dollars a night to some other travelers who had bargained for a better rate because they knew in advance that they would be staying for five or six nights. Obviously, it was to her advantage to keep things quiet."*

It's also possible to arrange accommodation in a private room through one of the various public or private tourist agencies. See the listings for accommodation agencies and tourist information offices.

Finding a teaching position

OVERVIEW

In Hungary, younger people frequently speak English or German as their second language, while those old enough to remember World War II will more likely speak only German. Out of all the peoples of Central and Eastern Europe, Hungarians speak the most English. This does not mean, however, that there is no demand for English teaching. In fact, to the contrary, the demand for English teachers is still increasing. Because Hungary has fully opened to the West, the burden to master the world's predominant business tongue is even greater now, especially for the younger generations who make up the bulk of the work force. In Hungary, being able to compete in the job market means being well educated, and Hungarians prize multi-lingual abilities.

Hungary may well be the most challenging of the four countries when it comes to finding a good teaching position in a well-established private school or a supportive public school environment. Many employers demand formal certification and, in some cases, prior teaching experience. For whatever historical reasons, Hungarians are appreciative of degrees, diplomas, and all manner of formal documentation. So an RSA certificate or any other recognizable teaching certificate will serve you well in Hungary. Expect to be asked early on in the interview process what sort of qualifications you possess. It will be to your advantage to talk about any kind of formal education that you have had that relates to English teaching in any way. If you can speak highly of a particular educational experience or perhaps a favorite professor, you just might impress your way into a job.

Believe it or not, in Hungary, there is a much greater chance that you will be competing with English-speaking Hungarians for teaching jobs. In this regard, several different factors set Hungary apart from the other countries under discussion. Prior to the revolution, Hungary's economy was far more decentralized than most of the other Eastern European countries, save for perhaps Yugoslavia. This economic decentralization informed the Hungarian sensibility, particularly in the relatively cosmopolitan environs of Budapest, by creating a more open and less repressive feeling. Because some private enterprise was allowed, many Hungarians felt less alienated from the West than their neighbors to the north. More people were able to learn English earlier than the Czechs or the Poles. Secondly, Hungarians are generally a homogenous lot, and therefore, are protective of their own. When the economy is not doing well, they are more likely to frown on people coming in from the outside in search of employment.

Formal prerequisites are not the only challenge that Hungary presents. Given the difficulty of the Hungarian language, holding court in the classroom can bring its own set of frustrations. Trying to explain complex grammatical structures often demands facility with the native language of your students. This is precisely the reason why many schools employ English-speaking Hungarians to teach English, even though they're not native speakers. The fact that a native speaker likely would be more effective at imparting correct idiomatic English is not lost on school administrators. But many schools do not have the resources to employ teams of native English speakers and English-speaking Hungarians in every classroom.

One thing you may notice in Hungary when you are applying for a teaching position is that many school administrators who speak English employ a very formalized and stilted style of speech. To the ears of younger North Americans, this may sound funny, or even pretentious. But it has little to do with personal choice. Most of these people studied English from older, often outdated British textbooks. And because Hungarian itself contains highly formalized structures, many English-speaking Hungarians who do not have the chance to use their English on a day-to-day basis with native speakers of English end up sounding very formal because they seem to naturally seek out what they believe to be higher forms of English.

Despite these idiosyncrasies, teaching English in Hungary isn't all about overcoming obstacles. Teaching is rarely easy on any level, so you just need to make sure you're aware of the specific requirements of each school.

In Hungary, some schools provide English teachers with a broad curriculum, but count on the teachers to plan and conduct individual classes. Though some teachers choose to give their lessons impromptu, without the benefit of careful preparation, better teachers usually spend a few hours preparing before each class. Scrambling for a new topic or improvising a hasty explanation for some important point of grammar is no way to impress your employer or your students. Education is taken very seriously in Hungary, often much more so than it is in the United States. Perhaps Hungary can be compared to Japan in this way. The vast majority of Hungary's population speaks Hungarian, and the population as a whole is relatively culturally homogenous. Thus teachers are not presented with the challenge of trying to bridge the gap between students of varying backgrounds. Most Hungarians are taught early on in life to respect their elders and superiors. Consequently, Hungarian students tend not to be vocal in class unless questioned

Teachers should be prepared to teach students about American culture, as well as the English language.

directly. This can mean that you will need to spend much of your energy establishing the kind of rapport with your students that encourages them to actively participate in the classroom. In order to encourage this, your lesson plans might include formal dialogues, question-and-answer sessions, discussions of current events, or explanations of popular culture in the United States and Canada. It all depends on you and your students.

If your students don't yet have a grasp of basic grammar or a simple, working vocabulary in English, you may teach in tandem with a native Hungarian who can translate for you when all else fails. Otherwise, you likely will be on your own in front of a class. Whether solo or tandem, the most challenging part of teaching English as a foreign language in Hungary has less to do with the formal mechanics of language and more to do with establishing an affective rapport with your students. Teachers should be sensitive, tactful, and adept at fostering a relaxed atmosphere for their students in the classroom.

WHERE TO START

If you know where you want to be—either the city or the region—you can start applying directly to the schools covered in the next section. Or you can take a less calculated approach and find out who's hiring through the newspapers or through newfound contacts locally.

The classifieds

The American-focused *Budapest Week*, the British-focused *Budapest Sun*, and the generic *Budapest Business Journal* are English-language newspapers that publish classified ads listing teaching positions and other available jobs. Most of the larger newsstands in Budapest carry all three papers, as do some of the businesses that serve English speakers, such as New York Bagels, IX. Ferenc Korut 20, and Bajcsy Zsilinszky ut. 20, phone (01) 131-8554; or Bestsellers bookstore, V. Oktober 6 ut. 11, phone (01) 112-1295. The contact information for these newspapers is:

Budapest Week
VI. Eotros ut 12
Phone: (01) 268-4002

Budapest Sun
XII. Alkotas ut 5
Phone: (01) 20-4002

Budapest Business Journal
V. Ferenciek ter 4
Phone: (01) 266-6088

There are also two popular Hungarian newspapers that are well known for their free classifieds, and classifieds from foreigners. Keep an eye out for *Expressz* (daily magazine) and *Hirdetes* (free classifieds).

Don't ignore ads that list requirements that you don't have, such as teaching certificates or experience. Though you may be intimidated by such demands if you don't fit the bill, it's worth a try anyway. There usually aren't enough qualified teachers to meet the demand, so you might be lucky and get hired by a school that needs to fill a position immediately. After all, teachers come and go—sometimes in the middle of a term, without giving notice to their employers. It's wise to pursue all possible leads, especially in the beginning and particularly if you don't have experience or a teaching certificate.

Advertising your services

Many English teachers post notices that advertise their services as native-speaking tutors on university job boards or other bulletin boards that cater to prospective students, such as those found in English-language bookstores and libraries, student lounges, and other businesses that serve the English-speaking community. If you use this method, post as many notices as possible.

The American Cultural Center in Budapest and the British Council English Teaching Center are excellent resources for English teachers and students alike. You will find small bulletin boards in the libraries or hallways of each place where you can post notices and perhaps even find ads for teaching positions.

American Cultural Center in Budapest
VI. Bajza utca 31
Budapest
Phone: (01) 142-4122, (01) 342-4122, or (01) 342-3156

British Council English Teaching Center
Benczur utca 26
Budapest
Phone: (01) 321-4039

Be creative and you might be able to make a small private tutoring business by advertising your services all over the city or town where you live.

Word of mouth

As in any part of the world, networking with your colleagues is one of the best ways to seek out employment opportunities. Many foreign teachers know students or friends of students who may be interested in your services. Be sensitive when discussing these matters with teachers who work for private schools. You don't want to get them into trouble for appearing to "steal" students from the school.

EMPLOYMENT OPTIONS

English-teaching jobs in Hungary are found everywhere, from cosmopolitan Budapest to small, rural towns. By far the greatest number of positions are found in the hundreds of private English-language schools scattered throughout the country. Public schools, colleges and universities, and even larger corporations hire native speakers of English to teach the classes they provide for their students or employees. Though these schools generally offer instruction with an emphasis on conversational English, the formalities of reading and grammar are still taken seriously. English teaching positions fall into the following general categories:

Private schools

Private schools range from reputable, long-established EFL institutions with thousands of students to small entrepreneurial outfits that spring up every year to meet the increasing demand. Jobs at these schools are the most numerous and easiest to find. Consequently, it's worth checking into your prospective employer before you accept a position. As previously mentioned, beware of fly-by-night businesses that care more for the money they can make than their students or teachers.

As in the other countries discussed herein, private school teaching jobs are generally the best source of good pay and reliable hours. You can expect to command rates of 1,200 *forints* per hour, which works out to roughly US$9. If you get paid a salary, you can count on 40,000 to 50,000 *forints* per month, or US$300 to $390.

Classes at private schools usually range in size from five to 25 students. Students may range in age from elementary school age to middle-aged adults, while the majority will likely be high-school and college students or business people. Classes usually last 50 minutes to an hour, depending upon the school.

The following schools hire native speakers, although their hiring requirements may vary:

Budapest
Ameropa Nyelviskola
Honfoglalas u. 22
Budapest H-1221
Hungary
Phone: (01) 371-0635
Fax: (01) 227-2164
North American staff: 3
Students per class: 1–8
Hiring requirements: Applicants should have teaching certification and experience.
Length of contract: Varies
Classes taught: Conversational English, preparation for the Hungarian State Exam
To apply: Send a resume and cover letter.
Comments: The school calendar runs from September through December, and from January through June. Intensive classes are offered during the summer.

Arany Janos Nyelviskola
Csengery u. 68
Budapest H-1068
Hungary
Phone: (01) 132-4580
Fax: (01) 132-7989
North American staff: 0

Total staff: 15
Students per class: 10 max.
Hiring requirements: Applicants must have a valid work permit.
Hourly wage: 700 *forints*
Length of contract: Five, ten, or fifteen weeks
Classes taught: Conversational English, preparation for the Hungarian State Exam
To apply: Send a resume, cover letter, and current photo.
Comments: Classes run from September through January, and from January through the end of May. Intensive courses are offered from June through August.

Atalanta International (Ausztral–magyar KFT)
Visegmadi u. 9
Budapest H-1132
Hungary
Phone: (01) 112-8349 or (01) 131-4954
North American staff: 1
Total staff: 120
Students per class: 12–15 max.
Hiring requirements: Applicants should have teaching certification and experience.
Length of contract: Semester
Classes taught: Conversational English, preparation for the Hungarian State Exam
To apply: Send a resume and cover letter. An interview is also required.
Comments: Classes run from mid-September through mid-December and from mid-January through the beginning of June. Intensive courses are offered in the summer.

Babilon Nyelvistudio
Karoly krt. 3/a
Budapest H-1075
Hungary
Phone: (01) 322-0433, (01) 322-3871, or (01) 269 5531
North American staff: 4
Students per class: 1–8
Hiring requirements: Applicants should have teaching certification and experience.
Hourly wage: 700 *forints*
Length of contract: Varies
Classes taught: Conversational English, preparation for the Hungarian State Exam

To apply: Send a resume and cover letter. Follow up by contacting the school directly.
Comments: They offer courses throughout the year. Intensive courses are offered during the summer.

Bell Iskolak
Tulipan u. 8
Budapest H-1022
Hungary
Phone: (01) 212-4324 or (01) 212-4190
Fax: Same as phone
North American staff: 20
Total staff: Approx. 40
Students per class: 1–12
Hiring requirements: Applicants should have teaching certification and experience.
Length of contract: One year
Classes taught: Conversational English, Cambridge (TOEFL equivalent), preparation for the Hungarian State Exam
To apply: Send a resume and cover letter. An interview is also required.
Comments: Semesters begin in September and January. Three-week intensive courses are taught during the summer. This school is a representative of Cambridge University Press in Hungary.

Berlitz
Vaci u. 11/B
Budapest H-1052
Hungary
Phone: (01) 266-3344
Fax: Same as phone
North American staff: 15-20
Total staff: 15-20
Students per class: 6 max.
Hiring requirements: Applicants should have a college degree, though not necessarily in teaching.
Length of contract: Negotiable
Classes taught: Berlitz English

Berlitz
Terez krt. 4
Budapest H-1066
Hungary
Phone: (01) 268-0488

Fax: Same as phone
North American staff: 15-20
Total staff: 15-20
Students per class: 6 max.
Hiring requirements: Applicants should have a college degree, though not necessarily in teaching.
Length of contract: Negotiable
Classes taught: Berlitz English

Berlitz
Semmelweis u. 2
Budapest H-1062
Hungary
Phone: (01) 137-0014
North American staff: 15-20
Total staff: 15-20
Students per class: 6 max.
Hiring requirements: Applicants should have a college degree, though not necessarily in teaching.
Length of contract: Negotiable
Classes taught: Berlitz English

Concord Nyelviskola
Nemet volgyi u. 34
Budapest H-1126
Hungary
Phone: (01) 155-8022
Fax: Same as phone
North American staff: 2–4
Total staff: 75–100
Students per class: 12
Hiring requirements: Requirements vary according to the requirements of the companies with whom they have contracted.
Hourly wage: 800–1,600 *forints*
Length of contract: Varies
Classes taught: Conversational English, TOEFL, preparation for the Hungarian State Exam
To apply: Contact them by phone.
Comments: This school caters to the business community. Generally, classes run from October through May, though this varies according to the requirements of the companies with whom they have contracted to teach.

Europai Nyelvek Studioja
Szentkiralyi u. 1/b
Budapest H-1088
Hungary
Phone: (01) 138-0730
Fax: (01) 138-1029
North American staff: 1
Students per class: 8 max.
Hiring requirements: Applicants should have teaching certification and experience.
Length of contract: Varies
Classes taught: Conversational English, preparation for the Hungarian State Exam
To apply: Send a resume and cover letter. An interview is required.
Comments: Classes run from September through December, and again from the middle of January through the beginning of June.

Fokusz Nyelviskola
Boszormenyi u. 8
Budapest H-1126
Hungary
Phone: (01) 156-2314
Fax: Same as phone
North American staff: 1
Total staff: Approx. 20
Students per class: 5–10
Hiring requirements: Applicants should have teaching certification and experience.
Hourly wage: 900–1,000 *forints*
Length of contract: Six months
Classes taught: Conversational English, TOEFL, GMAT/GRE, preparation for the Hungarian State Exam
Comments: Classes generally run from mid-September through mid-December, and from the second week of January through the end of May. These dates vary as required by the contracting companies.

Het Nyelv Oktatoi Kisszovetkezet
III. Lajos u. 123
Budapest H-1114
Hungary
Phone: (01) 168-2653
Fax: Same as phone
North American staff: 2–5

Total staff: 70–75
Students per class: 6–8
Hiring requirements: Applicants should have a college degree and some teaching experience.
Hourly wage: 950 *forints*
Length of contract: Varies
Classes taught: Conversational English, Cambridge course (TOEFL equivalent), preparation for the Hungarian State Exam
To apply: Send a resume, cover letter, and current photo via the American Embassy.
Comments: Twelve-week courses run from September through December and from February through April/May. Six-week intensive courses are also offered. This school is an extension of the same school at Bartok B. u. 27.

International House es Tanarkepzo kozpont
Bimbo u. 7
Budapest H-1022
Hungary
Phone: (01) 212-4010
Fax: (01) 212-4219
North American staff: 10
Total staff: Approx. 55
Students per class: 1–11 max.
Hiring requirements: Applicants should have ESL or RSA teaching certification and experience.
Length of contract: One year
Classes taught: Conversational English, TOEFL (if requested), Cambridge (TOEFL equivalent), English for business
To apply: Send a resume and cover letter. An interview is required.
Comments: Classes run from September through June, with intensive courses offered in the summer. This school also offers teachers an EFL certification program for teaching English as a foreign language to children. After completing this course, a teacher's pay range increases.

International Language School
Szemere u. 10
Budapest H-1054
Hungary
Phone: (01) 131-9556
Fax: (01) 131-9796
North American staff: Approx. 100
Total staff: Approx. 300

Students per class: 8–15
Hiring requirements: Applicants should have teaching certification.

Katedra Nyelviskola
Karinthy F. u. 4–6
Budapest H-1116
Hungary
Phone: (01) 165-5116 or (01) 186-8990
North American staff: 2
Students per class: 1–8
Hiring requirements: Applicants should have teaching certification and experience.
Length of contract: Varies
Classes taught: Conversational English, preparation for the Hungarian State Exam
To apply: Send a resume and cover letter. An interview is required.
Comments: Classes run year-round with intensive courses during the summer. Holidays are during Christmas and the second half of June.

Lingual School of English
Lajos u. 142
Budapest H-1036
Hungary
Phone: (01) 250-0270
Fax: Same as phone
North American staff: 1
Total staff: 30
Students per class: 8
Hiring requirements: Applicants should have teaching certification and experience.
Hourly wage: 650–800 *forints*
Length of contract: One year minimum
Classes taught: Conversational English, preparation for the Hungarian State Exam
To apply: Send a resume, cover letter, and photo. An interview is also required.
Comments: Classes run from mid-September through the end of December, and from mid-January through mid-June.

London Studio
Fadrusz u. 12
Budapest H-1114
Hungary
Phone: (01) 166-8137

Fax: (01) 181-1959
North American staff: 2
Total staff: Approx. 300
Students per class: 10–16
Hiring requirements: Applicants should have teaching certification
and experience.
Hourly wage: 700 *forints*
Length of contract: Typically one or two semesters
Classes taught: Conversational English, TOEFL (if requested),
Pittmann course (British), preparation for the Hungarian State Exam
To apply: Send a resume, cover letter, and photo. An interview and
completed application form are also required. Inquire in your cover
letter.
Comments: Teachers generally work 40 hours per quarter. Quarters
run from the end of September through January, from January
through March, from March through June, and from June through
August.

Magiszter Nyelviskola
Radvanyi u. 35/b.
Budapest H-1118
Hungary
Phone: (01) 185-0052
North American staff: 3
Total staff: 60–70
Students per class: 4–5
Hiring requirements: Applicants should have teaching certification.
Length of contract: One or two semesters
Classes taught: Special programs for companies and managers as
contracted

Mercedes Language School
Pannonia u. 88–90
Budapest H-1136
Hungary
Phone: (01) 129-5033

Novoschool Nyelviskola
Ulloi u. 63
Budapest H-1091
Hungary
Phone: (01) 215-5480, (01) 215-6496, or (01) 215-1068
Fax: (01) 215-5488

North American staff: 20–25
Students per class: 12 max.
Hiring requirements: Applicants should have teaching certification.
Length of contract: One semester
Classes taught: Conversational English, preparation for the Hungarian State Exam
To apply: Send a resume and cover letter. An interview is required.
Comments: Classes run from September 10 through mid-December, and from January 10 through early June.

Open University Business School
Fo u. 68
Budapest H-1027
Hungary
Phone: (01) 115-4090

Perfect–Poligott Studio
Rozsa u. 109
Budapest H-1064
Hungary
Phone: (01) 132-8137
Fax: Same as phone
North American staff: 3
Students per class: 1–8
Hiring requirements: Applicants should have teaching certification and experience.
Length of contract: Varies
Classes taught: Conversational English, preparation for the Hungarian State Exam
To apply: Send a resume and cover letter. An interview is required.
Comments: Classes run year-round with intensive courses during the summer. Holidays are during Christmas and the end of June.

Szoma Kepzesi Kozpont
Budaafoki u. 107
Budapest H-1117
Hungary
Phone: (01) 203-0106 or (01) 206-6772
Fax: Same as phone
North American staff: 2
Students per class: 8 max.
Hiring requirements: Applicants should have teaching certification and experience.

Length of contract: Varies
Classes taught: Conversational English, preparation for the Hungarian State Exam
To apply: Send a resume and cover letter. An interview is required.
Comments: Classes run from mid-September through mid-June with vacation from mid-December through mid-January. Intensive courses are offered during the summer.

Kecskemet
Babel Nyelvstudio
Vorosmarty u. 10
Kecskemet H-6000
Hungary
Phone: (076) 48 44 54

Coventry House
Budai u. 1
Kecskemet H-6044
Hungary
Phone: (076) 48 33 48

Pecs
Bognan Idegennyelvi Kozpont Bt.
Angster Jozsef u.2–7
Pecs H-7624
Hungary
Phone: (076) 31 33 63

Muller Nyelvstudio
Hunyadi J. u. 79/b.
Pecs H-7625
Hungary
Phone: (072) 32 64 31

Nyelvelde
Jokai u. 43
Pecs
Hungary
Phone: (072) 32 63 82

Relax Nyelvi Labor
Bercsenyi u. 7
Pecs H-7621
Hungary
Phone: (072) 31 90 14

Public schools

Though less popular among native speakers because of their lower pay and bureaucratic nature, public schools can be an excellent source of employment. Frequently, they offer benefits unmatched by even the best private schools, and they provide an opportunity to interact with the entire community, especially in smaller cities and towns. It's not uncommon to find public schools that offer accommodations as part of their compensation package, and getting effective assistance with work and residency permits is almost guaranteed. Yes, you might flinch at the following salary ranges. But don't fear, you can make it if you try. Remember, teaching in Eastern Europe isn't about getting rich. Public schools in Hungary pay from 25,000 to 30,000 *forints* per month. And if you really must know the dollar equivalent, it converts to approximately US$190 to $230 per month.

Because public schools are beholden to their community governments, most demand that their teachers be credentialed and experienced. As a general rule the farther you get from the larger cities, the more likely you will find schools that are more lenient about their requirements.

Several offices and agencies are worth contacting if a public school teaching position interests you:

Budapest Pedagogical Institute
(Fovarosi Pedagogiai Intezet)
VIII. Horvath Mihaly ter 8
Budapest
Phone: (01) 210-1030
(This organization recruits qualified teachers for Budapest.)

English Teachers Association of the National Pedagogical Institute
(Pedagogiai Alapitvany)
II. Boylai ut 14
Budapest
Phone: (01) 212-3865
(This organization recruits qualified teachers for outlying cities and towns.)

Orszagos Pedagogiai Intezet
VII. Reguly Antal ut 57/59
Budapest
Phone: (01) 210-0200
(This organization recruits qualified teachers for outlying cities and towns.)

Soros Professional English Teaching Program
888 7th Avenue, Suite 1901
New York, NY 10106
(212) 757-2323
(This organization recruits certified and experienced teachers for Hungary and other countries in the region.)

These organizations recruit teachers for placement in the Hungarian public school system. They act much like ministries of education, such as those in the Czech Republic, Slovakia, and Poland. In order to qualify for these positions, you must have both teaching certification and experience. If you possess a master's degree, you will be given even more favorable consideration. Remember, most Hungarians, especially in the field of education, appreciate formal qualifications. You shouldn't consider applying for a teaching position through the Pedagogical Institutes unless you are truly qualified to teach professionally.

Private tutoring

Teaching privately can be personally and financially rewarding. It's a great way to supplement your regular teaching salary—in fact, some enterprising teachers only teach privately. Private students can be difficult to find, however, because you often need to be introduced by a mutual acquaintance or friend, which alleviates any issues of trust or ability. Don't let this deter you from advertising or otherwise searching for private students. Meeting and gaining the trust of the right person can open the door to this well-paying niche. If one private student discovers your effectiveness, they usually are willing to introduce you to their friends and co-workers. This is especially effective when your student is well-connected or influential; you might try targeting an upper-level business person or a successful entrepreneur. An American woman who completed her teaching certification course in the United States related her experience in Budapest:

❝ *I began tutoring the children of a wealthy Hungarian businessman. What a great way to make good money and supplement my regular teaching job (in a private school). Though he spoke some English himself, he felt it was necessary for his kids to be tutored by a native speaker. He just expected me to come to his house once or twice a week to speak to his kids in English. At first, I was worried because I had never worked with kids so young, but it turned out to be a fun job.*❞

Private tutors also should consider teaching small groups. Some students feel more comfortable in a group setting, where the pressure to perform is spread out a little. In many ways, group tutoring takes some of the burden off of the instructor as well because a group is naturally social. Students can interact among themselves to practice dialogues, act out skits, or engage in other learning activities.

Setting up group lessons may not be as difficult as you think. Tell your prospective students that you are willing to hold group lessons.

They may feel more comfortable if they can get a friend or a sibling involved. In fact, kids often thrive when they are not alone in a lesson. Students in a group usually pay less than they would for an individual lesson, and this may appeal to the tremendous number of Hungarians who don't have much disposable income. And your earning potential will far exceed that of one-on-one tutoring.

You're probably aware by now that private tutoring usually commands the highest hourly wage. In Hungary, it's fair to charge between 1,000 to 1,500 *forints* per hour. Converted into United States dollars, this hourly pay range brings you between US$9 and $10 per hour. Once again, if you are willing to be flexible with your students, some won't balk at paying you closer to the upper end of the scale while others may only be able to cough up enough *forints* to pay you at the lower end of the range. If you assess your situation wisely, you will be able to make the kinds of arrangements that are fair to you and satisfactory to each of your students.

In-company instruction

Though the three most common forms of teaching have been outlined above, there is another approach worth mentioning. In-company teaching is language instruction that companies provide for their employees. Classes are usually set up "in office," either before or after work. In most cases, companies contract out to private schools who, in turn, provide the teachers. Or companies actually hire individual instructors independently.

In-company work can be financially rewarding and grueling at the same time. Not only do you have to adhere to the inflexibility of the company's business hours, you will likely have to contend with students of varying levels in the same class. While some companies may provide a curriculum, most ask teachers to design their own topics. Though the nature of the company's business may suggest appropriate teaching strategies, we recommend that only experienced and certified teachers pursue in-company teaching jobs.

With independent in-company teaching, the wages or salary you can command will depend upon your ability to negotiate with your prospective employer. If you know what a company would have to pay to contract with a private school, you can use that as a starting point. This doesn't necessarily mean that you should demand to be paid the same amount. Obviously, it would be difficult for you to provide the same services and resources that a well-established school could. Nevertheless, you should use whatever guidelines are available to you. Knowing the general wage ranges for different types of teaching positions should help you decide what is fair to both you and your prospective employer. Before you try to negotiate your pay, you should

EFL students are motivated to learn, even though the classroom atmosphere is often informal.

find out what the company expects of you. For example, if they expect you to be available at odd times during the day, this may detract from your ability to get other teaching jobs. Just make sure that your rate of pay reflects the demands of the job.

Full-time vs. freelance

Teaching full-time in Hungary does not mean teaching a class forty hours per week. Most of the time, full-time teaching demands only eighteen to twenty-four hours of classroom instruction every week. With preparation time, though, a teaching job can easily consume forty hours of your time.

There are several advantages to a full-time teaching job. Employers are more likely to help out with the work permit process and even assist in your search for accommodations (though this is hardly universal). Also full-time teachers tend to develop close relationships with their students, fellow teachers, and administrators. Another advantage is that their lives are relatively settled because they have at least part of every day planned out and spend less time in transit than those with several part-time jobs or private students. The main disadvantage of full-time positions is that they often pay less per hour than freelance tutoring sessions.

Freelancing means searching out your own students and managing your own tutoring times and lesson plans. Freelancers might work part-time at small, private schools and tutor privately at the same time.

Although this arrangement allows for greater freedom and potentially more money, it usually requires more initiative, patience, and dedication than most full-time employment. It can also become tiresome because of inconvenient and erratic work hours. Private students often feel less compelled to keep their lesson appointments because they feel that they have a closer, more casual relationship with their instructor. It would be wise to establish a policy regarding lesson cancellations and advance payment in order to protect yourself against your students' inconsiderate whims. After all, a few cancellations can affect your pocketbook as well as your schedule.

The best arrangement may be to combine a full-time job with a few freelance teaching sessions on the side (if they don't conflict with your full-time job). If you set things up this way, your workload will be varied enough that you will not get tired of either type of teaching.

ADVANCE PLANNING

Though we recommend traveling to Hungary before you begin your search for an English teaching position, it may be possible to begin your search in North America. This approach works best for qualified and experienced teachers who already have a sense of what kind of job they are looking for. Contact the following organizations for more information:

Budapest Pedagogical Institute
VIII. Horvath Mihaly ter 8
Budapest
Phone: (01) 210-1030
(This organization recruits qualified teachers for Budapest.)

English Teachers Association of the National Pedagogical Institute
II. Bolyai ut 14
Budapest
Phone: (01) 212-3865
(This organization recruits qualified teachers for outlying cities and towns.)

Orszagos Pedagogiai Intezet
VII. Reguly Antal ut 57/59
Budapest
Phone: (01) 210-0200
(This organization recruits qualified teachers for outlying cities and towns.)

Soros Professional English Teaching Program
888 7th Avenue, Suite 1901
New York, NY 10106
(212) 757-2323
(This organization recruits certified and experienced teachers for Hungary and other countries in the region.)

OTHER OPPORTUNITIES

Like most other countries in Eastern Europe (and for that matter around the world), Hungary's government does not like the idea of permitting foreigners to take jobs that its citizens could perform equally well. Obtaining a work visa is much easier if your stated aim is to teach English than if you are seeking employment with a construction company in Budapest, for example. After all, high unemployment statistics are a constant reminder to the government that there is plenty of room for improvement within Hungary's economy. At the same time, though, there are not many Hungarians who are highly experienced with jobs on the cutting edge of technology or in fields that demand an intimate knowledge of the subtle fluctuations of a market economy. Because of this, Westerners may be called on to lend their expertise in fields such as software engineering, marketing and advertising, computer graphics, power generation, environmental reclamation, and technical writing (in English).

" What they should be doing in Hungary is worrying less about how many English teachers are needed. Rather, they should hire one person to come in and set up a computer system which would allow them to manage people more effectively. In so many ways, they are still 40 years behind."

Generally, it is up to the job hunter to seek out, or even create, these kinds of opportunities. Budapest's English-language newspapers may occasionally contain help-wanted ads for jobs that fall outside the scope of English language instruction, but they shouldn't be relied upon as consistent sources of information. Most of the companies that advertise for positions that would attract skilled and educated foreigners are either partly or wholly foreign owned. Though there are some exceptions, Hungarian authorities make it much easier for foreigners to work for these kinds of foreign companies. (Under certain circumstances, a labor permit may not be necessary for jobs that involve work contracted to a foreign partner, etc.)

There are several tactics to consider when searching for a job that requires either technical knowledge or an advanced degree. If your area of interest or expertise is fairly specialized, it may be to your advantage to begin your job search in the United States or Canada. If you are hired in North America, you are more likely to be well compensated (i.e., paid a hard currency salary on a Western pay scale). If you leave for Hungary before you begin your search, contact the agencies listed below. But remember: no matter where you are, the best way for you to find work is to network as much as possible. Send out resumes and cover letters to companies that do business overseas, arrange to meet with someone who has worked or lived in Hungary, make contact with a Hungarian person who might maintain either business or family ties with Hungary, or consult the director of a foreign-exchange or study program in Hungary through your college or university. You might even find out if the city where you live has a sister city in Hungary. If so, make contact with the person who oversees the exchange, and explain your interest. Spread the word any way you can that you are interested in finding employment in Hungary.

The United States Department of Commerce in Hungary publishes a list of all American companies that do business in Hungary. This list will give you an idea of what kinds of positions might be available and who to contact to get more information. The list is available from the American Cultural Center in Budapest for a small fee. Visit the center or contact:

United States Information Service (USIS)
VII. Bajza utca 31
Budapest
Phone: (01) 142-4122, (01) 142-3717, (01) 342-3156,
    or (01) 342-4122

The USIS also provides a fairly up-to-date list of English schools throughout Hungary.

Another good source of information for job seekers is the American Chamber of Commerce in Hungary. They keep an up-to-date file of resumes of people who are seeking employment in Hungary, so that their members have access to a database of prospective employees. Though individual memberships cost US$250 for the first year, having access to all of their information can be very valuable, and attending events put on by the AmCham-Hungary is a great way to network with fellow business people. Contact:

American Chamber of Commerce in Hungary
VI. Dozsa Gyorgy utca 84/a, Room 406
Budapest H-1068
Phone: (01) 269-6016

Aside from English teachers, the vast majority of expatriates who reside in Hungary work for international or foreign concerns who do business with Hungary. Most of these jobs are found outside of Hungary, usually in the country where the company is based. The reasons for this are simple. When a non-Hungarian owned company wants to do business in Hungary, they send over a team of managers to set up their operation. This group usually sets about the task of hiring and training as many native Hungarians as are needed to keep the operation running once the management team has completed all of the requisite start-up tasks. And once the operation is up and running efficiently, the individuals who helped to get everything started are usually moved elsewhere, often to start up another branch or office in another part of the world. For most international companies it doesn't make sense to employ a Westerner where a native-speaking Hungarian could be trained to do the job at a much lower salary. Consequently, unless you possess some rare talent or expertise, the chances of finding a hard-currency (well-paying) position with an international company in Hungary are pretty slim. Such a position should be searched out back home in North America.

One American expatriate who lived for over three years in Eastern Europe explained:

66 *Many of the expatriates who showed up three or four years ago in places like Budapest and Prague were sent by larger companies who wanted to establish a presence in the newly opened markets of Eastern Europe. Now, their numbers are waning. These people are moving on or going home because they've completed their goals. The locals they hired have been trained and their operations are up and running."*

settling in

A PLACE TO LIVE

Finding long-term accommodations can be one of the most frustrating tasks for expats who want to settle in Hungary. Depending on what type of employment you seek, employers may provide little assistance when it comes to locating an apartment. English teachers are more likely to get assistance if they work for state schools (public) or if their private-school employer is large and well-established. For those who work in other fields, the same rule applies: the better established your employer, the more likely they will be to assist you. Obviously, if you accept an upper-level management job with a reputable company, they will have the wherewithal to locate appropriate accommodations. Whatever you do, though, it's best to take part in the selection process as much as you can.

Renting an apartment

Although finding an apartment in Hungary is difficult, most people who plan to stay for more than a few months do so. Don't rent an apartment until you are happily settled into a work routine, because if you make any sudden change of plans, the worst part of the change will likely be finding a new residence.

Though apartment and room rents in Hungary (yes, even in Budapest) are inexpensive by most standards in North America, they are not so cheap when you consider living on the Hungarian economy. In Budapest, it's possible to find rooms for the equivalent of US$90 per month and small apartments that start around US$200. You have to look long and hard, though, to find the better deals.

By far the best way to find long-term accommodations is through the people you meet—casual acquaintances, other teachers, co-workers. Make sure that you know the area so you can give people a good idea of where you would like to live. Though most places in Budapest are pretty safe by American standards, there are still important considerations, such as proximity to public transportation, availability of a telephone (for your personal use), furnished or unfurnished, etc.

Nightmarish stories about problems with accommodations are common throughout Eastern Europe. The best way to protect yourself from any prospective problem is to make certain that you set up a rental agreement that is understood by both you and your landlord. Have a Hungarian-speaking friend translate for you whenever you search for a room or an apartment. Many Hungarians jump at the chance to rent rooms or apartments to foreigners because they can charge rents that an average Hungarian wouldn't think of paying.

Consider the following before you sign an agreement to rent:

- Do you have good vibes about your prospective landlord? Your initial gut feeling should be a cue for your decision.
- Very few apartments in Hungary come with working telephones. Having a phone installed could take months or even years. Ask your landlord if you may have access to their phone on occasion. Will they be willing to take messages for you? This could be a sign of their friendliness and generosity.
- Apartments in Hungary are small relative to apartments in North America. Expect the basics and not much more, unless you want to pay a small fortune.
- The plumbing and heating systems often are antiquated. Make sure everything is in working order.

If money is an issue, you might want to consider finding a roommate or a private room in someone's home. Since much of your time probably will be spent out and about, exploring your new surroundings and meeting new people, why spend a bunch of hard-earned money on a place to sleep?

HUNGARIAN LANGUAGE

Hungarian is one of the more complex and difficult languages in the world. There are fewer than 11 million people worldwide who speak it. Considering the world's population is nearing five billion, Hungarian speakers are a small minority.

The history and evolution of the Hungarian language has fostered much controversy amongst linguists over the years. It's considered a Finno-Ugric language, which remotely resembles Finnish and Estonian. No other language in Eastern Europe is even remotely related. The Hungarians may have many Slavic neighbors, but shouting out a "Hi, how's it going?" (in Hungarian) over the fence is bound to be met with a quizzical stare.

Hungarian will always remain obscure when compared to the world's more widely spoken languages. Unless you have some specific (and perhaps masochistic) interest in learning to speak Hungarian, you would probably be better off learning a few simple phrases and leaving the rest to the natives. A small phrase book will come in handy in case of emergency, though.

Hungarian language schools

International Language School
V. Bajcsy-Zsilinszky ut 62
Budapest
Phone: (01) 131-9796

Studia Hungarica
Eotvos University
V. Pesti Barnabas utca 1
Budapest
Phone: (01) 121-1174

Katedra Language School
V. Veres Palne utca 36
Budapest
Phone: (01) 165-5116

Hungarian Language School
VI. Szinyei Merse Pal utca 1
Budapest
Phone: (01) 112-2382

HUNGARIAN FOOD AND DRINK

Compared to the other countries of Central and Eastern Europe, Hungary has several national dishes that are well-known throughout the West, and Hungarian food, in general, tends to be more flavorful and varied. It's still a meat-and-potatoes based diet, though, so vegetarians will have some difficulty.

Goulash (called gulyas in Hungarian), fish soup, and various paprika-laden concoctions are staples in the Hungarian diet.

If you stay in Budapest, there are plenty of different kinds of restaurants to choose from—Italian, Thai, vegetarian, etc. Cooking at home, on the other hand, will limit your choices because grocery stores, even in the big city, are not consistently well-stocked with different items from the various food groups.

Teetotalers are a rare breed in Hungary. Liquor such as vodka and apricot brandy, beer, and red wine are consumed in great quantities. In fact, Hungary is famous the world over for both red wine and a sweet, dessert wine called Tokaji.

" *I couldn't believe it. Many of the pubs in Budapest already were busy by eight-thirty in the morning. Even some of the construction workers were chugging on big bottles of beer well before noon."*

COMMON CUSTOMS

Hungarian customs will not seem nearly as foreign or incomprehensible as the language. In fact, if you have ever traveled in Western Europe you won't be too surprised by the ways in which Hungarians conduct themselves in everyday life. However, it's always wise to be

attentive to foreign customs so you don't offend anyone in the beginning. Consider the following:

- Hungarians tend to differentiate between those who are familiar
  to them (i.e., family and friends) and those who have yet to
  enter this realm. So when you are first introduced to someone
  make sure to call them by their appropriate title (e.g., Dr., Mr.,
  Mrs.) followed by their last name. When in doubt in Hungary,
  opt for formality.
- On business cards and the like, the last name precedes the first
  name.
- Handshakes are the common gesture of greeting, no matter how
  well you know someone.
- Expect to be offered both food and drink—and lots of it—when
  you enter someone's home. Always accept at least a modest serving of whatever is offered. If you're concerned about drinking
  too much, drink slowly and then politely decline the offer of
  another drink.
- Try to bring some kind of small gift when you are invited to
  someone's home.
- Hungarians are a talkative and passionate people. They frequently
  state their opinions in very direct terms. Expect lively and sometimes heated discussions.
- When in doubt, tip, much like you would in North America.
  Ten percent and upwards is a good, general rule for wait-people,
  bartenders, taxi drivers, hairdressers, etc.

SHOPPING

As far as Eastern-European cities go, Budapest is big and cosmopolitan. You won't have much trouble finding all the modern conveniences
there, but you may have to pay more for them than you would at
home. And, as a general rule, the farther you get from the larger cities
in Hungary, the more you have to worry about the availability of certain items. If you're worried about not finding what you need, consider bringing the following items:

- Birth control—don't rely on finding condoms and the like on
  short notice. Quality is obviously an issue here, too.
- Vitamins—if you're a health nut, bring your own goodies. They
  can be expensive in Hungary.
- Film—particularly if you require the more obscure varieties.
- Recorded music—the selection is limited in Central and Eastern Europe.

- Medication—even if it's sold over the counter at home, it may require a prescription in Hungary. And bring a note from your doctor, if you need to travel with prescription medication.

FINANCES

Hungarian banks often offer the best currency exchange rates and provide other useful services, such as cash advances.

Banks

OTP Bank
Vaci utca 19-21
Budapest

Ibusz
V. Petofi ter 3
Budapest
24 hours daily

Magyar Kulkereskedelmi Bank
V. Szent Istvan ter 11
Budapest

Dunabank
V. Bathory utca 12
Budapest

MAV Tours
Keleti Station
Budapest
Phone: (01) 182-9011

American Express
V. Deak Ferenc utca 10
Phone: (01) 266-8680

TELEPHONES AND MAIL

At best, telephones in Hungary are merely frustrating. Most of the time, though, they are outright appalling—even worthy of profane outbursts.

❝ *I had promised to call someone at three o'clock in the afternoon, when I was out and about in downtown Budapest. I covered several blocks and more than a few telephone booths before finding even one barely functional pay-phone, and it still took me three or four tries to get through."*

The telephone system is presently in the midst of a long-overdue overhaul. Numbers are changing to meet the specifications of the new digital system. And it's a mess.

Public telephones

- Public phones come in three colors: red (for long distance), silver (for local), and blue (for both).
- Look for the newer style of public phone. They work for both

domestic and international calls. You will need coins—at least five forint denominations, for most phones. Long-distance calls require 20 forint coins.

- For reliable pay phones try the main post office(s) in Budapest or your town of residence.
- Keep looking until you find one that works!
- Buy telephone calling cards. These will help keep you from dumping all your coins into the ill-working phones.

For long distance calls within Hungary: dial 06, wait for a dial tone, and then dial the city code and the rest of the number.

A central service for sending and receiving fax messages is available at:

Post Office No. 62
VI. Terez krt. 51
Budapest
Phone: (01) 112-1200
Fax: receiving (01) 153-4670
(You must pick up your faxes personally at the post office.)

Calling home

For international calls, try AT&T Direct. It's by far the most reliable way to use a calling card or call collect.

AT&T Direct Dial .... 00 (wait for tone) 800-011-11

or 00-36-0111

MCI WorldPhone .... 00 (wait for tone) 800-014-11

Mail

The Hungarian Postal Service is much more efficient than the telephone system. Airmail letters and small packages travel between Hungary and North America in roughly seven to ten days. If you don't have a stable address you can receive mail poste restante, or through the American Express office in Budapest, if you have an American Express card or American Express traveler's checks. (The services available through American Express can be invaluable, so get their checks or a card if you can.) Send or receive mail at:

Budapest

Send or receive mail
American Express
Deak Ferenc utca 10
Budapest H-1052
Phone: (01) 267-2024
   or (01) 266-8680

Post Office No. 62
VI. Terez krt. 51
Budapest
Phone: (01) 112-1200
Fax: receiving (01) 153-4670

Post Office Branch
Nyugati Station
24 hours

Post Office Branch
Keleti Station
Budapest
24 hours

Poste Restante
Main Post Office
V. Varoshaz utca 18
Budapest
Phone: (01) 118-4811
Weekdays, 8AM–8PM and Sat.,
8AM–3PM

HEALTH CARE

If you need medical attention, Hungary probably is one of the better places to be in Eastern Europe. Doctors generally are well trained and comparatively well equipped, as many Austrians will attest. It's not uncommon for people from Vienna to cross the border to find good quality yet less expensive medical and dental care in Budapest.

Public health care in Hungary is accessible to foreigners who contribute to the social security system via deductions from their wages or salaries. Of course, you must play by the rules and have your work permit in order before you are eligible.

Of course, you need to be able to communicate with your doctor in order to get proper attention, which is no small feat in Hungary given the complexities of the language. Both the American and British Embassies can refer you to well-trained English-speaking physicians.

Medical facilities and assistance

SOS Emergency Medical Service
VIII. Kerepesi utca 15
Budapest
Phone: (01) 118-8288
  or (01) 118-8012
(Provides English-language services)

International Medical Services
XIII. Vaci utca 202
Budapest
Phone: (01) 129-8423
  or (01) 149-9349

(Provides English-language services)

Belgyogyaszati Klinika
VIII. Koranyi Sandor utca 2/a
Budapest
Phone: (01) 133-0360
24 hours

Central State Hospital
Kutvolgyi utca 4
Budapest
Phone: (01) 155-1122
24 hours

Pharmacies

Pharmacy
II. Frankel Leo utca 22
Budapest
24 hours

Pharmacy
VII. Rakoczi utca 86
Budapest
24 hours

NOW HIRING!

Pharmacy
XXI. Kossuth Lajos utca 95
Budapest
24 hours

Pharmacy
XX. Tancsics M. utca 104
Budapest
24 hours

Pharmacy
III. Szentendrei utca 2/a
Budapest
24 hours

OTHER SERVICES

Embassies

United States Embassy
V. Szabadsag ter 12
Budapest
Phone: (01) 112-6450 (8:30 AM–noon, except Wednesdays)
Phone: (01) 153-0566 (after hours)

Canadian Embassy
XII. Budakeszi utca 32
Budapest
Phone: (01) 176-7686

Important telephone numbers

Budapest

Police emergency 07
Fire emergency 05
Ambulance .... 04 or (01) 111-1666
Police headquarters .... (01) 118-0800 or (01) 111-8668
Fire station ....(01) 121-6216
Directory assistance ....(01) 267-7111
International operator 09

LANGUAGE TIPS

Hungarian is one of the world's more complex languages, so don't expect mastery to come easily. To get started, though, make sure to put emphasis on the first syllable of every word. And remember to use your last name first when formally introducing yourself.

Numbers

one	*egy*
two	*kettó*
three	*három*
four	*négy*
five	*öt*
six	*hat*
seven	*hét*
eight	*nyolc*
nine	*kilenc*
ten	*tíz*

Important words and phrases

Yes	*Igen*
No	*Nem*
Good morning	*Jó reggelt kivánok*
Good afternoon	*Jó napot kivánok*
Good evening	*Jó estét kivánok*
Goodbye	*Viszont látásra*
Thank you	*Köszönöm szépen*
Please	*Legyen szíves*
Where is the bus station?	*Kérem, hol van a busz megálló?*
Where is the train station?	*Kérem, hol van a vasút állomás?*
Where is the toilet?	*Kérem, hol van a W.C.?*
Nice to meet you.	*Órvendek (hogy megismerhettem).*
I don't understand.	*Nem értem.*
I don't speak Hungarian.	*Nem beszélek magyarul.*

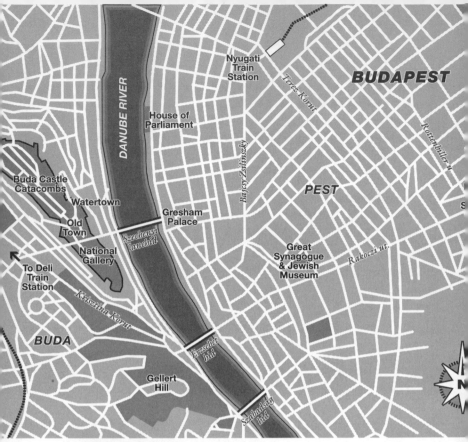

City Profiles

BUDAPEST

Budapest is the only metropolis in Hungary. As the capital city it stands out among all of the major cities of Eastern Europe as the most cosmopolitan and the most Western in its orientation. With a population of two million, and located in the center of the western half of the country, Budapest serves as the hub of commerce and culture in a country that is predominantly rural. Though there are a few medium-sized cities whose economies depend primarily on industry or agriculture, Budapest can boast of, among other things, an opera hall, several museums, many upscale shops, an exquisite cathedral, parks, and numerous restaurants and coffee houses. For the expatriate, Budapest offers almost anything that a city dweller could want.

Soviet influence

You won't easily forget its recent emergence from the shackles of Soviet repression, however, even though Hungary's capital suffered much less than Warsaw or Bratislava. Evidence of the old regime is less obvious here than in these other cities probably because the Kremlin gave Hungary a longer rope, allowing the local government to experiment with certain aspects of a free market economy long before the rest of Eastern Europe.

Places of interest

Between the metro, bus system, and tram lines, Budapest is relatively easy to navigate. And much of the city can be covered on foot. There are restaurants, pastry shops, and bars everywhere, and many of them cater to an expatriate clientele. If you want culture, there are plenty of theater and opera performances. And if you're after peace and tranquillity, you can venture over to the hilly Buda-side of the city to one of the venerated mineral baths that Budapest is famous for. For a terrific view of the city, go to the top of Castle Hill, where you will find the 13th-century Baroque Matthias Cathedral, the Royal Palace, which houses the Hungarian National Gallery, and Budapest's oldest bakery, Ruszwurm Cukraszda. Or check out the neo-Gothic Parliament building (Orszaghaz), which was designed by the Hungarian architect Imre Steindl and built by no less than 1,000 workers over a 17-year period (1885–1902).

Buda and Pest

Long ago, what is now Budapest was actually two different cities divided by the Danube river. Buda lay on the north side of the river—older with more rugged, hilly terrain—while Pest extended flat and plain-like on the south shore. Today, little evidence exists of those two historical incarnations, while the atmosphere and the cityscape of Budapest has retained both its human proportions and its nostalgia.

English schools

Number of staff	Number of students per class	Entry pay (forints)	Send resume/cover letter	
n/a	1–8	n/a	✔	Ameropa Nyelviskola Honfoglalas ut. 22 Budapest Hungary (01) 371-0635
15	10 max	700/hr	✔	Arany Janos Nyelviskola Csengery u. 68 Budapest Hungary (01) 132-4580
n/a	8 max	n/a	✔	Atalanta International (Ausztral-magyar KFT) Visegmadi u. 9 Budapest Hungary (01) 112-8349 or (01) 131-4954
n/a	1–8	700/hr	✔	Babilon Nyelvistudio Karoly krt 3/a Budapest Hungary (01) 322-0433, (01) 322-3871, or (01) 269 5531
30	1–12	n/a	✔	Bell Iskolak Tulipan u. 8 Budapest Hungary (01) 212-4324 or (01) 212-4190

Number of staff	Number of students per class	Entry pay (forints)	Send resume/cover letter	
75+	12	800–1,600/hr		Concord Nyelviskola Nemet volgyi ut. 34 Budapest Hungary (01) 155-8022
n/a	8 max	n/a	✔	Europai Nyelvek Studioja Szentkiralyi u. 1/b Budapest Hungary (01) 138-0730
20	5–10	900–1,000/hr	✔	Fokusz Nyelviskola Boszormenyi u. 8 Budapest Hungary (01) 156-2314
70–75	6–8	950/hr	✔	Het Nyelv Oktatoi Kisszovetkezet Ill. Lajos u. 123 Budapest Hungary (01) 168-2653
35	1–8	n/a	✔	International House es Tanarkepzo kozpont Bimbo ut. 7 Budapest Hungary (01) 212-4010
n/a	1–8	n/a	✔	Katedra Nyelviskola

Number of staff	Number of students per class	Entry pay (forints)	Send resume/cover letter	
				Karinthy F. u. 4-6 Budapest Hungary (01) 165-5116 or (01) 186-8990
30	8	650–800/hr	✔	Lingual School of English Lajos u. 142 Budapest Hungary (01) 250-0270
200	10–16	700/hr	✔	London Studio Fadrusz u. 12 Budapest Hungary (01) 166-8137
n/a	n/a	n/a		Magiszter Nyelviskola Radvanyi u. 35/b. Budapest Hungary (01) 185-0052
n/a	n/a	n/a		Mercedes Language School Pannonia u. 88-90 Budapest Hungary (01) 129-5033
n/a	8 max	n/a	✔	Novoschool Nyelviskola Ulloi ut. 63 Budapest Hungary (01) 215-5480, (01) 215-6496, or (01) 215-1068
n/a	n/a	n/a		Open University

Number of staff	Number of students per class	Entry pay (*forints*)	Send resume/cover letter	
				Business School Fo u. 68 Budapest Hungary (01) 115-4090
n/a	1–8	n/a	✔	Perfect-Poligott Studio Rozsa u. 109 Budapest Hungary (01) 132-8137
n/a	8 max	n/a	✔	Szoma Kepzesi Kozpont Budaafoki ut. 107 Budapest Hungary (01) 203-0106 or (01) 206-6772

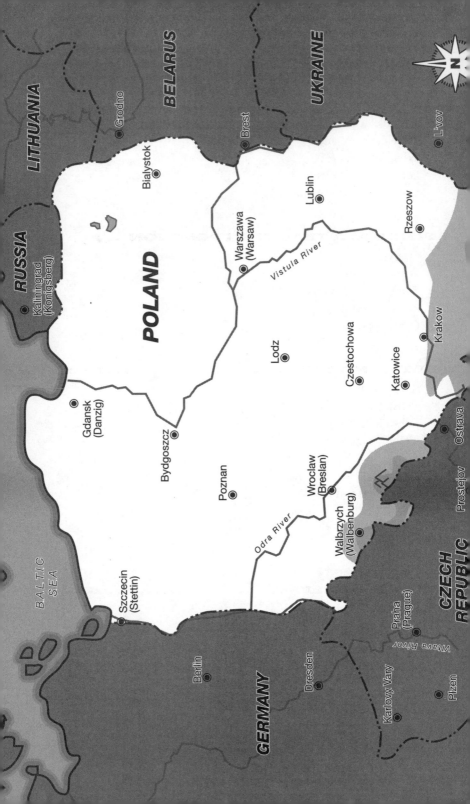

The lay of the land

A PROFILE OF POLAND

Population

Poland is by far the largest of the four countries covered in this book, with the biggest land mass and a population that hovers just over the thirty-eight million mark. The vast majority of Poland's people—nearly ninety-nine percent—are of Polish origin. The remainder are of either German, Ukrainian, Jewish, or Belorussian descent. Urbanization is a prevalent trend. Close to two-thirds of Poland's people choose the city over country living, mainly in the larger cities such as Warsaw, Poznan, Gdansk, Lodz, and Krakow.

Geography

With the Baltic Sea to the north, Poland shares its other borders with Germany (specifically, the former East Germany), the Czech Republic, Russia, the Ukraine, Slovakia, Belorussia, and Lithuania.

Aside from mountainous southern and southeastern border regions, Poland is generally flat. Given its consistently level topography, Poles can rightfully boast of their country's great tracts of arable land. Historically, though, the forbears of modern day Poles rarely passed quiet, pastoral lives. Invading armies made easy inroads into Polish territory because of the flatness of the North European plain. Poland's centrality on the European continent—combined with its gentle topography—has put it at the crossroads of many conflicts over the centuries; consequently, its population has been periodically ravaged and its borders changed, according to the desires of the victorious invaders.

Though the great North European plain may not attract travelers in search of rugged altitudes, Poland has more natural lakes than any other country except Finland. Several rivers also meander through Poland's countryside.

Climate

Though Poland's climate is temperate, winters can be wet and cold. Chilling winds whip across the great plain during the late fall and winter months and precipitation is common—expect plenty of rain and some snow. (Rain gear is recommended year-round.) Summers, on the other hand, are usually mild. Temperatures in July and August average in the high sixties and low seventies Fahrenheit.

Though weather is the principal consideration for most travelers, air and water pollution in Poland's major cities and much of its southern region is severe enough to be worthy of mention. Pollution-intensive industrial practices combined with the burning of brown coal for heat have tarnished much of Poland's countryside as well as its skies. Those who are particularly sensitive to airborne particulate matter should take caution, especially during the colder months.

In the Tatra and Sudety mountains, snow is common in the late fall, winter, and early spring. For those inclined toward winter recreation, there is plenty of skiing in the Tatras. Try the region surrounding the town of Zakopane in the southeast, about two hours by train from Krakow.

Politics

Like most of the other governments in the region, Poland is governed by a multi-party parliamentary democracy. A president is elected by the general population to act as head of state, while a prime minister (nominated by the President) and a cabinet are entrusted with executive powers.

Since the Solidarity uprisings and the revolution of 1989, Poland has been no stranger to political instability. As in other parts of Central and Eastern Europe, Poland has experienced the economic problems associated with the difficulties of building a market economy from the ruins of the Soviet system. Suffering from a combination of high unemployment, inflation, and perhaps a mistrust of the new political order, Poles have been politically indecisive—never seeming quite certain of the causes of their economic afflictions, or knowing which party or political philosophy might bring a cure quickly enough.

As in the other countries of Eastern Europe that were previously subjected to Soviet-style centralized government, certain aspects of the old status quo remain attractive to large sectors of the Polish population, especially amongst the older generations who have always looked to the state for various forms of social support, such as government-enforced price controls, housing subsidies, and health care. The attractiveness of freedom of expression and the pursuit of wealth under a system of private enterprise is frequently overshadowed by the more immediate and pressing questions: Who will pay for housing as price controls are lifted? Will the government have the wherewithal to provide care for the elderly? What is going to be done about the high rate of inflation? Will basic foods remain affordable to the average Pole?

Questions such as these are not easily answered when such major political and economic transitions are being made. For the foreseeable future, Poland will suffer the difficulties of a major economic transformation—essentially an enormous political, economic, and social experiment brought on by the vagaries of recent history. The economic

Mountain villages in southern Poland have developed a distinctive architecture due to heavy winter snows.

opportunities presented by Poland's newly emerging market economy are not lost on the rest of the world, however. Major foreign investments, which will help to invigorate the Polish economy, are announced regularly in the newspaper. And the Polish population, especially those in the younger generations, are well aware of the challenge ahead. Poland's universities are graduating students who are eager to make helpful contributions that will benefit the country as a whole.

Religion

Poland is predominantly Catholic. It's that simple. Nine out of every ten Poles belong to the Catholic church, and the majority—over sixty percent—attend church regularly. Pope John Paul II hails from Poland, so Catholicism's popularity and influence should come as no real surprise. In fact, the Catholic church has played an important political role throughout Poland's history. The Solidarity movement which brought about the revolution that toppled the communists owes much to the organizational forces and supportive underpinnings of the church leadership in Poland. Many Poles found refuge in the church's support during the repressive years of the communist regime.

Though predominantly Roman Catholic, Poland is home to other religious groups, such as Russian Orthodox and several Protestant offshoots.

History

Poland's early history follows closely the westerly movements of a set of early Slavic peoples known as the Polanie tribe. These predecessors of modern day Poles emerged as the most powerful group of Slavs in the region in the latter part of the tenth century. Their King, Miezko I, became a convert to Catholicism after his marriage to a Czech princess. Catholicism took hold very early on in Polish history.

Miezko was succeeded by Boleslav the Bold. King Boleslav's ambitious leadership formed the foundation of a dynasty that governed over a territory very similar to that of present-day Poland.

From the reign of Boleslav at the turn of the first millennium until the years preceding World War II, Poland experienced nearly ten centuries of unrest. Wars were fought, invaders raped and pillaged, governments came and left. Only from the fourteenth to seventeenth centuries, when Poland united with Lithuania under the Jagiellonian dynasty, did the country find stability and wield political power in Europe. This union made it one of the most powerful forces in the region at the time.

Throughout the seventeenth and eighteenth centuries, the map of Poland changed drastically several times. In fact, from 1795 until the end of World War I, Poland did not exist on the map of Europe.

Poland declared its independence as a modern republic in November of 1918, on Armistice Day. Independence did not, however, have a settling effect over the country. War with Russia ensued in 1920, ending in a victory for Poland which resulted in annexation of some of the territory from what is now the Ukraine and Belorussia. Expansion did not make for peace and quiet either, though. Political instability and unrest led up to military rule, which lasted until the beginning of World War II.

The Second World War ravaged Poland's territory and nearly decimated its population. The Nazis invaded from the west in 1939 at the beginning of the war. Over the course of six years of war, more than 20 percent of the entire population—six million people—perished. Of the six million, half were Jewish, murdered at the hands of the Nazis during the Holocaust. Poland suffered in other ways, too, losing much of its territory and material wealth. Over a third of all its industrial and agricultural resources were lost.

The destruction of Warsaw during the war serves as an analog to the rest of Poland's wartime experience. After the Jewish ghetto uprising of 1944, Hitler and the Nazis retaliated by deporting all 750,000 residents of the city to various destinations in the countryside. Jews were sent to the concentration camps, while the entire city was systematically leveled with dynamite. Warsaw was reduced to rubble in a matter of a few weeks, with virtually no buildings left standing—Poland's proud capital nearly wiped from the map on orders from Adolf Hitler.

The period that followed the Second World War brought continued unrest for Poland. Given the widespread destruction and lack of any solid political infrastructure, rebuilding the country was not an easy task for the Poles. After being liberated by the Soviets at the end of the war, Poland fell into the Soviet sphere of influence.

Though the Soviets wielded power over the Poles, their centralized form of government did not take hold in Poland in the same way it did in the other countries of the Soviet bloc. Acts of rebellion were organized against the communist authorities over the course of the four decades of Soviet domination in Central Europe. The Poles simply did not comply with many Soviet demands. Agricultural production was never successfully collectivized, and an independent intellectual life thrived under the auspices of the Catholic Church leadership. The Poles continued to demonstrate their independent ambitions through the late seventies and early eighties when the Solidarity labor union was formed. The strikes initiated by Lech Walesa and his Solidarity union in the Gdansk shipyards did much for the revolutionary causes in Central and Eastern Europe by attracting the attention of the rest of the world. In fact, the Solidarity movement was so successful at creating civil unrest that marshal law was declared in 1981 by General Jaruzelski. The Solidarity union leaders were jailed and their activities declared illegal.

Though the Solidarity movement did much to bring Poland to the brink of revolution and eventual political reform, the communist party leadership made significant contribution to their own downfall. By accumulating massive foreign debt over the years, the communists had sowed the seeds of eventual economic collapse. The cost of operating an enormous, inefficient centralized bureaucracy combined with the energy required to stifle the reform-oriented demands of an irrepressible population, forced the communists to bargain with the leaders of Solidarity, which resulted in General Jaruzelski's resignation and eventual national presidential elections.

In 1990, the new government instituted an economic program that was designed to "shock" the system into a speedy conversion to a free market economy. Though evidence suggests that this method of economic reform is the most effective means of economic conversion, it is by no means painless. After the new system was instituted, the standard of living fell and the country settled into a dreary economic funk. Unemployment rose above ten percent and inflation rates skyrocketed.

All is not lost, though. From the rubble of the old system, a burgeoning private sector is emerging. On the positive side, Poland has the advantage of having a relatively young, well-educated population, especially when compared to the other countries of Central and Eastern Europe. This bodes well for the future because many of these young people were not raised on the communist system, making it much easier for them to assimilate a new work ethic and lifestyle more adaptable to the demands of a free-market economy.

Today's Poland and expat life

Of all the countries in this book, Poland paints perhaps the most enigmatic picture for an expatriate who wants to settle in Eastern Europe. Like the Czech Republic and Poland, it's a Slavic country that shared in the large dose of Soviet repression which followed World War II. Both Poland's size and the economic difficulties it has experienced over the last five or six years make it an interesting place and yet less definable in terms of what possibilities it holds for expatriates.

Fewer expatriates seem to have chosen Poland than any of the other three countries, yet teaching jobs are widely available. Other business opportunities, however, are more difficult to find, unless you work with a large international corporation. But things are changing very rapidly in Poland, so it's still difficult to say what's going to happen with the economy.

In Poland's case, economic uncertainty hasn't meant that the doors are closed. To the contrary, it may mean that the country is ripe for opportunity. Poland's young people are not standing around worrying about their future. Many are pursuing higher education in order to ensure more secure futures. Some are starting small businesses. Regardless, all of this means that willing and energetic expatriates can help to bring about change in Poland. You only have to read the following interviews to see that persistence can pay off.

Compared to the Czech Republic, there hasn't been a sizable enough expat community anywhere in Poland to really set a precedent for the kinds of opportunities that might become available. It's hard to know exactly what kinds of obstacles there are to creating small businesses as well as other kinds of opportunities. But if you want to teach English, you shouldn't have much trouble, even without formal qualifications. Many school administrators seem to be willing to train native speakers if they agree to stay on and teach at their school.

Poland is large enough to present certain kinds of future opportunities that the other countries under discussion will never be able to. Sharing its western border with Germany and its eastern border with Russia, the Baltic states, and the Ukraine puts it at the crossroads of an enormous and quickly evolving region. With the Baltic Sea to the north, Poland has greater opportunity to trade with the Scandinavian countries, and greater access to sea lanes. What all of this means for expats who wish to stay in Poland remains to be seen, but it definitely means that Poland's stature on the international stage can only grow.

Of the expatriates who have settled in Poland, many seem to integrate better into the local communities and get involved in local activities than they do in places like Prague and Budapest, where it's relatively easy to avoid the locals by hanging out in places where only expats congregate. So if you want to find your own little niche among an ordinarily friendly and open people, Poland might be just the place for you. It will definitely challenge you in ways that the other countries won't simply because it seems more of a frontier than the Czech Republic or Hungary.

Introducing: Expats in Poland

Marty, a young, energetic American, teaches and pursues other ventures.

What brought you to Poland, and what has made you stay?

Well, that's a familiar question. First of all, my grandparents were from Poland so I grew up around the language, hearing stories of what it was like a long time ago. And since I'm from Chicago, an area where a lot of Polish immigrants settled, I have many memories of the kind of Polish life that took hold in the United States as it was expressed in the immigrant community.

I came here first in eighty-eight or eighty-nine, to meet my family. We had had contact via letters and packages, but I had never met them in person.

When I decided to come back here to stay after the first trip, people looked at me like I was crazy. They couldn't understand it. And, at that time, it was pretty difficult living here. It's gotten easier, but it still has its frustrations. The laws are such a pain in the ass: you have to do this, you have to do that, then you have to do it three more times in two different places. Bureaucracy is the universal problem.

I prefer the East as opposed to the West. I think I was born a hundred years too late, you know. I like nice things in life, but seeing traditional ways of life, the way people live in places like the Ukraine and Bulgaria—everything is totally different and interesting. Paris, London? Yeah, they're nice, but after that, what is there? Every place has a McDonald's, I hate that. It shouldn't be like that everywhere.

Enter Ben, a Brit who teaches English with Marty.

What do expats do in Krakow?

People play music. There is a lot going on in the music scene here. There are tons of different clubs around. I play guitar, jazz and blues. And I can make money at it, on the basis of the Polish economy anyway. It supplements my teaching job.

Krakow is a very busy cultural center. There is so much to do here. I was looking at the poster board at the university here and there are five or six musical things going on tonight alone. And I'm not even talking about other things like galleries and exhibitions. Every taste will be catered for at a reasonable price, a lot of it free. In fact, there is a sacred music festival going on at the moment in seven of the churches around town. You know, you can't get away with playing any old bollocks. There are some reasonable standards here, even among the buskers in the square. The general tenor here is that Krakow prides itself on its culture, and its architecture is the foundation for that. . . . The local people are really receptive to whatever you've got to offer. They're really wide open. But it has to be good—no bullshit.

Marty, what do you do other than teach English?

I operate a recording studio. I got into it through my work in radio. When I was a kid, I was always hanging around radio. My uncle was in radio, so I followed on his coattails into the business. I got into it here reading the news on one of the first independent radio stations in all of Poland, maybe even in all of Eastern Europe. Everything just kind of snowballed, the momentum carried me through.

I got together with a couple of friends of mine from the station who were working down in production. Like everybody, when you're young you want to do your own thing. So we scrimped and saved and put it together. We found a little hole-in-the-wall place and opened it. Started doing commercials and business started rolling in. We just added a second room, which we remodeled. The equipment is high technology; everything is digital, though I hesitate to use the words "state-of-the-art," but it is top-of-the-line.

The reason I think we're succeeding—forgive me for blowing our own horn—is that we're the only ones who are really creative. There are other recording studios in town. The ads you hear on the radio here are usually just straight reading, maybe with some basic music. But we're using Western imagination and creativity. We use sound effects.

Now we're making ads for radio stations around the country. And believe this or not—we were shocked—we've started doing commercials for Chicago, in both Polish and English. I am looking at the fax machine thinking, "What's going on?" People from Chicago want us to do ads for them?" The only thing I can think of is that it's cheaper. And they keep coming, so obviously they're satisfied. And to me, the proof is in the pudding. We're competent enough to meet Western standards, where you've got the most competitive radio industry in the world.

So I guess we're really riding this wave of privatization, in terms of radio and television. And I think we're really well-positioned.

So, you don't plan to teach English for much longer?

Well, I don't plan to do it for the rest of my life. There are bigger and better things. And I don't want to diminish teaching by saying that, because it's very important. But radio is where my heart is.

• •

TRAVELING TO POLAND

Being the largest country in Eastern Europe, Poland offers a number of destinations to a North American job seeker. Large cities dot the country. From the Baltic coast city of Gdansk in the north to the cultural capital Krakow in the south, Poland holds much in store for the city-minded. For those inclined toward a less hectic existence, smaller towns and cities are spread out over the entire countryside. Poland's rail and bus systems connect all but the most remote destinations.

Via airplane

It's possible to fly directly from the United States or Western Europe into Warsaw, Poland's centrally located capital city. There are reasonably inexpensive, non-stop flights from New York and Chicago to Warsaw on LOT, Poland's national airline. It's also easy to fly to Warsaw directly from many major European cities. Airlines with service to Warsaw include Air France, Aeroflot, Czechoslovak Airlines, Delta, Sabena, and Swissair.

Airlines with service to Warsaw and Krakow

Warsaw

Aeroflot	(02) 628-1710
Air France	(02) 628-1281
Al Italia	(022) 26 28 01
	or (022) 27 40 14
British Airways	(800) 247-9297
Warsaw	(02) 628-9431
	or (02) 628-3991
Czechoslovak Airlines	(022) 26 38 02
Delta	(800) 241-4141
Warsaw	(022) 26 02 57
	or (022) 27 84 61
LOT Polish Airlines	(212) 869-1078
Warsaw	(02) 630-5009
	or (02) 630-5007
Lufthansa	(02) 630-2555
	fax (02) 630-2535
Malev (Hungarian Airlines)	(02) 635-5841
Sabena	(02) 628-6061
SAS	(022) 26 12 11
Swissair	(022) 27 50 16

Krakow

LOT	(022) 22 50 76
	or (022) 22 70 78

• •

Via train or bus

Younger travelers to Central and Eastern Europe often choose to fly from North America to a major city in Western Europe and then travel the rest of the way by train or bus. Though considerably slower than flying, traveling overland has several advantages. If you want to save some money on airfare, traveling from North America to London, Amsterdam, or Frankfurt is usually the cheapest. Remember, though, that you have to add the cost of your train fare to your destination in Poland to your airfare in order to compare overall travel costs. International train and bus fares in Europe are not cheap, so if your budget is tight you may want to calculate the cost of the entire trip before you decide which route to take. Train or bus travel affords you the opportunity to see more of the European continent, and it gives you the ability to stop off in different places along the way. This is especially true of train travel—just make sure you have the kind of ticket that enables you to re-board without having to pay extra.

WHEN YOU ARRIVE

If you fly to Poland, you will likely land at Okecie, Warsaw's newly remodeled airport, which lies about four miles south of the city. If you travel to Warsaw by train, you will likely arrive at the main station: Warsawa Centralna. Because it's located right in the heart of the city, this is your best bet, unless you have a specific destination.

Airport

Though recently remodeled, Warsaw's Okecie International is not as large as most international airports. Nevertheless, many of the amenities you would expect to find at a major airport are available in the new terminal.

Negotiating your way around Okecie may actually be much easier than getting to and from it. Taxi drivers going to and from the airport sometimes try to take advantage of foreigners who aren't yet street savvy.

Train stations

Because Poland is a much larger country than the others dealt with in this book, you will find that you have a greater number of different train stations to choose from. Although Poland's train system generally runs efficiently, most train stations are old and often cluttered. Though first class is a designation that may be applied to certain train coaches, it does not apply to many train stations.

In the train stations of the larger cities, beware of pickpockets, thieves, and bands of children who can sleight you of your wallet with their tiny hands. You will be surprised at how quickly they can make off with the contents of your pockets and your backpack or handbag.

All major train stations post departure and arrival times on big reader boards that usually are situated above the main passageway to the train platforms. Arrivals are marked *przyjazdy*, and departures are marked *odjazdy*. Make sure to determine what kind of train you are boarding. Express and inter-city trains don't stop at all the little towns along the way, while local trains do. You won't travel quickly on a local train.

Because train travel is relatively inexpensive and therefore crowded, you should consider upgrading to first class on longer trips. You will be virtually guaranteed a quieter, more pleasant ride. First class cars generally are cleaner and less attractive to thieves, who tend to hang out in more crowded environs where they are less likely to be noticed.

LOCAL TRANSPORTATION

Local transportation in Poland is not as advanced as in the other countries of Eastern Europe. The larger cities do not have the extensive metro systems that you will find in places like Prague and Budapest. But don't let this dissuade you from settling in a town or city in Poland. Bus, tram, and train networks are effective means of getting around. As in other cities of Eastern Europe, inner-city transportation fares are cheap.

If you live in a larger city and commute frequently, you should consider investing in a monthly bus or tram pass. You will save both money and time. Because it's embarrassing to be "controlled" (caught without the proper pass or ticket) by a conductor, don't forget to carry your pass with you at all times.

Metro

Most of Poland's cities are not yet equipped with metro systems. Warsaw is the only exception. Given the success of the metro systems in several other of Eastern Europe's capital cities, it may come as a surprise that this is only a very recent development. Over seventy years in the making, Warsaw inaugurated its single metro line in the spring of 1995.

Though it's clearly a step in the right direction, a single metro line can't cover a city the size of Warsaw. Please refer to the following sections for further information on local forms of transportation.

Trams

You will find trams in many of Poland's larger cities. Though tram routes are usually not as extensive as bus routes, trams effectively complement other forms of local transportation, while lending their own charm to the urban environment.

Be sure to check whether or not the tram system in your city requires separate passes or tickets. Bus tickets will not always work on the trams and vice versa.

Buses

In Warsaw and in Poland's other cities and towns, buses are the most common and convenient mode of inner-city public transportation. In the larger cities, they are almost always crowded.

Buy tickets for city buses at the kiosks near the stop, and be sure to validate your ticket once you board the bus. It's a good idea to keep several extra tickets with you because not all buses sell tickets on board.

For longer trips, you can buy tickets at the station or on the bus if you're running late. Express buses take seat reservations, though they're not always required. If you absolutely have to be somewhere at a particular time, plan in advance and make a reservation.

These post-war apartment blocks in Kielce are not atypical of modern Polish architecture.

If you travel longer distances between larger cities, buses usually are slower than trains. Because buses travel to some of the more out-of-the-way places where trains don't venture, you will need to familiarize yourself with bus routes and schedules if you settle in a remote small town.

Taxis

Poland is like any place in Eastern Europe: if you aren't careful, many taxi drivers will not pass up the chance to relieve you of the heft of your wallet. Here are some tips to help you negotiate the shark-infested waters of Poland's taxi system:

- Taxi stops (where taxis line up and wait for fares) are the worst places to catch a taxi. The best way to get a taxi is to call ahead. Companies such as Halo-taxi and Radio-taxi are reputable and do not charge extra to pick you up.
- Settle on a price with the driver before you get in the cab. At least you'll have the option of turning down a fare that seems exorbitant.
- Once you board the cab, make sure the meter is in operation. If you can, try to determine the charge per kilometer.
- Familiarize yourself early on with the details of taxi travel in Poland, especially in the larger cities. You will save yourself both money and grief. Find out the shortest routes to and from places

where you frequently go, so you will know if a taxi driver is trying to run up the fare by taking the long way.

• If you can, make the driver aware that you know where you are going, he'll be much less likely to try to put one over on you.

Domestic trains

Warsaw may be the capital, but all trains do not lead there. A vast network of train lines criss-cross Poland (the national train service is known as PKP).

There are three types of trains in Poland: *Ekspres*, *Pospieszny*, and *Osobowy*—express, fast, and slow(est), respectively. Take these descriptions literally, or else you will find yourself pondering every tiny ripple in Poland's gentle topography as you ramble on the slowest train to Sosnowiec. The *Ekspres* and *Pospieszny* trains offer both first- and second-class cars. Reservations are obligatory on express trains and recommended on the fast trains, especially if you plan to travel in the crowded second-class compartments. Just to be safe, make reservations whenever possible, and particularly if your destination is several hours or more away.

SHORT-TERM ACCOMMODATIONS

Short-term accommodations are usually inexpensive and easier to find than long-term rental situations. Youth hostels, hotels, and private rooms all fall under the category of short-term accommodations.

Accommodation agencies can come in handy when you are in need of short-term housing, especially if you don't have the patience to find someone who speaks English well enough to assist you when you call to make reservations at a local hostel or hotel.

Accommodation agencies

Warsaw

Centrum Infromacji Turystcznej
pl. Zamkowy1/13
Phone: (02) 635-1881
Phone/fax: (022) 31 04 64

Informajca noclegowa (telephone service)
Phone: (02) 643-9592
or (02) 671-5825

Syrena Tourist Office
ul. Krucza 17

Phone: (02) 628-7540
Fax: (02) 628-5698

Krakow

Almatur
Rynek Glowny 8
Phone: (012) 22 67 08

INT Express Travel Agency
ul. sw. Marka 25
Phone/fax: (012) 21 79 06

Wawel Tourist
ul. Pawia 8
Phone/fax: (012) 22 19 21

Tourist information services

Warsaw

Tourist information by phone
Phone: (02) 635-1881

**Information on cultural events
by the phone**
Phone: (022) 29 84 89

Almatur
ul. Kopernika 23
Phone: (022) 26 35 12
    or (022) 26 26 39

Tourist Information Center
(Centrum Informacjii
    Turystycznej)
pl. Zamkowy 1/13
Phone: (02) 635-1881

ORBIS
ul. Bracka 16
Phone: (022) 27 01 72
    or (022) 27 07 30

ORBIS
u. Marszalkowska 142
Phone: (022) 27 67 66
Fax: (022) 27 11 23

PTSM
ul. Chocimska 28, Room 423
Phone: (022) 49 83 54
Fax: (022) 49 81 28

PTSM
ul. Szpitalna 5
Phone: (022) 27 78 43

PTTK
Podwale Srodmiescie 23
Phone: (02) 635-2752

PTTK
Rynek Staromiejski 23
Phone: (022) 31 05 44

Krakow

Tourist Office
ul. Pawia 8
(opposite the train station)
Phone: (012) 22 04 71
    or (012) 22 60 91

Almatur
Rynek Glowny 8
Phone: (012) 22 67 08

Fregata
ul. Szpitalna 32
Phone: (012) 22 41 44
    or (012) 22 49 12

INT Express Travel Agency
ul. sw. Marka 25
Phone/fax: (012) 21 79 06

ORBIS
Rynek 41
Phone: (012) 22 40 35

ORBIS
al. Focha 1 (in the Hotel
    Cracovia)
Phone: (012) 21 98 80
    or (012) 22 91 80

ORBIS
pl. Szczepanski 2
Phone: (012) 22 14 33
    or (012) 22 17 07
(tourism in Poland only)

Point Tour
ul. Przy Rondzie 2
    (in Ibis Hotel)
Phone: (012) 21 84 33

Youth hostels

Youth hostels in Poland are usually open only during the summer months, especially outside the larger cities. Because they are inexpensive and therefore crowded with young and restless travelers, youth hostels are not necessarily the best way to begin settling into a new home (however temporary). Unless you are oblivious to noise and don't value privacy, try to find a private room or an inexpensive hotel room. Depending upon your location, you might not save that much by staying in a hostel.

Warsaw

PTSM
ul. Chocimska 28
Phone: (022) 49 83 54
    or (022) 49 81 28
(Provides listing of youth hostels throughout Poland)

IYHF Hostels
ul. Smolna 30
Phone: (022) 27 89 52

IYHF Hostels
ul. Karolkowa 53a
Phone: (02) 632-8829

Hotel Studenski
ul. Smyczkowa 5/7
Phone: (022) 43 86 21
    or (022) 43 47 53
(May-Sept.)

Almatur International Student Hotels (main office)
ul. Kopernika 23
Phone: (022) 26 45 92
    or (022) 26 35 12

Krakow

Almatur
Rynek Glowny 7/8
Phone: (012) 22 67 08
(Provides information on new locations of student hostels)

Letni Student's Hostel
ul. Jana Pawla II 82
Phone: (012) 48 06 07
Fax: (012) 482-9277
(July-Sept.)

Summer Hotel Piast
ul. Piastowska 47
Phone: (012) 37 49 33
(July-Sept.)

Schronisko Mlodziezowe (HI)
ul. Oleandry 4
Phone: (012) 33 89 20
(Year-round)

Schronisko Mlodziezowe (HI)
ul. Kosciuszki 88
Phone: (012) 22 19 51
(Year-round)

Schronisko Mlodziezowe (HI)
ul. Szablowskiego
Phone: (012) 37 24 41
(July-Aug.)

Hotels

Inexpensive hotels are a good option if you value privacy and anonymity. Frequently you can find decent hotel rooms located near the larger train stations, or even in the center of town.

Finding an inexpensive room often takes perseverance, especially in the bigger cities and more popular tourist destinations. If you plan to find a room on your own, start early in the day. You also can book hotel rooms through a travel agency or booking service. Try any Orbis office, or if you're in Warsaw, American Express will find you a room for a small fee. Since it might take you the better part of a day to find a satisfactory room, especially if you don't speak Polish, the fee will be worthwhile. Besides, travel agencies or Orbis offices know much more than you can decipher from tourist guidebooks regarding which hotels are clean, affordable, and conveniently located. Not to mention the fact that someone will speak English.

Outside of Warsaw, European-style hotel rooms (with the toilet and shower facilities in the hallway) can be found for as little as US$10 or $12 per day, and perhaps less if you stay longer than five or six days. In the capital city, you might have to pay US$30 to $40 per night for a conveniently located hotel. Granted, none of the lesser-priced hotel rooms in Poland are going to approach luxurious, but they should be pleasant and clean.

Warsaw

Dom Nauczyciela
Wybrzeze Kosciuszkowskie 31/33
Phone: (02) 625-0571
    or (02) 625-2600

Hotel-Uniwersytet Warszawski
ul. Belwederska 26/30
Phone: (022) 41 13 08
    or (022) 41 02 54

Dom Chlopa
Powstancow Warszawy 2
Phone: (022) 27 92 51

Dom Literata
ul. Krakowskie Predmiescie 87/89
Phone: (02) 635-0404

Pensjonat Stegny
ul. Inspektowa 1
Phone: (022) 42 27 68

Metropol
Marszalkowska 99a
Phone: (022) 29 40 01

Krakow

Hotel Europejski
ul. Lubicz 5
Phone: (012) 22 09 11
Fax: (012) 23 25 29

Hotel Polonia
ul. Basztowa 25
Phone: (012) 22 12 81
    or (012) 21 12 33

Wisla
ul. Reymonta 22
Phone: (012) 33 49 22
    or (012) 10 15 35
Fax: (012) 37 37 60

Tramp
ul. Koszykarska 33
Phone: (012) 56 02 29

Pod Roza
ul. Florianska 14
Phone: (012) 22 93 99
    or (012) 21 75 13

Private rooms

Because Poland does not attract as many tourists as either the Czech Republic or Hungary, you won't find as many private rooms offered for rent when you arrive at the train station in Warsaw, Krakow, or for that matter, any other destination. It's not that the entrepreneurial spirit is lost on the Poles, demand is just not as high. There are, however, other ways to find accommodation in private rooms. As with hotel reservations, booking services that handle private room reservations can now be found in the larger cities. Many will have several thousand rooms at their disposal. Once again, make sure that the booking agent can show you the location of your prospective lodging on a map. Ask if it is convenient to public transportation and how long it takes to get to and from the center of town.

> 66 *If you talk to enough people you hear it all. So it's always difficult to sort out the truth when you're traveling. Ask one fellow traveler for advice about accommodation and you'll get an answer that will make you want to stay only in private rooms. Another person will tell you some horror story about all the inconvenience they endured because their host wouldn't leave them alone, or because they felt isolated on the edge of town. Whatever. I think you just need a little common sense, the kind of thing which separates the good traveler from the one who always ends up disappointed. I stayed in several private rooms when I first came to Poland, and I always had pretty good luck. I don't think it's that difficult—ask some questions, figure out where it is on the map, ask to see it first, and find out how much it is per night. Try to talk about the money so you'll know if that's all they seem to care about."*

No matter how you approach finding a room, keep a few rules in mind and above all else use common sense. Before you agree to anything, make sure you know the location and the price per night. If you plan to stay longer than a few nights, find out if you can make a deal—it's much easier for a landlord to rent you a room for a week or two than it is for him or her to track down new lodgers every couple of days. You could agree on a price per week, for example, which adds up to a dollar or two less per night than if you paid the daily rate. And never pay more than a night in advance, unless you've become friendly with your host and can rest assured that you will have your money returned to you if you have to depart earlier than planned.

Finding a teaching position

OVERVIEW

Poles are very proud of their heritage, and historically they have val-
ued education and all the attendant benefits of a high literacy rate.
Linguistic ability is no exception. Now that English has become the
foreign language of choice for young people, numerous public and
private schools offer English-language courses. And because most of
Poland is a less-popular destination for North American expatriates,
the demand for English teachers is high. Though experienced and
certified teachers are highly sought after, you don't have to have a
teaching certificate or experience to find a job.

Despite the fact that you may be able to get away without any
substantial formal qualifications in Poland, it would be to your advantage to get a RSA or TEFL certificate if you are able. As time goes by,
the job market will become more competitive so you'll want to stand
out from the teaching and tutoring rabble as best you can. One telling
indicator of what the future bodes for English teaching in Poland is
the international investment climate. Presently, big name multinational
corporations are making huge inroads into Poland so the demand for
Poles to learn English is ever increasing. As this escalates, the demand
for teachers increases and competition between schools becomes more
and more fierce. Though Poland may be behind Hungary and the
Czech Republic in terms of establishing a broad network of private
English schools, the demand is rapidly rising. More schools are pop-
ping up and more teachers are needed all the time.

Probably the main obstacle to finding a good, reliable teaching position is the Polish economy. Since the big turnover in 1989, both the
electorate and the government have had trouble deciding where the
country is going and who should be taking the helm. The economy
has suffered as a result. Naturally, Poles are slightly more concerned
about putting food on the table than coughing up enough *zloty* for
their English classes. None of this should come as any surprise, however, to anyone familiar with the predicament that each of the Eastern
European countries has confronted since the departure of the Soviets.
If you get too caught up in the possibility that things might change
quickly or that the situation in Eastern Europe should always be on
the up-and-up, you probably don't belong on the next flight to Poland, or anywhere else in the region for that matter. On the other
hand, if you can appreciate a little uncertainty or simply don't give a

To keep working year-round with a paid summer vacation, check out English language summer camps.

hoot about who the next Polish prime minister might be or what the rate of inflation is at any given moment, Poland could be just the place to chalk the chalkboard.

Whatever your approach, you should look forward to standing in front of a classroom full of eager Polish students. By most accounts, Poles are a friendly and gregarious lot who value education and respect their teachers. You can expect classroom discussions to be lively and open. And if you are able to befriend your students outside the classroom, you will find that the average conversation held over a beer or a cup of coffee often will progress beyond small talk. Don't be surprised to find yourself discussing some big social or political issues, and arguing passionately as the evening progresses.

In Central and Eastern Europe, public and private schools operate in a similar fashion. And Poland is no exception. A broad curriculum is usually provided by the school, and each individual teacher is generally held responsible for making adaptations that fit the specific requirements of the class. Most schools realize that a certain level of standardization is beneficial, but that each teacher has an individual style, and perhaps even unique teaching methods. Consequently, teachers are expected to abide by certain guidelines that may involve using specific lesson plans provided by the school. Regardless of a school's particular requirements, most devoted teachers spend time preparing for their classes, because no matter how experienced a teacher may be, improvising lessons is not easy. Teaching English anywhere demands patience and adaptability. Sufficient preparation allows you to focus your energies on the immediate needs of your students. As a teacher in Poland, much will be expected of you. So it's best to develop a teaching strategy that makes room for advance preparation. Consider the needs of each individual class. After all, it's difficult to answer a tough question on a sticky grammatical point if you're trying to make things up as you go.

As in Hungary, depending on the level and age of your students, there is the possibility that you might teach in tandem with a Polish-speaking person who can translate the finer points of grammar and nuance when you can't effectively communicate in rudimentary English. But because Polish is much less difficult than Hungarian, this happens with less frequency.

Even though Poles may prize education, Poland's public school system is still lacking when it comes to English language instruction. English is still not widely available at the elementary level in many areas, which means that in most cases students can't start to learn English in the classroom until much later in their schooling. Often, they must wait to reach the college or university level before English is offered. Though this may sound like a great opportunity given the demand for English language instruction, many areas still lack the resources to set up English language curricula in their public schools.

One thing is certain, the situation in Poland is changing rapidly and opportunities are being created at every turn, especially for optimistic, dedicated, and energetic prospective teachers. Unlike Hungary and the Czech Republic, you don't necessarily need to have formal certification to find teaching positions, but you may need to be more resourceful in other ways. After all, Poland is a newer frontier for English language instruction, especially if you venture outside of either Warsaw or Krakow.

WHERE TO START

Because Poland is so large, it's difficult to know where to start. You've got to narrow the focus of your job search to a manageable geographic region, preferably one city or town. And if you haven't been to Poland before, it's almost impossible to determine where you would like to end up. Read as much as you can before you go. If you can manage, travel around the country for a couple of weeks to get an idea of where you might like to settle. It's inexpensive and relatively easy to get around in Poland.

There are several sources of information that will aid you in your search for a teaching position.

The classifieds

Outside of Warsaw and Krakow it will be difficult to find an English-language newspaper that will provide classified ad sections with listings for teaching positions. Unlike Prague and Budapest, there is a dearth of English-language newspapers in cities as large as Warsaw. Perhaps the lack of a younger, well-established, cohesive expat community in Poland has made it difficult for international newspapers to make a viable business. Your best bet in Warsaw is the Warsaw Voice.

If you are truly eager to find a teaching job, follow up on every ad you find, even if you don't possess all of the qualifications listed. At least make a phone call to find out if you might be considered for the teaching position. Depending upon the time of year and fluctuations in the job market, there simply may not be enough prospective applicants to fill the demand. Besides, if you talk with an employer in person, you will definitely learn something about the job market. It doesn't hurt to get some practice early on in your search, so that you will know what to expect down the road.

Advertising your services

Posting notices that advertise your services as a native-speaking English tutor can be an effective means of rounding up a few private students, or even the beginning of your own small tutoring service. Various bulletin boards that cater to prospective students, such as those found in English-language bookstores and libraries, student lounges, and other businesses that serve the English-speaking community are generally good places to start. If you are truly ambitious, you could even advertise in the local newspaper's classifieds section. Of course, you would need to be settled enough to have a steady address or phone number (an unlikely scenario in most places in Poland).

The British Council English Teaching Center is a good resource for prospective teachers. By virtue of its name, it may sound like a place reserved for British teachers. The fact is that many expats, regardless of nationality, use the British Council library and its other teaching-oriented resources. At the very least, take a look at the bulletin board where notices for teaching positions often are placed. You can also leave your own notice there.

British Council English Teaching Center
Al Jerozolimskie 59
Warsaw 00-697
Phone: (02) 628-7401, (02) 628-7401, (02) 628-7403,
   or (02) 621-9955

If you're creative and resourceful, there is a good chance you will be able to supplement your regular teaching position with some tutoring on the side.

Word of mouth

Let everyone you bump into know that you are looking for a teaching job or for students to teach privately. Hang out in places where other expats or Polish students congregate, such as local pubs and coffee houses. Get to know people. Networking often is the best way to find out about all kinds of employment opportunities.

EMPLOYMENT OPTIONS

Teaching jobs are plentiful in Poland. And there are enough schools—both public and private—in the larger cities or more out-of-the-way places that you should be able to find something to your liking in a suitable environment. In fact, you will probably be more likely to find a good position if you stay away from Warsaw, where the competition is greater. As in the other countries covered in this book, if you lack formal teaching credentials and teaching experience, your chances of finding a teaching position are better the further you get from places like Warsaw and Krakow.

English-teaching positions in Poland fall into the following general categories:

Private schools

In Poland, the private sector provides the majority of English teaching jobs. Private schools operate all over Poland, although they are more likely to be found in the mid- to large-sized cities. Teaching jobs in private schools are generally less structured than those found in their public sector counterparts, both in terms of their curricula and the benefits they provide.

First and foremost, it's important to understand that private schools are businesses that aim to profit from tuition. Consequently, some private schools care more about the bottom line than they do about providing high-quality language instruction or about the teachers they employ. You will undoubtedly hear stories of schools that don't do much to support their teachers—perhaps they provide little in the way of support materials or guidelines for classroom curriculum. Though this should not dissuade you from pursuing work in private schools, be aware of the realities. Try to find a school that balances its priorities so that your aims are compatible with the school's overall goals.

For teaching positions in private schools, you should expect to be paid in the range of 20 to 25 *zloty* per hour. This amounts to between US$8 to $10 an hour. Bases on these hourly wage ranges, monthly salaries should fall between 2,400 and 3,000 *zloty*, or US$980 to $1,200.

Classes at private schools are usually forty-five or fifty minutes long, which counts as a teaching hour. Students run the gamut from young kids to middle-aged adults. Most, however, will be college-age or younger businesspeople who are eager to garner the benefits that proficiency in English will afford them in the world of international business.

The following schools hire native speakers, although the requirements may vary:

Warsaw
American English School
Kryniczna 12/14
Warsaw 03-934
Poland
Phone: (02) 617-1112
Fax: (02) 619-2774
North American staff: 5–7
Total staff: 50
Students per class: 11–13
Hiring requirements: Applicants should be experienced, certified teachers. The school will hire native speakers without certification, particularly if the applicant has some college background in the humanities.
Hourly wage: 15–20 *zloty*
Length of contract: One year; shorter for summer courses
Classes taught: Conversational English, TOEFL, Cambridge (TOEFL equivalent)
To apply: Send a resume and a copy of teaching certificate. A personal interview and trial lesson may be required.
Comments: Classes run from September through May. Two-week intensive courses are offered in the summer, as well as two-week summer language camps. Camp wages include free lodging in scenic surroundings.

American English School
Wilenska 27/3
Warsaw 03-934
Poland
Phone: (022) 27 26 54
North American staff: 5–7
Total staff: 50
Students per class: 11–13
Hiring requirements: See listing above.
Comments: This school is an extension campus of the American English School, Kryniczna 12/14.

Archibald Szkola Jezyka Angielskiego
Szpitalna 8/19
Warsaw 00-031
Poland
Phone: (022) 27 29 23
Fax: (022) 26 45 16
North American staff: 3
Total staff: 50
Students per class: 4–6
Hiring requirements: Applicants should have teaching certification.
Hourly wage: Varies
Length of contract: Monthly
Classes taught: Conversational English, Cambridge (TOEFL equivalent)
To apply: Applicants should apply in person and be prepared to take a test, interview with the school director, and teach a trial lesson.
Comments: Classes run year-round. Course lengths vary from intensive two-week sessions to four-month sessions.

British and American English School
ul. Noakowskiego 24
Warsaw 00-668
Poland
Phone: (02) 621-0222
Fax: (02) 625-1712
Students per class: 15
Hiring requirements: Applicants should have teaching certification, experience, and a work permit.
Hourly wage: 16–23 *zloty*
Length of contract: Three months renewable with initial one-month trial period
Classes taught: Cambridge advanced English (TOEFL equivalent)
To apply: Contact the school via phone, fax, or letter to arrange a personal interview.
Comments: This office oversees 15 subsidiary schools throughout Poland and should be able to inform about open positions at all 15 schools. These schools operate on a trimester system that runs from October through December, January through March, and April through June. There are also summer language camp opportunities, though these positions are often filled by permanent Polish teachers. This office also oversees Szkola Jezyka Angielskiego in Krakow (see listing below).

Edukacja Konsultingowo–Oswiatowa
Smolna 9/10
Warsaw 00-375
Poland
Phone: (022) 44 58 16 or (022) 27 86 59
Fax: Same as phone
North American staff: 5
Students per class: 10
Hiring requirements: Applicants should be native English speakers.
The school prefers those with experience or certification.
Hourly wage: 15 *zloty*
Length of contract: One semester minimum; typically one year
Classes taught: Conversational English, Cambridge (TOEFL equivalent)
To apply: Send a resume and cover letter from either the U.S. or Poland.
Comments: Classes run from September through June.

Greenpol–Signum Polsko–Byrtjska Szkola
Renesansowa 5/10
Warsaw
Poland
Phone: (022) 37 57 92 or (022) 35 77 60
Fax: (022) 31 04 45

Greenwich School of English
Zakroczymska 6
Warsaw
Poland
Phone: (022) 31 09 55
Comments: This school hires through the British Council in Warsaw.
Call the council at (02) 628-7401, (02) 628-7402, or (02) 628-7403. Also, this school cooperates with International House, a certification school for ESL teachers in Hastings, England, that also hires teachers.

Lexis School
Marszalkowska 60
przy Placu Konstytucji
Warsaw
Poland
Phone: (02) 625-5386 or (02) 625-7298
Total staff: 50
Students per class: 15

Classes taught: Conversational English (British), Cambridge (TOEFL equivalent), and advanced courses
Comments: They hire primarily British teachers. A knowledge of Polish is required for courses other than Conversational English.

Lingua Nova
Nowowiejska 37a
Warsaw 00-973
Poland
Phone: (022) 25 80 86
Total staff: 1
Students per class: Varies
Hiring requirements: Applicants should send a resume and cover letter.
Length of contract: Varies
Classes taught: Conversational English
Comments: This school was formerly the Linguarama school. Their courses run two to three months.

Linguae Mundi
Al. Jana Pawla 11/13
Warsaw
Poland
Phone: (02) 620-9049 or (02) 620-0351, ext. 258

Metodysci English Language College
Mokotowska 12
Warsaw 00-561
Poland
Phone: (02) 628-5348
Hiring requirements: Applicants should have teaching certification and a work permit.
Length of contract: One year minimum
To apply: Contact the school by letter or phone once you have a work permit.
Comments: This school does not like to hire people seasonally.

Poligota
ul. Dzialdowska 6
Warsaw 01-184
Poland
Phone: (022) 26 49 46
Fax: Same as phone
North American staff: 1

Total staff: 20
Students per class: 10
Hiring requirements: Applicants should be native English speakers with teaching certification. The school prefers experienced, professional teachers.
Hourly wage: 22–26 *zloty* per lesson hour
Length of contract: Varies; preferably one academic year
Classes taught: TOEFL, Cambridge (TOEFL equivalent)
To apply: Send a resume and cover letter once in Poland. A personal interview is required.
Comments: Courses run from October through June.

The Regency School of English
ul. Nowy Swiat 53
Warsaw 00-042
Poland
Phone: (022) 26 49 46 or (022) 27 92 41, ext. 245

School of Languages
ul. Krolewska 19/21
Warsaw 00-064
Poland
Phone: (022) 27 28 34 (3–7pm only)
Fax: (022) 27 69 08 (clearly indicate school name on cover)
North American staff: 0
Total staff: Varies
Students per class: 15
Hiring requirements: Certificate
Hourly wage: 15 *zloty* per teaching hour
Length of contract: Varies
Classes taught: Beginning Cambridge (TOEFL equivalent)
To apply: Contact the school by fax, mail, or phone to arrange an interview.
Comments: This school has changed its hiring requirements as of September 1995 and is encouraging native English speakers to apply. Classes typically meet twice a week for three hours and run from September through June. Semesters comprise 100 hours of class time. Intensive summer sessions last one month.

Top School
ul. Bonifacego 81
Warsaw 02-952
Poland
Phone: (02) 642-1351

Krakow
Celt
Konarskiego 2
Krakow
Poland
Phone: (012) 36 13 50

Gama Biuro Organizacyjne
Gama Gell School of English
Sw. Krzyza 16
Krakow
Poland
Phone: (012) 21 97 55 or (012) 21 97 22

International House Krakow
ul. Czapskich 5
Krakow 31-110
Poland
Phone: (012) 21 94 40 or (012) 22 64 82
Fax: (012) 21 86 52
North American staff: Varies
Total staff: 55
Students per class: 11–14
Hiring requirements: Applicants need RSA certification.
Hourly wage: Varies
Length of contract: Varies
Classes taught: Cambridge (TOEFL equivalent), intensive summer business English
To apply: Send a resume and cover letter preferably to the International House center in London, England, or directly the school.
Comments: Accommodation is provided. Two-week courses run from September through June.

Langart
Boleslawa Prusa 28
Krakow
Poland
Phone: (012) 22 26 65

School of English "York"
Burszlynowa 22
Krakow 31-213
Poland
Phone: (012) 12-31-14

Fax: Same as phone
North American staff: 3
Total staff: 13
Students per class: 9
Hiring requirements: Applicants should have teaching certification.
Monthly wage: 1,200 *zloty*
Length of contract: One school year: October through mid-June
Classes taught: Cambridge (TOEFL equivalent)
To apply: Send a resume and cover letter. An interview is required.
Comments: Classes run from October through mid-June. Holidays are during Christmas and Easter. Monthly wages fluctuate with holidays, which are unpaid.

Surrey Business and Language Centre Polsko–Brytyiska Spolka
Sw. Anny 9
Krakow 31-008
Poland
Phone: (012) 21 15 53
Fax: (012) 22 68 42
North American staff: 0
Total staff: 8
Students per class: 12
Hiring requirements: Applicants should have teaching certification.
Hourly wage: 12–18 *zloty* for each 45-minute class
Length of contract: One year with work permit; renewed monthly without work permit
Classes taught: All levels of Conversational English, Cambridge advanced (TOEFL equivalent), professional business English
To apply: Apply and interview in person.
Comments: The school year runs from October through June. Classes are four months long.

Szkola Jezyka Angielskiego
School of English
Jozefa Ignacego Kraszewskiego 9 Skawina
Krakow
Poland
Phone: (012) 76 39 53

Szkola Jezyka Angloamerykanskiego
Stanislawa Skarbinskiego 5
Krakow 30-071
Poland

Phone: (012) 23 54 84
Fax: (012) 23 79 15
North American staff: 3
Total staff: 22
Students per class: 10–15
Hiring requirements: Applicants should have a valid work permit and experience working with both kids and adults.
Hourly wage: 17 *zloty*
Length of contract: Three months (one trimester)
Classes taught: Conversational English, professional business English
To apply: Send a resume and cover letter.
Comments: Classes run on a trimester system from September through June. There are also summer camp teaching opportunities.

Szkola Jezyka Obcych "World" S.C.
Radziwillowska 28/3
rog ul. Mikolaja Reja
Krakow
Poland
Phone: (012) 22 16 82

Szkola Jezykow Obcych "Helix"
Al. 29 Listopada 32/1
Krakow
Poland
Phone: (012) 12 24 76

Kielce
Global Village
Szkola Jezyka Angielskiego
Plac Wolnosci 5
Kielce
Poland
Phone: (041) 61 50 39

Public schools

For teachers with formal credentials and experience, public schools in Poland are great places to find rewarding teaching positions. Though they rarely pay as well as the private schools in terms of cash compensation, the benefits they provide may more than make up for the difference in salary. Frequently, room and board are provided. And since public schools operate by the letter of the law, all of your social security taxes will be kept in order so that you qualify for all public health care benefits. Public schools are also more likely to help you arrange all necessary work visas and residency permits.

In Poland, as in other areas of Eastern Europe, public school teachers must somehow believe that less is more, at least when it comes to salaries. But Poland is as a good a place as any to make do on a small salary. Public schools pay about 1,200 *zloty* per month to English teachers. In some cases, your salary may be negotiable depending on your level of experience. The amount of money a school has left in its budget prior to your arrival may also affect what you'll take home every month.

As a teacher in a public school you will be better exposed to a broader segment of the surrounding community than you would in the private sector schools. For many expats, part of the experience of living abroad, especially if you pick a smaller city or rural area, is getting involved in the local community.

If you are interested in applying for a position in one of Poland's public schools, contact:

Ministry of National Education
Department of International Cooperation
Al. J. Ch. Szucha 25
Warsaw PL-00918, Poland
Phone: (02) 628-0461 or (022) 29 72 41, ext. 530 or 682
Fax: (02) 628-8561

Private tutoring

Taking on private students in addition to your regular teaching job in a public or private school is a means of balancing out your teaching schedule while making some extra money. Since it's often difficult to find enough private students to fill up your schedule and provide you with enough regular income, few teachers manage to make a teaching career of teaching only private lessons. Private students are generally hard to find, particularly if you don't speak Polish or haven't made contacts who can introduce you to prospective students.

Probably the best place to find private students is through your regular teaching job. Undoubtedly, one of your students will know someone who's schedule doesn't conform to the school's schedule of classes, so they will opt to take more flexible private lessons.

Once you become settled into your new digs in Poland, you'll be more likely to make a go of teaching privately. It's just hard to find enough people who can keep a regular schedule of lesson appointments. Private students are notorious for canceling their lessons at the last minute, or trying to reschedule when it's less convenient for you. And the economy is such that finding students who have enough disposable income to pay for private language lessons is a difficult proposition. Most experienced teachers would agree with this American in Krakow:

66 *I'm always glad that I have my regular teaching job, because even though I've found a few private students to teach on the side I wouldn't be able to count on them on a regular basis, and I wouldn't be able to make the same amount of money that I do at my school."*

Though it's certainly not the norm in Poland, it is possible to make private teaching the mainstay of your teaching career. You must be both tenacious and patient because it takes time and effort to establish yourself as a private tutor. You must find a place that has a big enough population of people who have both the money and the desire to take private English lessons. One way to assure a higher level of attendance when teaching privately is to conduct group lessons. If you can find upwards of three or four people to teach simultaneously, you usually can count on at least a few people showing up to every lesson. When you teach a group, you don't have to charge as much as you would on an individual basis, which alleviates some of the financial burden on your students.

Though some people prefer to learn one-on-one, language lessons are well-suited to groups because language is by its very nature social. So put out the word among all your students, friends, and other contacts that you are interested in setting up a few weekly group lesson sessions. You might even find another expat friend to help you, which would take some of the burden off of you and enable you to teach more people at the same time.

For one-on-one tutoring in Poland, you should be able to get between 15 and 20 *zloty* per hour, which roughs out to between US$6 and $8 per hour. You have the choice of setting a standard hourly price for your services, or setting up something along the lines of a sliding scale. If you think that you want to attract enough students to create a small business for yourself, consider what a little flexibility might do for getting more students interested in your services. After all, not everyone is rich enough to pay you at the upper end of the wage range.

In-company instruction

Given the transitional state of the Polish economy and the fact that over two million private businesses have been established in the last five years, entrepreneurs and business people all over Poland are competing to establish themselves as the leader in their field. At the same time, international businesses are investing in Poland. In order to compete internationally, many Polish companies are encouraging their employees to learn to speak English by offering language instruction. Some companies contract with private language schools while others hire teachers to teach in-house. Opportunities exist, but they are generally harder to find.

Compared to public teaching jobs, in-company work can be lucrative. What you can make is likely dependent upon how well you are able to sell yourself to company management. In-company teaching jobs will not fall into your lap very often. You must search them out. And though an in-company job may sound more prestigious than teaching on a private basis, chances are that you will have to meet the bureaucratic demands of the company. Many companies offer classes after the regular work day is finished which means you will have to make yourself available at odd hours such as late afternoon or early evening. Of course, in-company language instruction is usually business oriented, which may put limitations on the scope of your lessons.

Negotiating pay for an in-company teaching job could be a little trickier than you might think, especially if the company is new to the idea of providing English language instruction for its employees. Before you mention your going rate, make sure you know what the company expects from you. Your ability to supplement your in-company job with another position in a private school or even some private tutoring on the side will surely affect the terms of your pay. For a start, find out what a company would have to pay to contract with a private language school to provide English classes in-company. You shouldn't count on making this much a month, but at least you'll have an informed bargaining position. It's also a good idea to know what rates of pay other kinds of teaching positions command. Armed with all this information, you should be able to make a reasonable case when you negotiate your pay.

Full-time vs. freelance

Full-time teaching may require forty or more hours a week if you combine classroom and preparation time, but actual time spent in the classroom will rarely exceed eighteen to twenty hours per week, unless you make special arrangements to take on an abnormally large class load. In Poland, teaching jobs in the public sector usually demand eighteen units (forty-five minutes each) of classroom instruction, while the number of hours of preparation time is left up to the individual teacher. In private schools, roughly twenty hours per week of classroom instruction are expected. Since private schools are generally more flexible than their public sector counterparts, classes may be offered throughout the day and early evening. Don't be surprised if you are asked to teach at a couple of different locations or on weekends, usually Saturday.

Freelance teaching, on the other hand, means that you determine your schedule to a much greater degree than you would working for a school. Though that may sound appealing, you still have to teach at times that are convenient to your students. As a freelancer, you are more likely to be giving lessons at odd hours from early morning to late evening. This usually means that you spend more time commuting from one lesson to another, unless you are fortunate enough to convince all of your students to meet you at one convenient location.

ADVANCE PLANNING

It's not necessary to find a job before you leave for Poland. In fact, it's not even recommended, particularly if you don't possess formal qualifications and want to find a job with a private school. As with the other countries in Central and Eastern Europe, travel is inexpensive enough so that you should be able to visit different areas to determine where you might like to live for awhile.

If you want to teach at a state-run school, you are more likely to find leads by writing in advance. There are several organizations to contact. They should give you general information and some indication of what particular positions might be available:

East European Partnership
15 Princeton Court
53-55 Felsham Rd.
London SW15 1AZ
United Kingdom
Phone: (441-081) 780-2841

Academy for Inter-cultural Training
P.O. Box 2298
Georgetown University
Washington, DC 20057
Phone: (202) 687-7032

NKJO Network
c/o S. Pociecha
P.O. Box 1817
Wroclaw 46 50-385
Poland

Language for Eastern European Development (LEED)
41 Sutter Street, Suite 510
San Francisco, CA 94104
Phone: (415) 982-5333

Teachers for Poland
Hereford Education Centre
Blackfriars Street
Hereford HR4 9HS
United Kingdom
Phone: (441-04) 32 35 33 63

OTHER OPPORTUNITIES

Because of the economic situation in Poland, finding work opportunities outside the English teaching field can be a daunting task. A high rate of unemployment combined with the government's desire to create more jobs for unemployed Poles makes it difficult for foreigners to find work. In fact, for a foreigner, pounding the pavement in a city like Warsaw is more likely to result in depression and despair than it is to result in full-time, well-paid employment, unless you bounce back from rejection like one of those inflatable dolls weighted at the bottom with sand. Your chances are much better if you speak Polish and possess special skills or a high level of expertise in a field where Polish people have not yet excelled.

❝ *Few foreigners can create the types of job opportunities here which make them want to stay for longer periods of time. Unless you work for an international company, there isn't much to choose from on today's open job market in Poland. We're still trying to figure out how to recover from four decades of communist rule.*"

If you are determined to find work in your field in Poland, you will be much better off making inquiries about job openings prior to your departure. The fact that the Polish people have voted some of the old communist leadership back into office does not bode well for expats who want to compete with Poles for the few positions available. The new government is unlikely to create policies that favor foreign workers.

Said an employee of the American Cultural Center in Warsaw:

❝ *Those who work for foreign ventures account for almost one hundred percent of the expat work force in Poland.*"

There are several tactics to consider when searching for a job that requires either technical knowledge or an advanced degree. If your area of interest or expertise is fairly specialized, it may be to your advantage to begin your job search in the United States or Canada. If you are hired in North America, you are more likely to be well-compensated (i.e., paid a hard currency salary on a Western pay scale). If you leave for Poland before you begin your search, contact the agencies listed below. But remember: no matter where you are, the best way for you to find work is to network as much as possible.

Most of the younger expatriates who work outside of the teaching field create opportunities for themselves, usually in concert with a Polish partner. It's much easier to get a small business venture started if you've got an inside track, that is a local resident who will make fewer waves with the authorities when applying for the requisite business licenses. A native-English-speaking Polish-American woman who was offered work through friends when she was visiting Poland contributed:

❝ *Poland is a place where it's good to know people if you want to find work. And businesses there need people who understand Western styles of business management. . . . They are especially receptive to energetic young people."*

Send out resumes and cover letters to companies that do business overseas, arrange to meet with someone who has worked or lived in Poland, make contact with a Polish person in the United States or Canada who might maintain either business or family ties with Poland, or consult the director of a foreign exchange or study program in Poland through your college or university. You might even find out if the city where you live has a sister city in Poland. If so, make contact with the person who oversees the exchange, and explain your interest. Spread the word any way you can that you are interested in finding employment in Poland.

The United States Department of Commerce in Poland publishes a list of all American companies that do business in Poland. Peruse this list to determine if your field of interest is represented by an American company doing business in Poland. Contact:

American Cultural Center
Senatorska 13/15
Warsaw 00-076
Phone: (022) 26 70 15

Another good source of information for job seekers is the American Chamber of Commerce in Poland. They keep an up-to-date file of resumes of people who are seeking employment in Poland, so that their members have access to a database of prospective employees. Individual memberships cost US$500. Joining the Chamber of Commerce is expensive, so you should make an appointment to speak with someone about the benefits of joining. Contact:

American Chamber of Commerce in Poland
Pl. Powstancow 1
Warsaw 00-950
Phone: (022) 26 39 60
Fax: (022) 26 51 31

No matter what` kind of work you decide to pursue, it's important to understand that relative to the other countries under discussion Poland is a big place. The economic situation varies from city to city, and from place to place. If you expect to find work outside of English teaching, your best bet is the larger cities.

She continued:

66 *Poland, for the most part, is really rural. Once you leave the major cities, the situation really changes. People's attitudes about the economy really depend on where they are from. People in Warsaw can be pretty optimistic, whereas people in a smaller place like Lublin can be much more negative. They are much less likely to have had a change of attitude. It's hard to break the old habits—many of these people worked for state-subsidized industry (prior to the fall of the communists), and they don't adapt easily. If you want to find opportunities, you have to go to either Warsaw, Krakow, or Gdansk."*

Settling in

A PLACE TO LIVE

It's the curse of most of Central and Eastern Europe, and Poland is no exception: finding long-term accommodations is perhaps the most difficult task for foreigners. The only advantage that some foreigners have over the average Pole is that they are accustomed to paying a lot more in monthly rent. Said one teacher in a school in Krakow:

❝ *The bottom line is you won't get what you want when looking for accommodation, unless you're very lucky. Finding accommodation is the single biggest problem for foreigners in Krakow, and I would imagine all over the rest of Poland, too. . . . If you find something, take it."*

The teacher went on to say that connections are important when looking for accommodation. It's fair to say that you should spend as much time in the beginning looking for a place to live as you do looking for work. Unless you find a job in a public school, most schools do not assist you in finding accommodations.

Renting an apartment

Because finding an apartment can be a tiresome task, take what you can get, provided it meets your basic specifications. And don't expect to find an apartment equipped with a phone, as they are rare. When you do, it's probably not worth the extra expense.

Though apartment and room rents in Poland are inexpensive when compared to what you pay at home, they will probably require about the same percentage out of your pay. Expect to pay upwards of US$350 per month for a studio apartment.

By far the best way to find long-term accommodations is through the people you meet—casual acquaintances, other teachers, co-workers, etc. It's a good idea to search out a Polish-speaking person who can help you in your search for accommodation. Most landlords in Eastern Europe boost their rents considerably when they rent to a foreigner, and Poland is no exception.

Consider the following before you sign an agreement to rent:

- Apartments in Poland are small, cramped, and often short on amenities of any sort. They are usually measured in terms of square meters, and are designated one room, one-and-a-half rooms, two rooms, etc. A one room apartment is the rough equivalent of a studio. One-and-a-half rooms means that there is a small room or area between the sleeping quarters and the kitchen area, and so on.
- The plumbing and heating systems are often antiquated. Make sure everything is in working order.
- Most landlords who rent to foreigners don't report their rental incomes to the tax collector. It is advisable to get some sort of written receipt from your landlord just in case there are any problems. Whether or not the landlord does choose to file with the tax authorities, chances are the full amount of what you pay will not be reported.

POLISH LANGUAGE

Like Czech, Slovak, Russian, and a host of others, Polish is a Slavic tongue. If you travel throughout Central and Eastern Europe you will notice many similarities between the Slavic languages, though they are not necessarily mutually comprehensible. All of the Slavic languages are difficult because of their inherent grammatical complexities. Pronunciation is no simple task either. You will notice lots of unusual punctuation symbols, and a high ratio of consonants to vowels. On the good side, Polish is completely phonetic, and once you've mastered the sound combinations, you're well on your way.

POLISH FOOD AND DRINK

Slavic cuisine is heavy on meat and starch and not much else, and thus rarely elicits gasps of gastronomic rapture. Put another way, the Poles will never threaten the French or the Italians in any kind of culinary battle. Salivation is rarely, if ever, the motivation for anyone to visit Poland.

If you're an avid drinker of distilled spirits, Poland is much closer to heaven. The Polish national drink is vodka, and lots of it. Beer is becoming increasingly popular, as well.

Just because Poland's cuisine has never quite attracted international attention doesn't mean the Poles are short on hospitality. In fact, quite the contrary. When visiting a Polish home expect to be treated like a VIP. Your hosts will undoubtedly expect you to ingest great quantities of heavy food and strong drink.

Teaching older students and professionals carries the advantage of learning more about the country's culture and history.

COMMON CUSTOMS

Though the Polish people have struggled over the centuries to keep hold of their territory, Polish culture is rich with customs and tradition because Poles have been too stubborn to let history's vagaries quash or dilute their identity. The following are customs that you would do well to observe:

- Bring a bouquet of flowers if you are invited into someone's home.
- Shake hands when you greet people (both men and women), and opt for the formal greeting when addressing someone, unless you know someone or have mutually agreed on using first names.
- Poles love to drink—often late into the night. Expect interesting and lively conversations, often about politics and other controversial social concerns.
- Keep both of your hands above the table while you're eating.
- Catholic conservatism dictates the way many Poles think, so be careful about offending people by expressing strong religious views that may run counter to tradition. In other words, keep your atheism to yourself.
- If you visit a church, take off your hat.
- Don't make fun of the pope!

SHOPPING

Poles seem to have a well-developed taste for Western goods, and stores are becoming better stocked all the time. If you choose to live in any of the larger cities, you shouldn't have much trouble finding the things you need. Luxury items, though, are harder to find. You might have to search out certain stores that consistently stock your favorite items. Be prepared to find Western prices on these items, as well as stereos, and some clothes.

Folk-craft items such as hand-knit clothing, hand-stitched leather goods, and custom jewelry often are inexpensive and widely available. Many Polish cities feature open-air markets where such items are available. In fact, Krakow is famous for its public market, located right in the middle of its town square. Fine crystal glassware is also a favorite gift idea of many visitors to Poland.

Bring the following items if you are concerned about either their cost or availability:

- Birth control. Poland is a Catholic country, so don't count on finding your favorite contraceptive products at the corner drug store, especially at the last minute.
- Film. Particularly if you require the more obscure varieties
- Medication. If it's prescription, make sure it's labeled, and bring a note from your doctor so you're able to set things straight if you're questioned by a Polish pharmacist (or a suspicious customs official).

FINANCES

Though the Polish equivalent of the IRS may not inspire the same level of fear or anxiety as its American counterpart, you are required to pay taxes on your income when you work in Poland. Your employer should deduct the appropriate amounts from your pay. Keep in mind that Polish employers sometimes find other things to do with your tax money, so it's important to ask whether or not taxes are being properly deducted from your pay.

Even though you may not be making enough money (over US$70,000) to pay taxes to the IRS back home, you are still required to file a tax return.

New zloty

You should be aware that two currencies are now in circulation in Poland. On January 1, 1995, the National Bank of Poland knocked off four zeros from its currency, creating a new *zloty* worth 10,000 old *zloty*. The bank also introduced a new series of coins and banknotes based on the new nominal value of the *zloty*. Both currencies will be in use officially until December 31, 1996.

Unfortunately, some exchange centers are taking advantage of the situation. When presented with foreign currency for exchange, these centers are handing out old 50, 100, and 200 *zloty* notes—worth mere pennies—instead of new *zlotys* worth from US$20 to $80. So, be careful. You should check that notes purchased are dated 1994 or later.

Banks

As you might imagine, the banking system in Poland does not compare to what you're accustomed to back home. Don't despair, though, because you'll still find them to be useful when you need to exchange money or get a cash advance.

Warsaw

American Express
ul. Krakowskie Przedmiescie 11
Phone: (02) 635-2002

Bank PKO Rotunda
ul. Marszalkowka 100/102
Phone: (022) 26 00 61

Bank Inicjatyw Gospodarczych
ul. Kopernika 36/40
Phone: (02) 657-5185

Bank PKO S.A
pl. Bankowy 2
Phone: (02) 637-1000

Krakow

American Express (at ORBIS)
al. Folcha 1
(in the Hotel Cracovia)
Phone: (012) 21 98 80
or (012) 22 46 32

American Express
Rynek 41
Phone: (012) 22 11 57

Bank PKO S.A.
Rynek 31
Phone: (012) 22 60 22

TELEPHONES AND MAIL

Telephones

Yes, you guessed it—the Polish telephone system sucks. You will be lucky to find a public telephone that works properly. As a general rule, use telephones that require phone cards. They are newer, and therefore more likely to work. Of course, you will need to buy a phone card.

Long-distance calls cannot be made from any pay phone. You must go to the post office phone bank. For long distance calls within Poland: dial 0, and then dial the area code and number. For international calls, try AT&T Direct. It's by far the most reliable way to use a calling card or call collect. Dial 0-0104800111 for an AT&T operator. If you use a phone card, it will cost you two units.

Calling home

AT&T Direct Dial .... 0 (wait for tone)
010-480-0111
MCI World Phone 010-480-0222

Operator-assisted calls can be made from the main post office and from US West, on the southwest corner of the intersection of ul. Nowogrodzka and ul. Poznanska. US West also provides telex and fax services.

Mail

Poland's postal system (PTT) may be more efficient than its telephones, but don't expect too much. Airmail letters and small packages to and from Poland take a week or two, at the very least.

Poste restante is your best bet if you don't have a stable address, or if you expect to receive larger packages. Make sure you're going to the main post office to pick up your poste restante mail, unless the sender knows to specifically designate the nearest post office (particularly important in the larger cities).

If you have an American Express card or carry American Express traveler's checks, you can receive mail (letters and small parcels only) at any American Express office.

Warsaw

Send or receive mail

Main Post Office
ul. Swietokrzyska 31/33
Warsaw 00-001
Phone: (022) 26 60 01, (022) 26 04 11, or (022) 27 04 77
Fax: (022) 30 00 21
(Faxes can be sent from here as well. The branch at the main train station also has 24-hour telephone service.)

American Express
ul. Krakowskie Przedmiescie 11
Warsaw 00-069
Phone: (02) 635-2002

Poste restante
Main Post Office, Window 12
Address letters:
Your Name
Poczta Glowna
ul. Swietokryska 31/33
Warsaw 00-049
Poland
Poste Restante

Krakow

Send or receive mail
Main Post Office
ul. Westerplatte 20
Krakow 31-045
Phone: (012) 22 03 22
Fax: (012) 21 43 31

American Express (at ORBIS)
al. Focha 1
(in the Hotel Cracovia)
Phone: (012) 21 98 80 or (012) 22 46 32
(Will hold mail for a fee)

American Express (at ORBIS)
Rynek 41
Phone: (012) 22 11 57
(Will hold mail for a fee)

DHL
ul. Raclawicka 56
Phone: (012) 33 80 96

Express Mail Service
pl. Kolwjowy 5
Phone: (012) 22 40 26

Express Mail Service
ul. Westerplatte 20
Phone: (012) 22 66 96

Courier services

Warsaw

UPS
ul. 17-go Stycznia 2
Phone: (02) 606-6350
Fax: (02) 650-4544

Poste restante
Main Post Office, Window 7
Address letters:
Your Name
Main Post Office
ul. Westerplatte 20
30-960 Krakow 1
Poland
Poste Restante

DHL
al. Jerozolimskie 30
Phone: (022) 26 32 92

HEALTH CARE

Public health care in Poland is accessible to foreigners who contribute to the social security system via deductions from their wages or salaries. Of course, you must play by the rules and have your work permit in order before you are eligible. And unfortunately, eligibility doesn't necessarily translate into the same kind of care that you receive in the United States or Canada. The economic transformations in Central and Eastern Europe have not been kind to health care systems. Hospitals and clinics are often under-staffed and poorly equipped. In this regard, specialized care definitely suffers more than routine treatments.

For English-speaking medical help, consult the American or British Embassy. They keep lists of doctors who can assist foreigners, and they will also have information on private medical clinics for foreigners.

Following are some medical information and assistance facilities:

Medical facilities and assistance

Warsaw

Health Info Line (Information about health services)
Phone: (022) 26 27 61
or (022) 26 83 00

24-hour service and ambulance
ul. Hoza 56
Phone: (02) 628-2424

Emergency room at Hospital Szpital Srodmiejski
ul. Solec 93
Phone: (02) 625-2231
or (02) 625-3327

Marriott Hotel Medical Center
al. Jerozolimskie 65/79
Phone: (02) 630-5115
or (02) 621-0646

J.J. Capricorn Ltd.
Podwale II
Phone: (022) 31 86 69
Phone/fax: (022) 31 06 07
(24-hour medical assistance)

Centrum Medychn
Domiana I cenmed sp.zoo
Walbrzyska 46
Phone: (022) 43 51 53, (02)
    644-3313, or (02) 644-3314

Krakow
Private doctors are available
    at:

Profimed
Rynek 6
Phone: (012) 21 79 97

Profimed
ul. Grodzka 26
Phone: (012) 22 64 53

Pharmacies

Warsaw

Apteka
ul. Grojecka 76
Phone: (022) 22 28 91

Swiss Pharmacy
al. Roz 2
Phone: (02) 628-9471

Krakow

Pharmacy
Rynek 13
Phone: (012) 22 41 90

Other medical services

Warsaw

**24-Hour Psychological Help
    Line**
(Not always available in English)
Phone: (02) 628-3636

Women's Hotline
(Not always available in English)
Phone: (02) 635-4791

AIDS Hotline
(Not always available in English)
Phone: (02) 628-0336

OTHER SERVICES

Embassies and consulates

Warsaw

United States Embassy
al. Ujazdowskie 29/31
Phone: (02) 628-3041

Canadian Embassy
ul. Matejki 1/5
Phone: (022) 29 80 51

Krakow

United States Consulate
ul. Stolarska 9
Phone: (012) 21 67 67

Laundromats

Warsaw

Laundromat
ul. Karmelicka 17
Phone: (022) 31 73 17

Important telephone numbers

Warsaw

Police emergency	997
Fire emergency	998
Ambulance	999
Police headquarters	(022) 26 24 24
PolCard (a 24-hour number for reporting lost or stolen credit cards)	(022) 27 45 13 or (02) 611-3060

Krakow

Police emergency	997
Fire emergency	998
Ambulance	999
Police headquarters	(012) 21 00 20 or (012) 10 71 15
Directory assistance (all of Poland)	913

● ●

LANGUAGE TIPS

Polish is a member of the Slavic language family. Though none of the Slavic languages are considered easy, Polish is completely phonetic. Once you have mastered the various sound combinations, pronunciation comes easily.

Numbers

one	jeden
two	dwa
three	trzy
four	cztery
five	piec
six	szesc
seven	siedem
eight	osiem
nine	dziewiec
ten	dziesiec

Important words and phrases

Yes	Tak
No	Nie
Good morning	Dzien dobry
Good evening	Dobry wieczór
Goodbye	Dowidzenia
Thank you	Dziekuje
Please	Prosze
Where is the bus station?	Gdzie jest stacja autobusowa?
Where is the train station?	Gdzie jest stacja kolejowa?
Where is the toilet?	Gdzie jest toaleta?
I don't understand.	Nie rozumiem.
I speak only English.	Mówie tylko po angielsku.
My name is _____.	Nazywam sie _____.

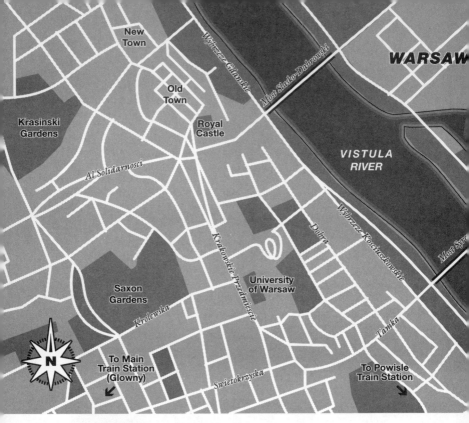

City Profiles

WARSAW

Though Warsaw may be an old, historically important capital city, it doesn't possess the time-honored charm of its other Eastern European counterparts. Hitler's army destroyed to rubble all of the buildings that would have allowed Warsaw to claim its share of architectural wonders. Even the Old Town Square in Warsaw is a reconstruction from the ruins of the original.

Commerce

In this city of 2.4 million people, Western commercial influence is recent and rampant. If you can get beyond the tacky, commercial, and grim architecture, Warsaw is actually a bustling and lively metropolis. There are plenty of bars and restaurants offering international cuisine or fast food, but don't expect either the level of quality in food or service that you would get in the West.

City psyche

Residents of Warsaw do the majority of their socializing in their own homes. This holds true even for most expatriates. Rising costs in Warsaw have had an impact on residents. High prices have created a "nouveau-riche" Warsaw society that frequents the flashy establishments, which most Poles and expatriates can't afford. You will, however, find many people in Warsaw frequenting the numerous theatrical, music, and arts festivals that take over the city every year. The annual jazz festival and the Chopin festival are just a couple of examples.

A large university keeps the city feeling young. And there is a great deal of international trade going on in Poland's capital. This can bring with it changes that can be seen as both positive or negative. The changes have brought some of the finer things in life to the shops of Warsaw, but it is very much a city of business. Because of all the international trade and diplomatic activity, Warsaw's expatriate crowd tends to be a little older and more sophisticated.

Travel and weather

Conveniently, Warsaw is located in the central region of Poland's great plain. It's easy to travel to and from by train or air. Consequently, it's fast becoming a major transportation hub for all of Eastern Europe, which makes it a good home base for the adventurous expatriate. A train ride west will take you to Berlin, while a train to the east will eventually arrive in the Ukraine or the Baltic states. The climate tends to be a little more severe in its hot and cold extremes but good planning can keep you comfortable.

In the words of one of Warsaw's veteran expatriates, "Warsaw is a great city to live in, but you wouldn't want to visit."

English Schools

Number of staff	Number of students per class	Entry pay (złoty)	Send resume/cover letter	
50	11–13	15–20/hr	✔	**American English School** Kryniczna 12/14 Warsaw Poland (02) 617-1112
50	11–13	n/a	✔	**American English School** Wilenska 27/3 Warsaw Poland (022) 27 26 54
50	4–6	varies		**Archibald Szkola Jezyka Angielskiego** Szpitalna 8/19 Warsaw Poland (022) 27 29 23
n/a	15	16–23/hr		**British and American English School** ul. Noakowskiego 24 Warsaw Poland (02) 621-0222
n/a	10	15/hr	✔	**Edukacja Konsultingowo-oswiatowa** Smolna 9/10 Warsaw Poland (022) 44 58 16 and (022) 27 86 59

Number of staff	Number of students per class	Entry pay (*zloty*)	Send resume/cover letter	
n/a	n/a	n/a		**Greenpol–Signum Polsko–Byrtjska Szkola** Renesansowa 5/10 Warsaw Poland (022) 37 57 92 or (022) 35 77 60
n/a	n/a	n/a		**Greenwich School of English** Zakroczymska 6 Warsaw Poland (022) 31 09 55
50	15	n/a		**Lexis School** Marszalkowska 60 przy Placu Konstytucji Warsaw Poland (02) 625-5386 or 625-7298
1	varies	n/a	✔	**Lingua Nova** Nowowiejska 37a Warsaw Poland (022) 25 80 86
n/a	n/a	n/a		**Linguae Mundi** Al. Jana Pawla 11/13 Warsaw Poland (02) 620-9049 or (02) 620-0351, ext. 258

Number of staff	Number of students per class	Entry pay (złoty)	Send resume/cover letter	
n/a	n/a	n/a	✔	**Metodysci English Language College** Mokotowska 12 Warsaw Poland (02) 628-5348
20	10	22–26/hr	✔	**Poligota** ul. Dzialdowska 6 Warsaw Poland (022) 26 49 46
varies	15	15/hr		**School of Languages** ul. Krolewska 19/21 Warsaw Poland (022) 27 28 34 (3-7PM only)
n/a	n/a	n/a		**The Regency School of English** ul. Nowy Swiat 53 Warsaw Poland (022) 26 49 46 or (022) 27 92 41, ext. 245
n/a	n/a	n/a		**Top School** ul. Bonifacego 81 Warsaw Poland (02) 642-1351

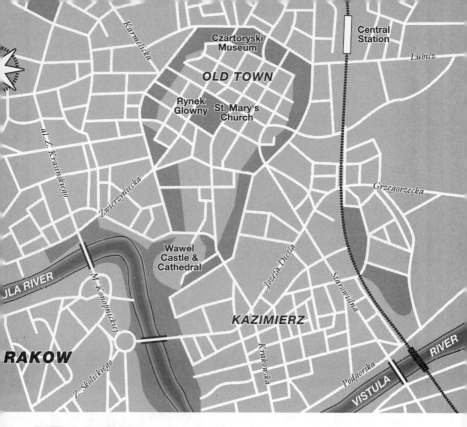

KRAKOW

While Warsaw may be the political capital of Poland, Krakow is definitely the cultural center of the country. Nearly 1.2 million people live in Krakow and its outlying city limits. Architecturally—with its enormous old town square, numerous churches, meandering cobbled streets, ancient city wall, palaces, and houses—the Renaissance, Romanesque, Gothic, and Baroque periods stand side by side. Krakow is legendary as a mystical city—once a center of magic and astrology—where Faustus began his studies. Unlike Warsaw, Krakow had the advantage of not being decimated during the second world war.

City life

For a lesser known place, Krakow's teeming social life resembles Prague's, albeit on a slightly smaller scale. As in Warsaw, a major Polish university keeps the city feeling young and energetic. After dark, just off the old town square, the sounds of rock, jazz, and classical music can be heard filtering out of the nightclubs and restaurants. During the day, in the middle of the square, a public market attracts tourists and makes good money for the locals. Tourism brings a certain vitality to Krakow's economy, that most travelers and expats will appreciate. (An absolute must-see in Krakow is Leonardo da Vinci's "Lady with Ermine" at the Muzeum Czartoryskich—on a sidestreet off of the Rynek Glowny. There are those who find this piece way cooler than the Mona Lisa, with no crowds or bullet-proof glass to deal with.)

Surrounding area

For the expatriate, Krakow's location in southern Poland has both advantages and disadvantages. The country's southern stretch is notoriously polluted, and yet at arm's reach of some of its more beautiful terrain. The Tatra mountains, with their ski areas and hiking trails, lie just an hour and a half or so to the south. Slovakia and the Czech Republic are a short train ride away. And the town formerly known as Auschwitz lies just a half hour bus ride away from Krakow. The museum that commemorates the grim atrocities committed there still attracts thousands of visitors every year.

If Prague, Budapest, and Warsaw sound too settled with Western familiarities for your liking, Krakow is perhaps one of the more desirable places to live and work in Eastern Europe. And if, for whatever reason, you end up going elsewhere, make sure to plan a visit to this splendid city.

English schools

Number of staff	Number of students per class	Entry pay (zloty)	Send resume/cover letter	
n/a	n/a	n/a		**Celt** Konarskiego 2 Krakow Poland (012) 36 13 50
n/a	n/a	n/a		**Gama Biuro Organizacyjne Gama Gell School of English** Sw. Krzyza 16 Krakow Poland (012) 21 97 55 or 21 97 22

Number of staff	Number of students per class	Entry pay (zloty)	Send resume/cover letter	
55	11-14	varies	✔	**International House Krakow** ul. Czapskich 5 Krakow Poland (012) 21 94 40 or 22 64 82
n/a	n/a	n/a		**Langart** Boleslawa Prusa 28 Krakow Poland (012) 22 26 65
13	9	1,200/mo	✔	**School of English "York"** Burszlynowa 22 Krakow Poland (012) 12 31 14
8	12	12–18/hr		**Surrey Business and Language Centre Polsko-Brytyiska Spolka** Sw. Anny 9 Krakow Poland (012) 21 15 53
n/a	n/a	n/a		**Szkola Jezyka Angielskiego School of English** Jozefa Ignacego Kraszewskiego 9 Skawina Krakow Poland (012) 76 39 53

Number of staff	Number of students per class	Entry pay (zloty)	Send resume/cover letter	
22	10-15	17/hr	✔	**Szkola Jezyka Angloamerykanskiego** Stanislawa Skarbinskiego 5 Krakow Poland (012) 23 54 84
n/a	n/a	n/a		**Szkola Jezyka Obcych "World" S.C.** Radziwillowska 28/3 rog ul. Mikolaja Reja Krakow Poland (012) 22 16 82
n/a	n/a	n/a		**Szkola Jezykow Obcych "Helix"** Al. 29 Listopada 32/1 Krakow Poland (012) 12 24 76

Teaching English as a second language

FOSTERING A NATURAL ABILITY TO LEARN

Millions of people around the world learn to speak a foreign language without ever having looked up a word in a dictionary or attended a language class. How do they do it?

Members of some African tribes may marry only outside of their language groups; it is considered incestuous to marry someone who speaks the same language. All newly married brides and grooms are therefore required to learn each other's language. When asked how they were able to learn their new languages, most couples said that after listening for a while they were able to catch on and, later, to communicate. They took it for granted that they would be able to learn the language naturally over time; they didn't doubt their ability or dread having to learn a new language.

People learn a new language with the greatest ease when they want to be able to communicate with the speakers of that language and when they feel that it will be natural for them to do so. Needless to say, most language teachers don't have the luxury of immersing their students in environments where they are intensely motivated to communicate, nor do most students believe that being able to speak English will come naturally to them. We can't send our students to any magical place, or change their deep-seated beliefs overnight. The next best thing is to create a learning environment conducive to language acquisition. The basic concepts involved in teaching a foreign language all tend to lead back to this fundamental goal. Consider this perspective from anthropologist Margaret Mead:

> ❝ *I have worked now in many different cultures. I am a very poor speaker of any language, but I always know whose pig is dead and, when I work in a native society, I know what people are talking about and I treat it seriously and I respect them, and this in itself establishes a great deal more rapport, very often, than the correct accent. I have worked with other field workers who were far, far better linguists than I, yet the natives kept on saying that they couldn't speak the*

language, although they said I could! Now, if you had a recording it would be proof positive I couldn't, but nobody knew it. You see, we don't need to teach people to speak like natives, we need to make the natives think they can, so that then they will talk to them and then they will learn."

HOW STUDENTS LEARN

Affective filter

How did you feel when your teacher called on you during the first week or two of beginning Spanish and waited expectantly for you to answer her question? Something about being in a foreign language classroom can make even the most confident person want to fade into the background.

It is important for your students to feel comfortable in your classroom. When people are under stress or feel anxious they get a mental block. This block is known in the ESL field as an affective filter. It prevents language from entering and being assimilated into your students' minds. The more your students are able to relax in your class, the easier it will be for them to understand what you are saying and thus begin the process of acquiring English. Aim for your students to be in a state of alert relaxation.

If you notice that your students are beginning to feel anxious, it is a signal for you to change the pace of your class in some way. You can have your students get out of their seats and do an activity that requires them to mill around the room; you can play some music and change the focus of your lesson; you can tell a joke or two to help your students lighten up.

Comprehensible input

Children begin learning language by listening to people tell them about things in their immediate environment. When you talk to a child you talk to him about objects or events that he can see, hear, or touch. You use easier vocabulary, more exaggerated inflection, and more animated expressions than you would if you were communicating with another adult. You speak clearly and purposely. You don't talk about yesterday or tomorrow; rather you talk about the here-and-now: your clothes, a glass of water, the light switch. You don't expect a one-year-old child to talk back to you at length about the light switch just after you told him all about it; neither should you expect this from your students.

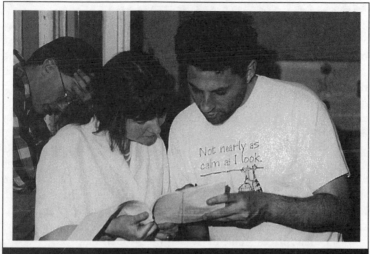

Class planning and student participation are important elements of successful teaching.

Key concepts from the field of first-language acquisition transfer easily to the field of second-language acquisition. Listening skills develop first in children, and they develop first in people learning a new language. Likewise, when you teach English to beginning students you talk about here-and-now events and objects. You are more animated (or expressive) than usual. You speak clearly and with purpose.

Your aim when talking to your students is for them to understand what you are trying to communicate. You do this not only with words but also with objects, pictures, gestures and drama. Talk with students at a level that is just above their current ability. Language at this "just-above" level is called comprehensible input. Comprehensible input facilitates language development whether for first- or second-language learners.

When you think about it, doesn't it seem that toddlers understand a lot more than they are able to say? And you wouldn't feel anxious if a toddler couldn't speak in complete sentences, right? Likewise, it is crucial that you do not expect your students to produce language immediately upon entering your classroom. Expect a silent period. People need to warm up for a good amount of time before running a marathon; so too do your students need time to build language in their minds along with self-confidence. Provide your students with the opportunity to absorb language with minimal expectations from you. Allow students to have this silent period until they begin to feel comfortable using the language little by little on their own.

Natural order of acquisition

There seems to be a natural order to acquiring mathematical ability. We start with recognizing numbers, counting, and adding, and move on to subtracting, multiplying, and dividing numbers. Most of us end somewhere between adding fractions or figuring out percentages and doing advanced calculus. No one would consider teaching a preschooler how to figure out the sale price of a sweater marked forty percent off. That kind of mathematical calculation doesn't come naturally to young children.

People acquire language structures in a fairly set order, too. People learning English acquire the 's' plural as in "I have five sisters" and the -ing ending for verbs in the beginning stage of language study. For reasons not clearly understood, these grammatical points stick with new learners of English. Conversely, the 's' possessive as in "John's sisters are pretty" and the third-person-singular 's' as in "John enjoys going to new places" tend to be acquired much later on. No one knows for sure the exact order of acquisition for every grammatical structure. The order of acquisition theory states, however, that students will acquire language in a somewhat predictable sequence. Therefore it will be useless to try and get your beginning students to learn complex grammar. They just won't be able to acquire it; it won't stick.

A good rule of thumb when it comes to grammar is to target those structures that the students are attempting to use to communicate now, or those your students need for basic communication, such as the tenses.

Acquiring language is a process of one step forward and two steps back. On Monday your student may use the third person singular 's' correctly. On Wednesday he may not. Give your students plenty of language input with a modicum of correction, and trust their individual learning processes. If you would like more information on the natural order of acquisition, consult a book on second-language acquisition.

Language monitoring

If you ask a pianist how she is able to play the piano so beautifully she may well respond, "I don't know. I just do it." She has acquired the ability to play the piano after having had hour upon hour of musical input and practice. Highly skilled musicians listen to great music often. Listening to music shapes them into great musicians. When a new musician practices she produces a lot of off-key plunks and clangs. She may hear how badly she sounds, but she doesn't give up. She has in her mind a melody she aspires to replicate, and she is confident that eventually she will be able to play it as well. If she does get frustrated and gives up, she will never become the pianist that she wants to be.

Creative class projects help keep students interested and motivated.

It is important that your students do not become self-conscious when they are speaking English. What would happen if you stopped yourself in the middle of typing and started to think about every letter as you typed? Naturally you would slow down and your typing would become choppy rather than fluent. Likewise, the more your students have to stop and think about the language they are using, the more choppy and stammering they will become. You can have your students shut their eyes and imagine themselves speaking English fluently and with ease. This exercise is useful when your students are thinking about their language too much.

You will find that some of the English your students produce is fluent and they are relaxed and confident as they use it. They have acquired that language. They don't have to think about what they are saying while they are saying it. Other times, your students will speak slowly and carefully and will be thinking about what they are saying. This is language that they are learning, but have not yet acquired. When students think about what they are saying and the grammatical forms they are using, they are monitoring their language.

Monitoring takes time. When you are in a conversation you don't have time to think of grammar rules or to plan out what you want to say. When it's your turn to talk, you talk, or else you rapidly lose track of the conversation.

Most language learners do monitor themselves from time to time. It is appropriate to do so during grammar time in class. It is inappropriate to use it when participating in authentic communication. An over-reliance on monitoring will prevent the learner from becoming fluent in the language. At some point every language learner must jump off the diving board into the water and trust that they are going to be able to swim.

How can you help a group of students from over-monitoring their language? Provide them with a lot of comprehensible input, so that they feel confident in understanding the language. Keep the language learning environment relaxed yet engaging by providing plenty of authentic language learning tasks, such as interviewing one another in class in order to make a bulletin board display, playing cards together, or teaching each other a new recipe. These activities require that students concentrate on meaning rather than form.

YOUR ROLE IN THE LEARNING PROCESS

Correction

When is it appropriate for you to correct your students' grammar? Certainly a student who has been studying with you for some time will be aware of the third person singular 's'. He has heard it and you have told him about it. But every time he starts a sentence with "My friend . . . ," he neglects to add the third person singular 's' to the verb. You can correct him, and chances are one of two things will happen. Either he will thank you, and if he is ready to acquire that structure, he will internalize the correction and use the verb form comfortably and correctly; or he will feel ashamed of his error, freeze up, and start speaking more slowly and with practically visible pain. It is this second situation that you should avoid.

One of the primary language milestones for beginning students is to be able to start communicating in English. This communication will not be grammatically correct, but over time it will improve to that point. If you and other native speakers who are not ESL teachers can understand what your beginning students are saying, and your students seem confident of their abilities, you are doing something right in your classroom. Again, going through a lot of grammar drills is not going to speed up your students' language acquisition process.

There are two ways to go about correcting students' grammar. The first is to repeat back what a student says to you and tag on an extra piece of information. If your student says, "My aunt going to movie yesterday," you can say, "Oh, so your aunt went to a movie yesterday, what did she see?" The value of this form of correction is that students are receiving good language input and the emphasis is on continuing communication rather than on correction. In other words, this form of correction is not as direct a hit as if you said, "Vaclav, when you want to talk about the past use the past tense. In that sentence you should have used 'went' instead of 'going'."

Another way to handle correction is to correct the class as a whole. Listen for errors that the majority of students are making. Bring up the error to the class in a light hearted manner such as, "I hear a lot of you saying 'He go' instead of 'He goes.' Remember, after he and she there needs to be a 's' on the verb." You might then have the students come up with a few examples of their own which you then write on the board. This form of correction is the "We're all in the same boat" approach. No single student's language ability is singled out.

The errors you choose to correct should relate to grammar that you have already studied in class, or that you are currently studying. Correct your students' grammar during their focused grammar study time, not otherwise. Don't ever be a correction machine, "fixing" each and every error your students make.

Contextual learning and relevance

Were you one of the many students who was bored stiff in high school? You may have wondered what ancient history had to do with getting a job or growing up. Then again, maybe you took part in a project at school that really mattered to you and you jumped out of bed excited to get to school every morning. School was relevant to you; you were getting something out of it. Perhaps you could see that what you were learning was connected to your everyday life and future goals.

It is crucial that language learning activities be both relevant to the student and placed within a context. For example, all language learners will need to go shopping if they spend any time abroad, thus they are motivated to learn about shopping. Shopping for food becomes the context in which you teach all of your English skills. It is an excellent context for teaching count and non-count nouns, vocabulary related to food and money, and phrases such as "How much does this cost?" and "I would like . . . ."

Find out what contexts or topics interest your students. They may be interested in how to write a business letter or how to use transportation systems or what to do in case of an emergency. Incorporating your students' learning goals into your curriculum will enhance their interest in learning English. And when they are motivated to communicate, they are less likely to monitor their language as conveying meaning takes precedence over correct form.

Integrated skills

Teaching in an integrated fashion, where students listen, read, speak, write, and learn grammar in the context of a particular topic, takes contextual learning one step further. It allows your students to take the language out of the classroom and into the real world. For example, you can build a whole lesson plan around an imaginary visit to an American restaurant, having students listen to a conversation with a waiter, read the menu, talk about other restaurants in their neighborhoods or about their favorite foods, and write a letter to the restaurant owner complaining about a fly in the soup (they'll be learning about using the past tense at the same time).

You will have to place extra emphasis on listening, for that is how language learners get their language input. They won't be able to talk about eating in a restaurant, for example, until they have heard the language associated with it. And they will need to hear that language at least a few times before they will feel comfortable communicating with others.

A language learner's listening comprehension is higher than her speaking ability and her reading comprehension is higher than her writing ability. Listening activities should take up a large portion of time in your beginning ESL class. Getting plenty of comprehensible language input is crucial to your students' success.

Introduce a language context by talking to your students about various objects and pictures related to that context. You can have them repeat the language, and answer questions based on the objects that you brought into the classroom. They can read a dialogue you have written on the board showing two people communicating in that context. They can practice this dialogue a few times with a partner. They can then write their own dialogue with a partner and act it out in front of the class. Your students thus hear, read, write, and communicate using language that was previously new to them.

Grammar instruction

A linguist may be able to tell you everything you would ever want to know about the Czech language—its history, its sound system, its vocabulary, and its grammar—without being able to speak a word of it. It's much like the couch potato who knows all about football from watching it every Sunday, but wouldn't last a minute out on the field on the line of scrimmage.

Some of your Eastern European students will have learned about English grammar in junior high and high school but will be unable to utter a simple sentence. They learned *about* English grammar; they didn't learn how to use it as a tool to aid them in communication.

It is important for you to teach grammar in a context. Let's say your class has been talking about shopping. You can introduce the future tense by telling your students about what you plan to buy next month when you go home to America for a vacation. Then you can write "I am going to buy" on the board and provide your students with a fifteen-minute lesson on the future tense. Then give them several more examples of the future tense. "I am going to go out tonight." "I am going to watch football this Sunday." "I am going to call my parents tomorrow." Have your students tell you what they are going to do in the future and write what they say on the board. Give them worksheets to do on the future tense as homework.

It is important to spend time in grammar class teaching your students how to form questions. When your students are in an English-speaking environment and know how to ask questions, they are then able to seek information, get more language input, and keep conversations going.

In order to teach future-tense questions you should spend several minutes telling your students what you are going to do tomorrow and then asking them, "What are you going to do tomorrow?" You ask them this question several times before you write it on the board. You then have them repeat the question several times before you have them break into groups of four to six people and have them ask each other the question. And there should be an authentic purpose to their questions. Perhaps the purpose of this activity is for them to find out what each has in common in terms of how they are going to spend their free time tomorrow.

During grammar activities your students will monitor their language. Worksheets of any kind call on students to think about form. When you have students repeat sentences that contain the targeted grammar point they also think about form. When they use the new grammar with each other they will think about form. Any correct grammar that your students have not yet acquired will have to be monitored when it is used.

In short, grammar instruction should not be an end in itself. Direct grammar instruction should connect with real-life communication. To acquire grammatical correctness, your students will benefit most from hearing immense amounts of authentic language again and again.

Review

Students who learn English in an English-speaking country have an advantage over students who learn English abroad, in that they are surrounded by authentic language. They hear it in music, on television, in snatches of conversations around them. They read it on the bus, in newspaper headlines, and on menus. In short, they have a built-in language review at every turn.

Producing a play is one way to focus learning toward a practical result.

When you teach abroad you think about the language you used in class previously when you design your future lesson. Perhaps two weeks ago you provided your class with language related to shopping such as, "I bought a few loaves of bread" and "Where can I find the bananas?" They are likely to hear similar phrases occurring naturally in your speech or to read them from time to time. But because your students are not in a language-rich environment, you need to provide review experiences for them that encompass the past language they have studied.

Two weeks ago, your class learned English in the context of shopping. Now your context is getting medical help. Students will hear you say things such as, "Where can I find a good skin doctor around here?" and "I went to a skin doctor in the United States and he told me to try a little of this lotion" (you hold up the lotion). Your students are placed in a new language context but are using language they have learned in a previous context (in this case, "Where can I find . . . ?" and "a little"). They may find it helpful if you point out these connections.

Other sources of English

For achieving language acquisition goals, one or a combination of outside "speakers"—language tapes, guest speakers, music lyrics, and books—fill an important need in the ESL classroom. For one, these other sources of English will introduce language different from your own. Your students understand your English because it is purposeful and direct; you edit and simplify your English because your goal is for them to understand it. Your students get used to your English, but as is often the case, they are unable to understand any other native speaker's English. Other speakers speak more quickly, use varied vocabularies, idiomatic expressions, and grammar, and include pauses, gestures, and expressions that your students are not used to. Other English sources will help students broaden their comprehension of the language.

It's a good idea to start using tapes of general dialogues and to bring in guest speakers when your students are high beginners. Tapes and guest speakers should be a staple of your ESL classroom from then on. It is important that the students understand the communication context and its goals prior to listening to the tapes, reading the passage, or listening to a guest speaker. Understanding context is always important.

Tips to remember

- Purchase some ESL books that can give you more ideas on the kinds of activities you can do with your students in the classroom, and seek out more training if you feel it is necessary.
- Provide your students with initial and ongoing assessment. Find out what it is your students want to study as well as their actual abilities in English. From time to time reassess their abilities and help them to become aware of the progress they are making. Check in with your students to see how they feel about the class and if there is anything new they wish to study.
- Check for real understanding. Students may look at you and nod their head without understanding a word you have said. Make sure they understand you by asking them a question using the language you wish to target.
- Try to recognize boredom. Student boredom can indicate that the students don't understand you, you've been talking for too long, or that they need to get out of their seats and do something different.
- Bring real objects into your classroom. It is more interesting to talk about an authentic box of cereal than simply looking at a picture of a box of cereal.
- Give your students homework to do, including those grammar worksheets. Don't waste class time doing work that students could do on their own. Their class time is better spent listening to your English and participating in real communication.
- Allow for occasional translation. If all except for a few students

understand an abstract word or a particular phrase, allow for a quick translation. It saves time and will help to keep everyone up to speed. (Note the word *occasional*.)

- Allow your students to speak freely without correcting their mistakes. Let your students know that you will be correcting their mistakes during grammar time but not outside of it.
- Put your students into small groups to practice what they have learned, to carry out tasks, and to exchange information.
- Accommodate a variety of learning styles in your classroom. Some people learn best by reading, others by hearing, others by doing. In addition to providing your students with plenty of comprehensible input, be sure to write new vocabulary, grammar points and phrases on the board for those students who absorb information best by seeing it. To accommodate those in your classroom who learn best by doing, incorporate role-play and get your students to talk to one another standing up. Moving around also relieves tension.

Recommended reading

Communicative Competence: Theory and Classroom Practice by Sandra Savignon. Addison-Wesley, 1983.

Instructed Second Language Acquisition by Rod Ellis. Oxford University Press, 1990.

Memory, Meaning, and Method: Some Psychological Perspectives on Language Learning by Earl Stevick. Newbury House, 1976.

The Language Teaching Controversy by Karl Diller. Newbury House, 1978.

The TESOL Quarterly. Available from TESOL Central Office, Suite 300, 1600 Cameron Street, Alexandria, VA 22314; telephone (703) 836-0774.

Understanding Second Language Acquisition by Rod Ellis. Oxford University Press, 1986.

● ●

SAMPLE LESSON PLANS

Sample plan I (one hour)

1. Greet your students and tell them an amusing story about an experience you've had in their country. This serves to break the ice.
2. Tell the students what they did the day before in class.
3. As a review activity, have students interview each other using language learned a day or two previously.
4. Tell a story that introduces the language you wish to target for that hour. Use real objects and drama.
5. Check for comprehension by asking questions.
6. Using the language, create an authentic dialogue on the board. Recruit a student to act out the dialogue with you several times in front of the class. Check for comprehension. An example of an authentic dialogue would be:
   Customer: Excuse me, where can I find the oranges?
   Clerk: They are in the produce department in the back of the store, next to the apples.
   Customer: Thanks a lot.
7. Students copy the dialogue into their notebooks, and then practice it with a partner.
8. Show the students how to create their own dialogue similar to the one written on the board. (You need only to change a few words; in this case, instead of looking for bananas you could be looking for soup. The soup might be on aisle five rather than in the produce section.) In pairs, students create their own dialogue.
9. Students act out their dialogues in front of the class.
10. Have the students tell you what it is they learned for the day. Act out a situation where they have to supply the language, hold up an object and have them name it.

Sample plan II (one hour)

1. Greet the students and show them something you found in their country that you can't understand. Have them explain what it is.
2. Ask the students what they did the day before in class, and have them respond.
3. Tell your students that you are interested in finding out about the habits of people in their country related to the topic of XYZ (in this case we'll use clothing as a topic). Write six to eight yes–no questions on the board. For example:

a. Do you wear the current fashion?
b. Do you dress like your friends?
c. Does your family approve of your clothing?
d. Should people over thirty dress differently than people under thirty?
e. Do you like to wear dark colors?
f. Would you dress differently if you met your friend's parents?

4. Have students divide into groups of four or five. Each person takes a turn answering the questions. One person is in charge of writing the group's number of yes or no answers following each question.

5. Groups (or if there are too many groups, just a few) briefly report back their attitudes concerning clothing. (Show them how to report back quickly.)

6. Hand out a short half-page reading selection on "Clothing Attitudes of Young People." Read it aloud to the class. (Assume that the students will be able to understand at least eighty percent of the story.) Check for comprehension.

7. Students break into pairs. Each person takes turns reading two sentences at a time. On a separate piece of paper they compile words or phrases that they can't figure out. The class as a whole shares the words and phrases, and either you or the students provide the meanings.

8. Hand out questions related to the story for the students to answer for their homework. Have them ask another person the same survey questions that they answered in class.

9. The next day students share how the interviewees outside of class responded to the survey questions.

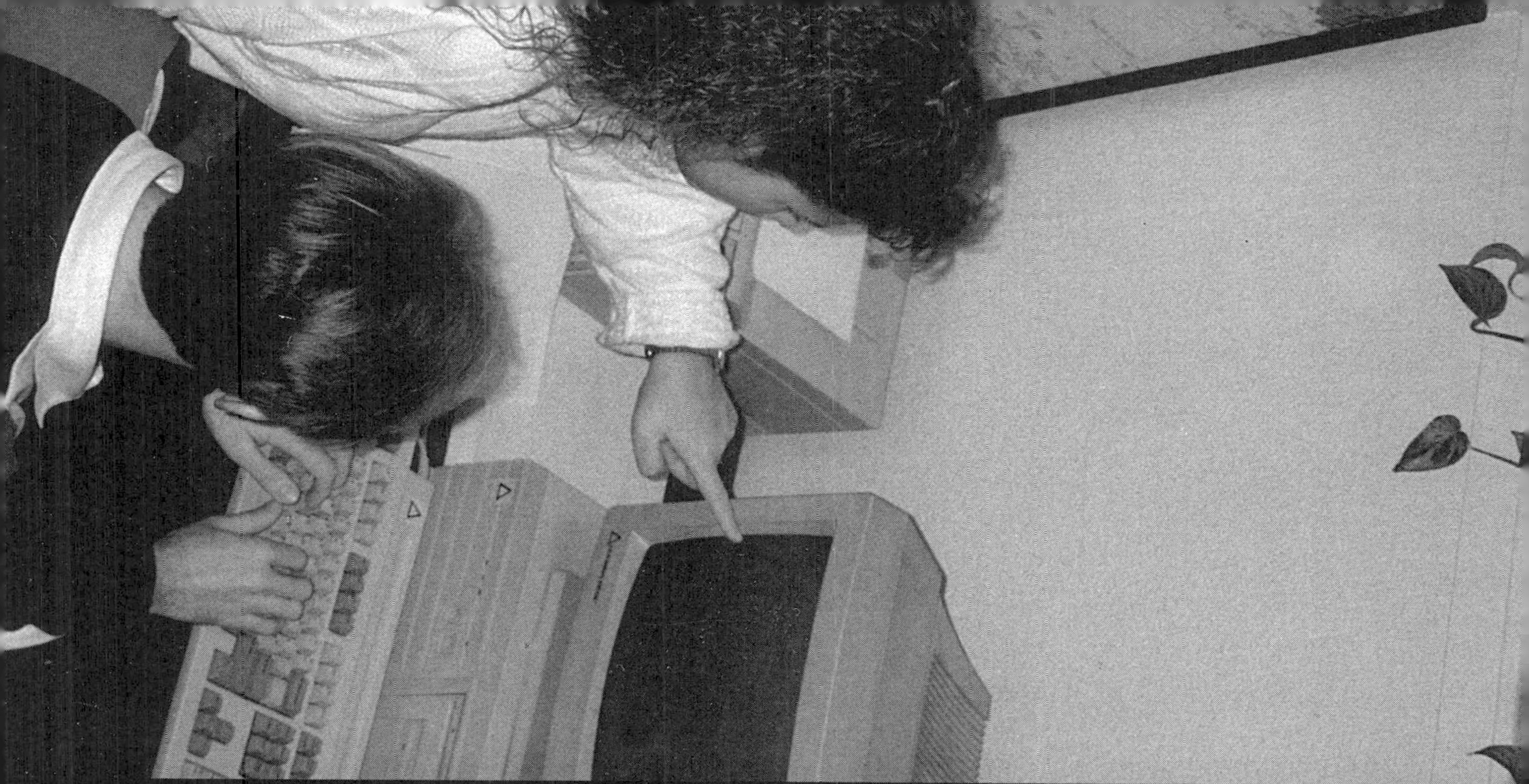

JOB HUNTING TOOLS 7

Applying for a job

Although the employers in this book have varying hiring practices, there are a few strategies that can help you in almost any job search. While the advice in this chapter may not be essential to every prospective position, it will come in handy if you're applying for a teaching position with a discerning private school or another kind of company that prizes professionalism. Application requirements for these jobs could include sending a resume and cover letter, arranging for letters of reference, or attending an interview.

THE RESUME

Writing a resume is a fundamental part of any job search. This single sheet of paper is especially important when it represents you to an employer hundreds of miles away. Like any other resume, your language instruction resume must be clear, concise, and the best advertisement of your skills and experience. It must also express your interest in education and your ability to work well with people.

Take some time to put together a resume that portrays you as an enthusiastic instructor, ready to take on a whole classroom full of eager students. What are language-school employers seeking? As we've said earlier, they are not looking solely for formal qualifications. Most of the employers we list are interested in your tutoring experience and your personality. These public and private schools are looking for responsible people who inspire their students.

On your resume, highlight any experience in which teaching skills were a key component of your job performance, whether or not you were paid for them. Emphasize any volunteer or work experience you have tutoring privately or helping out in the classroom. What are your relevant qualifications? List any experience with study, work, or play in an educational setting. Do you volunteer with a local school? Have you worked as a teaching assistant? Maybe you've done extensive ESL tutoring, or you've worked as a volunteer where you utilized your bilingual skills. Including these details in your resume could be your ticket to a sought-after teaching position.

What if you have no experience relevant to teaching English? Write a resume anyway. This will indicate to employers that you are committed to finding a job. Show them that you have the capacity and desire to learn new skills and will do so if given the opportunity.

Step one

Brainstorm. List any and all of your jobs, skills, achievements, hobbies, and your educational background. Which are the most relevant to communicating, educating, and working as a team? Which are the most relevant to living and working in Eastern Europe? Which show that you are a dedicated and trustworthy employee?

Step two

Start writing. Take each entry on your list and elaborate. Use action verbs. What did you learn, achieve, or master in each area? Be aware that in explaining these experiences, you are trying to persuade an employer that you can achieve the same results for him or her. Make sure your sentence structure is simple and straightforward. Use the dictionary to check your spelling and word usage. Remember that you may be writing for someone whose first language is not English.

Step three

Organize. Present the information you have so industriously acquired in a concise, readable, and persuasive format. In most cases, the employer will only skim the resume, so use eye-catching headings and keep the document to a single page.

You can use one of several styles to create your resume. If your experience is tailored to working in the teaching field, you'll probably want to use the chronological resume. This is the most traditional format for resume-writing, especially when all experience is pertinent to the job at hand. At the other end of the spectrum is the functional resume. When you lack relevant experience, the functional resume allows you to elaborate on abilities and accomplishments while downplaying actual training and expertise. The functional resume shows the employer that you have potential, if not hands-on experience. The third style of resume-writing is the combination resume. If your experience is somewhat related to teaching, and you have other noteworthy skills, you can list both aspects of your background. See the following examples of each resume style.

Step four

Polish, perfect, and present with style. Using a word processor will speed up the resume and cover letter writing process considerably. If you don't have access to a computer, check out a nearby copy shop. Copy shops often rent computer time by the hour. Use a laser printer and high-quality paper to produce your self-styled sales pitch. Never hand-write your resume.

Functional resume

Pat Doe
123 State Street
El Paso, TX 79968
(915) 123-4567

Abilities:

- Proven organizational and interpersonal skills.
- Demonstrated ability to communicate well with clients.
- Ability to solve problems and pay attention to detail.
- Successful implementation of effective learning environment.
- General understanding of intermediate-level Czech.

Accomplishments:

- Managed a customer-service team for over two years.
- Developed and implemented a comprehensive teacher training program.
- Maintained excellent rapport with long-term clients, encouraging repeat customers.
- Coordinated ordering and inventory for one year.
- Drew up school policy on classroom standards.

Work History:

1989-Present University of Texas libraries, El Paso, TX. Assistant research librarian.

1988-1989 Volunteer tutor at University of Texas at El Paso. Helped international students with their writing and composition skills.

1985-1989 Private tutor, El Paso, TX. Worked with ESL students from several different countries.

Education:

1989 University of Texas at El Paso
Bachelor of Arts Degree in English.
Emphasis on Contemporary Literature; G.P.A. 3.1

References available upon request.

● ●

Chronological resume

Pat Doe
123 State Street
Ann Arbor, MI 48104
(313) 123-4567

Education:

1989	University of Michigan Bachelor of Science Degree in English. G.P.A. 3.2

Experience:

1989-Present	Mid-Michigan Community College English literature teaching assistant.
1987-1989	University of Michigan Private Biology tutor for undergraduate students.

Environmental Activities:

1985-1989	Member of University of Michigan Environmental Club. Knowledge of environmental issues. Member of The Nature Conservancy.

Leadership Activities:

1988	University of Michigan Environmental Club Organized and coordinated monthly meetings.
1987	University of Michigan Implemented World Hunger Awareness Day.
1986	University of Michigan Coordinated all-University Blood Drive.

References available upon request.

Combination resume

Pat Doe
123 State Street
Seattle, WA 98109
(206) 123-4567

Education:

1989   University of Washington
            Bachelor of Science Degree in Biology
            G.P.A. 3.2

Abilities:

- Proven ability to communicate with clients.
- Effective organizational skills in team management.
- Demonstrated interpersonal skills.
- Ability to solve problems and pay attention to detail.

Experience:

1989-Present Environmental Protection Agency, Seattle, WA
              Public Relations Assistant
1986-1988   University of Washington
              Tutored international students in Biology and Zoology.

International Activities:

1992   *Community Weekly*
            Wrote articles for local newspaper concerning the international Earth Summit in Brazil.
1988-1989   *The Daily*, University of Washington
            Wrote several articles for school newspaper concerning global issues.

References available upon request.

Don't forget to include your first and last name, address, and telephone number (if you're lucky enough to have one). If the prospective employer can't get in touch with you, your efforts will have been in vain. Have someone proofread your resume; another person's perspective can be valuable.

THE COVER LETTER

Many resumes look alike, especially to people who read five to ten a day. Consequently, it is crucial that you draw attention to yours. This is the primary function of a cover letter. It allows you to communicate directly with the employer in a creative, open manner. Employers do not want to be tied up reading your life story; they want to know about your goals and why you are interested in their school or company. Limit yourself to between a half and one page. Write to hold the attention of the reader through your entire letter and lead him or her on to your resume.

Prepare a form letter and alter successive copies slightly to make each look like a personal letter addressed to an individual. Address your letter to a real person whenever possible and do anything you can to individualize it. "To whom it may concern" will not catch anyone's attention. Be sure to spell the addressee's name correctly (double check for Slavic names, triple check for Hungarian).

Your statement of intent should be simple. Try to make it more interesting than, "I am a native speaker of English looking for a teaching job." Once again, you need to set yourself apart from the average applicant. Explain briefly why you want to live and work in Eastern Europe, or why language instruction holds special interest for you. Be straightforward; getting to the point quickly will be appreciated.

THE PACKAGE

Finally, you are ready to send your packet out to prospective employers. Remember to double-check everything to make sure that it is perfect. Here is what your package should include:

- Cover letter
- Resume
- Original copy of your teaching certificate and/or your degree (if you have one)
- Letters of recommendation (if you have any)

Put your materials into an 8 1/2" x 11" envelope, and either send it off by mail or deliver it in person.

Keep copies of everything you send out so that you can follow up with the right person. Make sure that you follow up your application with a personal visit or phone call to the hiring director.

Sample cover letter *

Pat Doe
123 State Street
Seattle, WA 98109
[U.S.A. if sending abroad]
(206) 111-2222
May 3, 1996

John Smith
ABC English School
123 Street
Prague 1 111 11
Czech Republic

Dear Mr. Smith,

I am writing to inquire about a position teaching English with [school].
As you can see from my resume, I have a Bachelor of [type] in [degree] from [college], and I would like to enhance my present skills and experience by teaching English in [country] with [school]. I have extensive experience working and communicating with people, and I am a diligent and conscientious worker. I hope you will consider my qualifications and experience for a position with [school]. Please feel free to contact my references. I look forward to hearing from you at your earliest convenience. Thank you for your time and consideration.

Sincerely,

[sign name here]

Pat Doe

* DO NOT COPY THIS LETTER. The information herein is designed to demonstrate the style of a cover letter. If an employer receives several identical or similar letters, they may disregard them.

THE INTERVIEW

Most interviews only last thirty minutes and involve between ten and fifteen questions. Try not to get hung up on figuring out the "correct" answers to an employer's questions. Rather than trying to read the interviewer's mind, realize that the interviewer is looking to see if you are a good communicator. Listen carefully, think about your reply, and then answer the question as clearly as you can.

There are a number of steps an interviewee can take to have a successful interview. Remember, you only get one chance to make a good first impression. The hiring officer is going to be evaluating each person on the basis of their personality, manner of dress, experience, and communication skills, as well as attitude towards being interviewed. The content of the answers to questions asked is really secondary to your ability to communicate something positive about yourself to the employer.

Always dress formally and look your best for an interview. You might want to consider wearing a suit or sport coat, if you have one, and a tie if you are male, though this may not be necessary in all school situations. Shine your shoes. Dress and act professionally. You want to give the impression that you are serious about yourself and your work.

Finally, attend to personal hygiene. Trim your fingernails, comb and style your hair, put your make-up on carefully, and brush your teeth. Bring some breath mints to the interview, and if you are chewing gum, be sure to get rid of it before you go inside.

Make sure that you arrive early for your appointment. Since it can be difficult to find your way around in new and unfamiliar surroundings, know where you're going in advance of your appointment. Consult a map, or scope out the school's location in advance. Most employers will appreciate your prompt arrival, and some may even be surprised that you didn't seem to have any difficulty locating them.

Interview tips

- Maintain eye contact with the interviewer. You don't have to stare the person down, but try to talk directly to her.
- Do not overuse hand gestures when answering questions because this indicates to the interviewer that you are not altogether comfortable. Make an attempt to keep your hands folded loosely together in your lap. Periodically use them to animate your answers.
- Sit forward in you chair and be very attentive instead of sitting back in a passive manner. If you do this, it tells the interviewer that you're listening carefully and that you are confident.

- When the interviewer asks you a question, he wants you to answer that specific question. Listen to the question and then think before answering.
- Think about your posture. Try to sit up straight in the chair and at the same time stay loose.
- Don't leave the premises without making sure that you know the full name of the person who interviewed you. Do your best to pronounce her name correctly.

Sample interview questions

Use the following sample questions for practice, but learn to think on your feet by having a friend or a family member make up and ask you other interview questions. The key is to sort your thoughts quickly and respond clearly and accurately. You want to avoid becoming flustered if the interviewer asks unexpected questions. Answer these questions to start the thinking process, and go over the information on your resume and in your notes and know it cold. You will also want to have in mind sample lesson plans for both a beginner class and an advanced/conversation class.

1. So, what is it that interests you about teaching English?
2. Tell me a little bit about the kinds of responsibilities you had with your last employer.
3. Tell me about a problem you've had with a student and how you dealt with it.
4. What do you see yourself doing in the future?
5. How long will you stay in Eastern Europe?
6. What assets do you possess that would help you in your job?
7. Give me a brief history of your teaching experience.
8. Have you ever worked with people with different cultural standards?
9. What can you contribute in the classroom that will make you an asset to our school?
10. Why do you wish to work in this industry in Poland, Hungary, the Czech Republic, or Slovakia?
11. Tell me what techniques you employ to prepare yourself for an upcoming class?
12. What do you anticipate missing the most while living abroad?
13. Tell me about yourself.
14. How would those who know you describe you?
15. What do you think you'll be doing if you get the job you're applying for?
16. Do you speak any other languages besides English?
17. Do you have any questions I can answer for you?

18. What teaching materials have you used in your preparation and classes?
19. How will you spend your time outside of class?
20. Why did you come to Poland, Hungary, the Czech Republic, or Slovakia?

THE WAIT

Once you have walked out the door, it is time to begin your follow-through. Within five days of completing an interview, send your interviewer a thank-you letter (avoid personal phone calls.) You do this to bring your name back into the interviewer's mind and to show that you are professional and responsible. Today a follow-up letter is standard procedure. Keep it short and to the point and address it to the person with whom you spoke.

In a short time, the employer should respond with information regarding a second interview or information about your hiring. Turn-down letters are also part of the game, but don't get discouraged! Always accept a rejection gracefully and keep working. You have to be persistent in a competitive job market.

ENVIRONMENTAL DONATION PROGRAM

Our environmental policy

Thank you for purchasing *Now Hiring! Jobs in Eastern Europe*. Deeply rooted in our corporate philosophy is the belief that both individuals and corporate entities must share in safeguarding our world's ecosystems and in restoring the health of the planet. Our commitment begins with our use of recycled materials and with our efforts to reduce our company's consumption of energy and natural resources.

ADOPT AN ACRE

In addition to minimizing our environmental impact as a corporation, we donate a portion of our profits to the Nature Conservancy's Adopt an Acre Program, through which individuals and companies assist in protecting critical natural areas.

A football field-sized section of Latin American temperate forest is "axed for timber, burned for cultivation, or clear-cut for cattle grazing every second of the day." The TNC's Adopt an Acre Program allows individuals and corporations from around the world to become involved in the effort to preserve these forests. With every dollar donated, TNC is able to:

- Work with local partners to purchase lands deemed critical for the survival of endangered species and ecosystems.
- Educate local citizens about the importance of sound environmental management.
- Hire, train, and equip forest rangers to more effectively manage natural areas.
- Arrange for the exchange of debilitating debt burdens for threatened lands through "debt for nature" swaps.

Over 15 million acres in Latin America have been protected by TNC and its local counterparts in those countries. Our corporate contribution, made possible in part by your purchase of *Now Hiring! Jobs in Eastern Europe*, will help TNC protect even more of these threatened lands.

Perpetual Press is proud to be playing a part in TNC's Adopt an Acre Program, and encourages its customers, suppliers, and employees to redouble their efforts to conserve the precious natural resources that we all need.

ABOUT THE NATURE CONSERVANCY

The Nature Conservancy was founded in 1951 as a non-profit, tax-exempt corporation. Their mission is to "preserve plants, animals, and natural communities that represent the diversity of life on earth by protecting the lands and waters they need to survive." The Nature Conservancy works within the U. S. and abroad to ensure the survival of all types of plant and animal life, primarily through the purchase and careful management of threatened areas.

For more information or to become a member of the Nature Conservancy, please call (800) 628-6860.

SHARE YOUR EXPERIENCE...

Please complete this survey and receive a 25 percent discount off the purchase of any Now Hiring! book when bought directly from Perpetual Press. See the order form on the next page for more information. If we quote you in a future edition we'll give you a free book.

Personal profile

Name: _____
Address: _____
City: _____
State: _____ Zip: _____
Phone: _____
Age: _____ Gender: Male   Female
College student?   Yes   No   Graduated?   Yes   No
Where did you hear about the *Now Hiring!* series? _____
_____
What newspapers or magazines do you read regularly? _____
_____

Job search/travel

What kind of job did you get? _____
_____
How long did it take you to find your job? _____
_____
What procedure did you follow? _____
_____
After you got your job, how did you travel there? _____
_____
How long did you stay? _____

Employer data (company 1)

Company: _____
Address: _____
City: _____ Country: _____
Hours worked per week: _____ Wage: _____
Number of American workers: _____
Your duties: _____
_____
Where did you live? _____
What did it cost? _____
What expenses did you have? _____
Would you work for this company again?   Yes   No
Why or why not? _____
_____

Employer data (company 2)

Company: _____

Address: _____

City: _____ Country: _____

Hours worked per week: _____ Wage: _____

Number of workers: _____

Your duties: _____

_____

Where did you live? _____

What did it cost? _____

What expenses did you have? _____

Would you work for this company again?   Yes   No

Why or why not? _____

_____

General information

Other employment available in the teaching field that is not listed in
  our book: _____

Comments about teaching in general: _____

_____

Now Hiring! Jobs in Eastern Europe critique

Did our book help you find your job?   Yes   No

Positive aspects of our book: _____

_____

Negative aspects of our book: _____

_____

Other employment available in the country in which you worked
  that is not listed in this book: _____

What should be added or changed: _____

Other comments: _____

May we contact you for additional information?   Yes   No

May we quote you in future editions?   Yes   No

Send your completed survey to:

Perpetual Press
P.O. Box 45628
Seattle, WA 98145-0628

If ordering other *Now Hiring!* books, please enclose completed survey,
order form, and payment and you will receive twenty-five percent off
your order.

   Note: All Now Hiring! books are also available at bookstores throughout the U. S. and Canada.

LOOKING FOR ADVENTURE?

Check out other
titles in our

NOW HIRING!
SERIES

NOW HIRING! SERIES

If you would like to order additional copies of books from the *Now Hiring!* series, fill out the order form below. Please include $2 postage and handling for the first book and $1 for each additional copy.

_____ $17.95   *Now Hiring! Jobs in Asia*
_____ $17.95   *Now Hiring! Outdoor Jobs*
_____ $17.95   *Now Hiring! Destination Resort Jobs*
_____ $14.95   *Now Hiring! Jobs in Eastern Europe*
_____ $14.95   *Now Hiring! Ski Resort Jobs*

Also from Perpetual Press:

_____ $9.95   *The Global Adventurer's Handbook*
_____ $9.95   *The Courier Air Travel Handbook*

_____ Total copies

$ _____ Total amount
$ _____ Postage and handling
$ _____ 25% discount (if completed survey is enclosed)
$ _____ Total enclosed

Send check or money order with this form to:

Perpetual Press
P.O. Box 45628
Seattle, WA 98145-0628

Name: _____
Address: _____
City: _____
State: _____ Zip: _____
Phone: _____

All Perpetual Press titles are available at bookstores, or use the order form provided.